NEWS

The Evolution of
Journalism in Canada

Andrew M. Osler

Graduate School of Journalism and the
Department of Sociology
University of Western Ontario

Copp Clark Pitman Ltd.
A Longman Company
Toronto

ISBN *0-7730-5193-7*

Executive Editor: Jeff Miller
Editor: Maral Bablanian
Typesetting: Heidy Lawrance and Associates
Printing and binding: John Deyell Company

Canadian Cataloguing in Publication Data
Osler, Andrew M. (Andrew Martin), 1938–
    News: the evolution of journalism in Canada

Includes index.
ISBN 0–7730–5193–7

1. Journalism – Canada – History. 1. Title.

PN4904.086 1992   071'.1   C92–094900–2

An honest attempt has been made to secure permission for all material used, and, if there are errors or ommissions, these are wholly unintentional and the Publisher will be grateful to learn of them.

Copp Clark Pitman Ltd.
2775 Matheson Blvd. East
Mississauga, Ontario
L4W 4P7

Associated companies:

  Longman Group Ltd., London
  Longman Inc., New York
  Longman Cheshire Pty., Melbourne
  Longman Paul Pty., Auckland

Printed and bound in Canada
1   2   3   4   5   5193–7   97   96   95   94   93

for Linda's children

"…ye can discern the face of the sky; but can ye not discern the signs of the times?" (Matthew 16:3)

T
A
B
L
E

O
F

C
O
N
T
E
N
T
S

Preface

As a young reporter in the mid-1960s, my editor at the *Globe and Mail* sent me off to cover a speech by Daniel Johnson at Toronto's old King Edward Hotel. Johnson was the last *Union Nationale* premier of Quebec. Sovereignty association and the referendum of 1980 were still several premiers and a decade and a half away, but anglo-Canada already was becoming aware of restiveness in Quebec society. Someone had coined the phrase, "the quiet revolution," and the news media were beginning to chronicle the words and actions of senior Quebec politicians with lively interest. Johnson's speech that evening was routine and not especially newsworthy; something of a disappointment to the assembled scribes. But after his talk, he gave a brief press conference that he artfully (and with the perfect timing of a man long-experienced in the ways of reporters) converted into the sudden squall of a full-blown news scrum. The ever-smiling political countenance darkened in well-timed anger, and he demanded to know who in the crowd was from the *Globe and Mail.* Someone pointed my way, and the great man rounded on me, theatrically furious about an editorial the paper had run a day or so earlier.

Suddenly, the reporter was no longer gathering the news, but part of it. It seemed to me as though the premier and I were at the centre of a tight pressure chamber that had not existed moments earlier— reporters' pencils flashing under our chins, swarms of microphones jabbing at our nostrils, photo strobes blinding us and making it difficult even to breathe as they punctuated the glaring heat of the powerful lights that accompanied television cameras in those days.

An old political pro, Johnson was used to it all. But for a young reporter who had been part of the scrum often enough, but never its object, this was an utterly new experience. And an entirely disorienting one. The whole episode may have lasted sixty seconds in all. Nothing more consequential than the subject matter of an amusing anecdote to be retold in later years. But it was this experience that first set me to wondering about the dynamics of journalism in society; the nature of the power it wields, and the effects of media publicity on individuals and institutions. In a modest way, the experience provided an inspiration that led me on to a career as a media teacher, researcher, and critic; and eventually to the writing of this book.

Recently I've learned that my experiences in this regard are not unique. In 1960, I was privileged to be taken on at the *Toronto Star* as one of half a dozen university students hired to work as reporters for the summer. Most of us went on to work as journalists for a time, some making lifetime careers of it. Among our group of that summer, Sid Adilman went on to become one of the country's finest entertainment writers and critics; Tom Curzon became a senior editorial executive at the *Star*. Equally interesting, are the experiences of those of us who eventually left the craft—myself, Stuart Adam who went on to become chair of the School of Journalism at Carleton University, and Terry Keenleyside who became a professor of political science at the University of Windsor. Like myself, Adam and Keenleyside had experiences (I learned in reminiscences with both of them many years later) that turned them away from the practice of journalism. This was not in any profoundly traumatic sense, but privately and in a manner like my own experience that turned them not so much away from the craft, but toward a good critic's sense of caring concern. Hopefully, all of us, those who stayed and those who left, have made useful contributions.

These are the people who were my first colleagues in journalism, and I'm grateful for the experiences we shared; also for the editors at the *Star* who taught us and made it all possible, Ray Timson and especially Ralph Allen. Later at the *Globe and Mail*, I learned much from Richard Doyle, Clark Davey, and others. Their ideas, too, have influenced what has emerged in these pages as did the ideas of Ron Neilly, public affairs producer at CBE Radio in Windsor, Ontario, where I broadcast weekly commentaries for a number of years.

I'm grateful for the support of colleagues, initially at the University of Windsor and in later years at the University of Western Ontario, especially that of Stuart Selby who always knew that the book would be written eventually. Criticisms of the original manuscript by Stanley Cunningham, Eugene Tate, and Jay Weston were invaluable, and many of their good ideas are incorporated in the final version. David Lepofsky's advice and comment on matters relating to the law in chapter 6 are especially appreciated. I am also pleased to acknowledge with appreciation the kind cooperation of Benjamin Singer. Chapter 7 in this book is, in part, a revised version of my article "To Thomas Kent and Beyond: The Evolution of a National Press Policy in Canada," in *Communications in Canadian Society*, ed. Benjamin Singer (Toronto: Nelson Canada, 1991).

My thanks as well to Richard Bywaters who read the manuscript with intelligence and care, to Michele Goddard who kept me alive, and to Maral Bablanian who edited the work. If problems remain; if there are errors or omissions evident to the discerning reader, then these are my responsibility alone, and in no way to be laid at the feet of any or all of the excellent people who did their best to make this book a useful one.

News: A

Mirror to

Ourselves

C
H
A
P
T
E
R

1

Everyone who lives in the developed democracies of the Western world is exposed to a daily flood of mass-mediated news, analysis, features, documentaries, and commentary of one sort or another. This is the substance of journalism, flowing incessantly from endless printed pages and cluttered airwaves into every corner of our psyches. A commonly applied metaphor likens the news system to a gigantic social mirror into which we must look for most of our knowledge of the world and for most of our images of reality. As with most metaphors, that of the "media-as-mirror" has its limitations. One is obliged to recognize that we are dealing with a mirror of most peculiar properties.

Here is a mirror that does indeed reflect much that exists around us. But unlike any other looking glass, this one has an odd way of simplifying the images it reflects back to us, of leaving out whole components, complexities, and subtleties. Stranger still, this mirror selects what it chooses to reflect; more often than not, it ignores whole components of society's reality, completely failing to reflect many images.

Very often, too, what the media mirror reflects, it also tends to distort. All of this will become more evident to the reader in the chapters that follow. But for the moment, it is enough to make the basic point that the degree of influence these images may have on us (reflected as they may be in that strange mirror that is our media system) and the degree to which they may be distorted in random or patterned ways are matters of great social importance.

News and all the related components of printed and electronic journalism provide an embracing presence in our lives. They tend to breed in us, not amazement or discomfort at the remarkable influence they manifest in shaping and defining human existence in the mass society, but rather, a comfortable sense of contempt that we reserve for those things that are utterly familiar and utterly encompassing.

And journalism is nothing if not a phenomenon of ubiquitous familiarity. Like the atmosphere we breathe, its outpourings are so much a part of modern existence that we tend to take them for granted, rarely thinking about what they are, how they get there, or what effects they may have upon us. Apart from an occasional casual reference, perhaps to one of those romantic and mostly inaccurate Hollywood images about reporters that most of us store in the back of our minds, we hardly ever consider news and the news system as being of consequence in themselves and in their own right.

Ironically, it is precisely when journalism's offerings are most vital and most dramatic (in the circumstances of a major political crisis, or a breaking war, perhaps) that we are least likely to consider the processes by which it comes to us. When thousands of Chinese students demand democracy in Tiananmen Square, and then face terrible retribution at the hands of a cruel state, we understandably become completely involved as empathizing fellow humans. We become much too involved in the actual news, to pay much analytic attention to the intricate system of human, mechanical, and electronic components that identified the events as being "newsworthy" in the first place; editorially processed them; established their priorities relative to other elements in the public information mix; and ultimately brought them to print, television, or radio as the dominating news of the day. Returning once more to the mirror metaphor, here is a looking glass into which we intently look, seeking images and information, but often without paying attention to the qualities and characteristics of the mirror itself.

One important explanation as to why such a circumstance prevails is simple enough: of all the human stories it relates, journalism consistently does the poorest job of telling its own. The growing ombudsman and press council movements in the newspaper industry, a number of well-publicized government studies of the news media in recent decades, and an increasing interest evident among broadcast regulators with regard to the quality of radio and television news content may eventually lead to greater public awareness and understanding of how the news system works. But that day has not yet arrived.

The reality of the moment is that journalists rarely take the time or trouble to explain why one piece of information, or human situation, should be neglected while another situation—one that may seem unimportant to the unschooled observer—may galvanize journalists to the feeding frenzy of the "scrum."

Whether one views journalism from the perspective of the individual who suddenly becomes a source of the news, or simply from that of the media consumer trying to keep abreast of events through the content of the news media, one's attitude is generally guarded and even sceptical. Quoting a poll in his *Toronto Star* ombudsman's column some years ago, Borden Spears observed:

> Critics of the press, rejoice. The American opinion pollster Lou Harris has discovered that 51 per cent of the U.S. public have faith in their garbage collectors, but only 16 per cent trust the press.
>
> It's just the figures that are new, of course. Newspapers have been condemned as purveyors of misinformation and prejudice

since the first one was established. What Harris reports is a widening of the credibility gap in recent years.[1]

In the same column, Spears correctly noted that journalism is, in fact, a process that serves us best when it stands apart, and this may explain at least some of that guardedness and uncertainty in the public mind. The distancing phenomenon sometimes costs journalism its friends when integrity requires the reporting of bad news about otherwise good individuals and organizations. Spears also stated that the journalistic system itself (the newspapers and magazines, television and radio stations, and the people who produce their content) often become inextricably and confusingly associated in the public mind with the bad news it produces. This is a problem that dates to the ancient Persian illogic of killing hapless messengers foolish enough to bear bad news to the feet of those in power.

Such explanations, however, are only part of the reason for the increasingly difficult relationship between journalists and the general public.

The Psychology of the Source

The most immediate consequence of a generalized state of public ignorance and misinformation about journalism and its processes, is that most people tend to be unprepared, and find it an unnerving experience, to suddenly discover themselves the objects of journalistic interest as sources of news.

Despite the romanticized Hollywood images first conjured by Adolphe Menjou and Pat O'Brien in *The Front Page* nearly sixty years ago, and kept alive by the likes of Robert Redford and his 1970s film *All the President's Men* about the *Washington Post*'s assault on the Watergate presidency of Richard Nixon, most news people don't realize what the public thinks of them at all. Generally, they are stereotyped as a romantic breed, perhaps a bit wild and somewhat dangerous when they come too near.

Actually, most journalists see their jobs as routine and underpaid nine-to-five affairs most of the time, and they are quite unaware of how unsettling their attentions can be, especially on the unwary and inexperienced news source. Showing a rare insight among working journalists, Sandra Precop, who used to write a lively column for the *Windsor Star*, once offered this bit of bemused wisdom on the subject: "People get a bit afraid when a news person comes around. It's as though a big neon sign had gone up over the house saying, 'Joe Blotz

Howard Hughes' *The Front Page* was one of the first Hollywood movies to depict our stereo-typed images of journalism. (Museum of Modern Art, Film Stills Archive, New York City)

lives here, and his name is in today's paper.' It makes people feel quite uncomfortable."[2] Uncomfortable, indeed. And it is a discomfort that can become frightening when an encounter with the media includes two or more reporters, especially those who come equipped with intimidating cameras, microphones, and the related electronic para-phernalia of the broadcast media. It is one of the oddities of the unin-hibited journalism practised in the modern Western world that so few reporters seem sensitive to the information-distorting reality inher-ently present in the very processes by which they reach out to their news sources.

The dishing out and receiving ends of journalism are different worlds, a truth that many news people can live a lifetime without fully appreciating. To most reporters, the newsgathering process is routine. But to the news source on the receiving end of journalism's attentions, whether said source is being swamped with unwanted probing (as was sprinter Ben Johnson, for instance, in the wake of being stripped of his 1988 Olympic gold medal) or ignored when he or she actually would like a little attention, meeting the news media can be traumatic. Facing the media as sources of news is an experience that a surprisingly large number of otherwise ordinary people eventually come to share. Instead of making people media-wise and informed in the ways of newsgatherers, and instead of encouraging the development of public wisdom about media manners and morals, for the most part the process merely adds to that wall of mystery that surrounds journalism in the eyes of the public.

Such a consequence, of course, is more typical among those who ordinarily live private lives, and rarely have occasion to meet the media head-on. Well-known politicians, stars of the screen and the sports arena, and other public figures who encounter the media on a day-to-day basis, usually are wiser in the ways of the news media but even these people have their difficulties.

Richard Gwyn has described, for instance, Pierre Trudeau's uneasy relationship with the news media, a phenomenon often given dramatic expression in Trudeau's case but hardly unique among our most senior and visible political and social leaders.

> In 1968…Trudeau called the press "instruments of oppression" because they got everything wrong; in 1969, he called reporters who accompanied him to London (for a Commonwealth conference) "crummy" because they interviewed a talkative blonde whom he had taken to lunch. Near the end of his term, he told aides, "The press tried to destroy me in '72 and in '74 and they failed. They'll try again."
>
> Trudeau always considered most reporters "crummy," collectively and individually. Except for some women reporters whom he admired for other reasons.[3]

Defining News

News is no less a mystery from the point of view of the consumer. It is unfortunate that most of us usually pay scant attention to news as a phenomenon in its own right. The news system is a powerful cultural artifact, a product of human hands. The peculiar social mirror that it conjures for us can be imperfect. It can—and does—generate remarkable distortions in the way we see the world.

Generalities and opinions about news abound. But since these tend either to be vague in the case of generalities, or frequently to disagree with each other in the case of opinions, their collective effect is not especially helpful. This is not to suggest that there isn't a good amount of wisdom, or an abundance of interesting ideas on the subject. The American sociologist, Harold Lasswell, suggested (among other purposes, including serving as educator, and giving people a connected and holistic sense of what is happening around them) that the prime function of democratic journalism is the "surveillance of the environment."[4] Lasswell's ideas about news and journalism, first offered in the late 1940s, have inspired a generation of journalism professors and city editors to explain the idea of news not as a mirror, but as a social searchlight. The newsroom organization is seen standing as a lighthouse, casting its penetrating beam back and forth across the social landscape, and pausing wherever there are aberrations.

Implying illumination in a somewhat different manner, the 1981 Report of the Royal Commission on Newspapers speaks about journalism "having as its ideal the quest for what is true and right."[5] In a similar philosophic vein, Walter Lippmann once wrote these words about news and where it is found:

> Usually it is the stereotyped shape assumed by an event at an obvious place that uncovers the run of the news. The most obvious place is where people's affairs touch public authority. *De minimis non curat lex.* It is at these places that marriages, births, deaths, contracts, failures, arrivals, departures, lawsuits, disorders, epidemics and calamities are made known.
>
> …News is not a mirror of social conditions, but the report of an aspect that has obtruded itself. The news does not tell you how the seed is germinating in the ground, but it may tell you when the first sprout breaks through the surface. It may even tell you what somebody says is happening to the seed underground. It may tell you that the sprout did not come up at the time it was expected. The more points, then, at which any happening can be fixed, objectified, measured, named, the more points there are at which news can occur.[6]

Without recourse to any metaphor, but succinct and representative of attempts at practical definition found in the generally dull fare of "how-to" journalism textbooks, Mitchell Charnley, has described news simply as "the timely report of facts and opinion, that holds interest or importance, or both, for a considerable number of people."[7]

Charnley's definition may be helpful in a general way to working journalists mining their course through the vast ore of information generated worldwide each day, seeking to discover the few nuggets of news that it may contain. Certainly the rich literature of philosophic comment gives substance to the endless process of journalism school seminars and after-hours press club reflection on the nature and purpose of news in the mechanisms of democratic journalism. It seems likely, however, that the actual work of journalism is more guided by instinct and feeling, and by the myths and traditions with which the craft is richly endowed.

Few modern journalists will admit to it, but most half believe that there is something very special about them, something in their genes. Call it talent or an innate sense of what is newsworthy—it is a quality that sets news people apart. In reality, a good sense of language, a lively curiosity, the ability to observe intelligently, and perhaps a touch of P.T. Barnum's sense of showmanship, are journalism's special skills. They are shared by many people and it is only training in the daily use of such skills, participation in the traditions of the newsroom, and imbibing the heady infusions of journalism's 300-year-old mythology that really set journalists apart. Appropriately, Phyllis Wilson has written this about journalism's mythic traditions: "There is a belief widespread in the news world, that the recognition of news is intuitive, that it is a faculty with which the select are born, not bred, that a Geiger counter clicks in the heads of a gifted few in proximity to the uranium of news."[8]

Though Professor Wilson's words are tongue-in-cheek, they describe very accurately the feeling many news people share about their craft and its essential skills. Unfortunately, romantic fancy does little to help journalists (let alone the reading, viewing, and listening public) in seeking some sort of precise measure of what journalism's role is, or ought to be, especially with regard to the central matter of defining and describing the mysterious thing called news.

The Ingredients of News

A small group of us researched this question about news in 1976 and 1977 for the Ontario Royal Commission on Violence in the Communications Industry, chaired by Judy LaMarsh.[9] We found that very few among a sampled group of thirty Ontario news people could produce from conscious thought or memory even such simplistic definitions of news as Charnley's, cited above. Instead we found news people much better able to provide individual news stories and situations that had excited them, and that they understood at the time, almost intuitively, to be news scenarios of the first magnitude.

One very senior Toronto editor, who like almost all his colleagues in the research sample was hard pressed to give an abstract working definition of news, was able to claim with absolute certainty that Israel's 1976 commando raid on the Ugandan airport at Entebbe undoubtedly was the greatest news story of that turbulent decade. "We responded in this newsroom with every resource we had, and just kept it going for days and days to show people how there may not have been anything comparable carried out even in World War II." He went on to describe the event as having "very, very high drama. [There was] the national dedication of the Israeli rescue squad; the underlying principle of a country under siege deciding it wouldn't pay blackmail, and going to fantastic lengths to pluck the source of the ransom away from the ransomer."[10]

This man knew with certainty what news was when he saw it, as did all the other people we interviewed. Collectively, they provided an exciting list of scenarios including a would-be bank robber wrapped in dynamite who blew himself up inside a Northern Ontario bank branch, a comparatively prosaic list of hurricanes, epidemics, and sundry natural disasters, and a suspenseful (but thankfully botched) attempt to kidnap the daughter of a prominent Toronto merchant family. But none of these news people was able to offer a solid abstracted description of news itself, a definition set apart from the actual examples that all provided so readily.

What this means (and it is a fundamental point that must be grasped if one is to understand the psychology of journalism) is that most news people perceive the newsworthiness, or lack of it, in any given situation more or less unconsciously. The process is one of intuition; it is emotional rather than rational. There seems to be little room for such reasoned and logical considerations such as whether priority given to a news item is appropriate relative to other items in the news mix; whether the item has intrinsic social importance; whether the style in which the piece is written—its tone, and the emphases given to the various information elements it contains—will best and most accurately inform the reading, listening, and viewing public. Instead, news selection and preparation tend to be based on the emotional "feel" of a situation.

Few scholars or media critics have directly addressed the question of news definition, but most who have would agree with the views that have been expressed here. Herbert Altschull, for instance, notes that "reporters, editors and journalism teachers have been struggling with the problem ever since there have been reporters, editors and journalism teachers. But the concept of news remains a puzzlement." In 1973, Altschull interviewed a number of Washington journalists on the subject of news, and offered this comment about his findings:

> Each respondent said it [news definition] was a matter of news judgement, but no one was able to define news judgement. One said news was "what is important to me as a father, as a husband, not only as a correspondent, but also as a taxpayer." Another said decisions about news were based on "cues you get from outside sources, including press agents, your peers, what others are writing about." Still another said: "It all boils down to one's own judgement and perhaps—I hate to say biases because that puts a political slant on it—but basically I would say it's judgement."[11]

In the same article, Altschull reminds us of David Brinkley's famous exasperated dictum on the subject: "News is what I say it is." But for the moment, the last word goes to Gaye Tuchman who has likened news reporting to the telling of fairy tales.

> "Once upon a time" announces that what follows is myth and pretense, a flight of cultural fancy. The news lead proclaims that what follows is factual and hard-nosed, a veridical account of events in the world. But, ultimately, both the fairy tale and the news account are stories, to be passed on, commented upon, and recalled as individually appreciated public resources. Both have a public character in that both are available to all, part and parcel of our cultural equipment. Both draw on culture for their derivation....Both take social and cultural resources and transform them into public property: Jack Kennedy and Jack of beanstalk fame are both cultural myths, although one lived and the other did not.[12]

None of this is intended to suggest that the news process is merely random and chaotic—far from it. News has a subconsciously derived rationale of its own. When one gathers enough graphic examples of news situations that journalists themselves have described as exciting and newsworthy, as in the study for the LaMarsh Royal Commission, a definite pattern emerges and the pieces of a definition of news begin to filter through from the journalistic subconscious. What follows is a listing, and not especially a scientific description, of the more crucial pieces as we found them. Among other things, news must be important, interesting, graphic, and immediate.

Important

News should be about events and situations that are important for a lot of people to know about. Accounts of the significant public activities of politicians and government officials; information about important trends in society; accounts of scientific and medical innovation of immediate consequence; the day's stock market activity; and, of course, prognostications relating to tomorrow's weather. All of these situations and activities are "important"; unfortunately, being merely important is not always enough to guarantee an item's publication or broadcast.

Interesting

Information may be important to know about, but if it isn't interesting as well (and by interesting, most news people seem to mean entertaining) it may be downplayed or ignored altogether.

The patriation of Canada's constitution from Great Britain, provided a package of information that was important for Canadians to know about during the late 1970s, as did the troubled Meech Lake Accord, and the Free Trade pact a decade later. The ongoing daily, weekly, and monthly detail about local municipal works tenders, mill rate adjustments, and demographic statistics relating to hospital planning and population age distribution are also important. Unfortunately, such information is not interesting in the sense of its being entertaining to read or view. All other things being equal, it will tend therefore to receive relatively lower priority in competition with a news "event" that contains inherent properties of drama and excitement, even though such an event may not be nearly so important in the long-term and historic scheme of things. Merely important information that cannot be ignored for the simple reason that it is very important (the Meech Lake Accord, the continuing reactive constitutional processes of the 1990s, and the Free Trade pact are fine examples) may be distorted in several ways. This is especially true in the often convoluted seeking out of the obscure sub-themes of controversy or confrontation, that are then are used quite literally to force and twist the subject into a journalistically entertaining mold.

The upshot is that we learn more from our news media about the drama than about the substance of Quebec's frustrations with the constitutional process; more about the fact that a group of native people in traditional dress staged a protest or a drum ceremony on Parliament Hill than about the precise constitutional proposal that concerned them.

News people often refer to a certain entertainment quality in news information as "human interest." There is a dash of Walter Mitty's spirit in all of us, and news people know from long years of experience that nothing engrosses the reader, viewer, or listener quite so intensely as a news story with which he or she can identify on a personal and emotional level. Call it daydreaming or escapism, we all experience it. The raid on Entebbe was a story rich in human interest; readers and viewers identified with the avenging Israelis joining in the fray on the wings of imagination. Every disaster or dark human drama, be it flood, act of war, epidemic, or highway accident, brings out the darker side of an intensely human capacity to identify with the stressful experiences of others: to imagine through the anguish of a safely distanced and impersonal figure in a newspaper or television story, precisely what it might be like to watch one's family swept away in a hurricane; to see one's community savaged by war or famine; to be engulfed by the fire and agony of an air disaster. In some intense and peculiar way, people seem to want to know and feel such things, and the news media, knowing this, play to it with enthusiasm.

Happily, there is also a brighter side. Who, alive and sentient at the time, failed to identify with Hillary on Mount Everest's summit, or with Armstrong on the moon, or more recently with the Woods Hole divers when the Titanic's bow loomed above them from the ocean floor? The Walter Mitty spirit (James Thurber not only described it first, but best as well, through the daydreams of his famous character) can even ennoble us occasionally as when, for instance, we read of the touch of Mother Teresa's gentle hand in the horrific slums of Calcutta.

Directly, or indirectly, all news stories are about people, and this means that there is a human interest element hidden in most story situations waiting for the enterprising journalist to dig out and refine.

Unfortunately, journalism's powerful imperative to entertain (an imperative that is becoming increasingly intense in today's ascendant television news environment) frequently means that the human interest element and other entertainment values in the news can distort the news as we read, view, and listen to it. One of the most powerful sources of distortion in our media mirror, a strong human interest element can twist the reality of both the noble and the obscene. Or more often, it can elevate the merely inconsequential to a position of prominence far beyond its inherent social worth. By the same token, a dry and abstract story in which human interest or other entertainment values are only minimally present, can be relegated to obscurity among the comics and advice columns without regard to its worth in terms of any absolute standard of importance.

Writing with obvious frustration about the information selection patterns of journalists covering the business of the federal government in Ottawa, the authors of the 1969 report of the Task Force on Government Information left us this extreme but lasting observation:

> There is a lot of federal government information that never gets to Canadians who might be able to put it to great personal use, and the reason it's failing to get there is not that someone is suppressing it but simply that this information does not help in the peddling of papers. Nor does it build the sort of mass media interest upon which radio and television stations nurture themselves.
>
> ...A Gresham's law of mass media starts to operate with bad communication driving out good. Complex issues and events lose out to simplification. Harmony is eroded by emphasis on discord. Faith is undermined by day-to-day emphasis on the attention-getting substance of crisis, lust, incompetence and sloth.[13]

Graphic

Closely related to journalism's passion for human interest and other entertainment values, is the craft's insistence on graphic qualities in the news. Basically, news people tend to shun abstract information apparently on the grounds that if it can't be seen, touched, or kicked, it probably isn't newsworthy. The problem is evident especially in television, with most every journalist in the medium feeling powerfully constrained to fill the insatiable little screen with a parade of active people and moving things.

Print shares the problem, with every press reporter preferring to write stories that require picturesque adjectives, busy verbs, and nouns that label real things and visceral actions. And if a great news photo is there to accompany the copy, so much the better. The presence of television as print's overwhelming news competitor in the modern media environment, has intensified the search for the graphic in print.

Citing the extreme case, Pierre Péladeau (whose Quebecor Inc. publishes the very successful and highly sensationalized morning tabloids *Journal de Québec* and *Journal de Montréal*) has suggested that the formula for publishing profitable daily newspapers is simply to follow and supplement television coverage of events. "Publishers in

Péladeau's tabloid newspapers seek to imitate TV-style news coverage by using rounded corners on photographs. (Le Journal de Montréal)

North America think a great deal of themselves. They forget television. Newspapers are not the most important medium."[14] Péladeau's papers are rich in photographs, often with rounded corners reminiscent of a TV screen, providing an affirmation today in print of what the reader viewed last night on television.

A talking head on television mouthing worthwhile abstractions, or a print story in a similar vein, can turn an alert audience into a gently snoring one. The implied dilemma here has more to do with an impoverished journalistic imagination, than with any inherently negative qualities in abstract information as such. The abstract can be written in a bright and interesting manner with, for instance, careful use of metaphor and example. As Curtis MacDougall has written: "There is nothing that cannot be made interesting in the skillful telling."[15] The sort of writing MacDougall has in mind demands hard work and sweated creativity, however, and few reporters seem prepared to make the effort. At least, they are not prepared to do so as long as there are plenty of easy-to-write-about disasters and theatrical House of Commons confrontations with which to play journalistic games.

Immediate

News must be about something that is happening right now. An event that occurred twelve hours ago is almost out of the time frame demanded by the competitive nature of electronic journalism, unless it can be updated and given fresh life by some amazing new development. One of the results of this crushing concern with "now" is that our yesterdays, our sense of history, and our appreciation of cause and effect relationships over extended periods of time tend to be lost in the rhythms of modern journalism.

Immediacy has another sense, a geographic one, and this is also an important component of journalism's sense of newsworthiness. All other things being equal, the news that happens closest to home receives the biggest billing in the local media. A local train derailment in a medium-sized city, for instance, will receive coverage in the home town press equal to a much more serious rail accident half a continent away in which human life perhaps has been lost.

In summary, these are the basic ingredients of news: audience interest potential (especially in the sense of a news scenario's "human interest" potential, but in terms of other entertainment qualities, as well); graphic elements that lend themselves to dramatic, concrete description; immediacy in time and place, and the sense of urgency that immediacy naturally stimulates in the reader's or viewer's imagination; and finally there is that neglected factor, inherent importance.

A Problem of "Narrowness"

Such a definition is too narrow to serve as a realistic guide in the daily selection of news information that members of an informed society ought to know about themselves and their psychological, spiritual, and physical environments. But for better or worse, that is the journalistic tradition. Only those starkly dramatic, concrete events properly fit the definition—volcanic eruptions, air disasters, bank robberies, and indeed the whole range of greater or lesser human agonies that one can imagine. Fortunately for society (if not for journalism) these are very much aberrations, and not always especially significant ones in the flowing and shifting of those long-term patterns that are much more descriptive of, and important to, our individual and social existences.

The problem remaining with such a definition is that very little that happens in the world actually meets the criteria of newsworthiness. Thus, there is a continuing creative struggle in every newsroom to force information into a mold that rarely fits. Borden Spears once suggested in his *Toronto Star* ombudsman's column that this practice is so well entrenched that a term for it exists in the jargon of the craft—"hardening" the news values. Spears described the process as being one of "pushing a statement just a little farther than the facts will warrant...usually in removal of qualifications; the part becomes the whole. It happens most frequently in headings, but almost as often in the first paragraph of a story when an editor considers that the essential point [of the story] is obscure."[16] In other words, shades of gray are removed, and information is presented in simplified (and therefore much more dramatic) blacks and whites. A man suffering a significant hearing loss becomes deaf in the journalistic telling of an industrial accident story, as Spears points out in his column. His example is a simple one, but when one considers that hardening of news values is a widespread practice in news information, the potential for distortion becomes very real, and very significant.

The problem becomes especially worrisome when already hardened news values in an original news account become harder still in the story's reworking and retelling through the national news system. Canada's two elite newspapers, the *Globe and Mail,* and Montreal's *Le Devoir,* provided a classic example of the process in their coverage in 1979 of social scientific research findings at McMaster University in Hamilton, Ontario, that compared Canadian anglophone and francophone values.

Among other things, this research looked into attitudes toward work and the workplace among 1700 Ottawa hospital employees. The study suggested that anglophone workers might be more interested than their francophone co-workers in career-related matters such as promotion and the prospect of acquiring greater workplace responsibility, as sources of satisfaction in themselves. Francophones, on the other hand, tended to view their employment (statistically somewhat more frequently than their anglophone colleagues) not as an end in itself, but as a means to support lifestyle and family-related values. The research, it should be noted, had been reported in a reputable academic journal before it was picked up for milling into news by the daily press.

Hardening from the original tone of the research report was obvious in the lead paragraph of the *Globe and Mail*'s front page story: "French-speaking workers in Canada may first need some extra training in the Protestant work ethic if they are to be promoted up the management ladder, according to a McMaster University study of worker motivation."[17] Responding a few days later (with no evident attempt to clarify matters with the original source) one of *Le Devoir*'s editorial writers further hardened the values of this news situation almost beyond recognition. The original *Globe* story, and the research it reported, was described as "a barely disguised political attack on Quebec so noticeably without scruples that all normal standards of journalistic ethics are ignored." The editorialist dismissed the research itself as "an intellectual cover to ordinary social prejudice."[18]

Several days later, the principal researcher in the McMaster work complained with admirable academic understatement in a letter to the *Globe and Mail*: "In spite of my cautionary remarks (to a reporter with regard to certain variables, and the inappropriateness of generalizing from the specific context of the research) the February 27th story provided many inaccurate and misleading pieces of information."[19]

The hardening of news values as a means of forcing inappropriate information into the narrowly defined news mold of journalistic tradition is a very common practice. Distortions both great and minor in the news consumer's perceptions of reality logically follow. While serious enough as a general phenomenon, it is precisely these traditions of hardened journalism that also lead to one in which violence in its various forms and guises, is routinely over-represented.

The Violence Question

It is an unfortunate reality that of all the information scenarios one might imagine as lending themselves to the processes that shape news, none lends itself so readily as one in which social or natural violence provides the strong and central theme. A bank robbery, an industrial explosion, a plane crash, the explosive and deadly arrival of a summer tornado in suburban Edmonton—these are events with inherent information elements that perfectly fit journalism's traditional definition of news.

Consider the case of a bank robbery. All the needs of news are there. It is, by its nature, an isolated event of short duration and therefore by definition it has temporal immediacy. It also is immediate in that it psychologically conveys a sense of physical proximity; a block away or a world away, a bank robbery is information with immediate meaning to the home town reader. More importantly, its very essence is action, with real people doing real things. The robbery is concrete, rich in details lending themselves to graphic description. Above all, with its abundant dramatic qualities (danger, the potential for death or martyrdom, for heroism or cowardice) a bank robbery is an event saturated with that mysterious news ingredient, human interest.

Of course, the scenario does not have to be a bank robbery. The same essential ingredients are present at a serious motor accident, a house fire, a construction site cave-in, or at an Iraqi battlefield during Operation Desert Storm. Nor does the scenario have to be one in which human beings run either afoul or amok within their environment. The ingredients of news can be as powerfully present, even more so on occasion, when nature unleashes a hurricane or volcano, or capsizes a drilling rig in a sudden North Atlantic gale. It is interesting that the natural event that threatens no human life, or damages no property, is rarely seen as newsworthy. (The journalist has no difficulty with the philosopher's conundrum about the tree falling in the forest. From the reporter's point of view, if no one is there to hear it, then the tree makes no sound as it falls. Most certainly, it makes no news.)

It is clear to anyone who reads the papers, listens to radio, or watches televised news programming that violence attracts journalistic attention. The notion of the violent event as the ideal news scenario may not be so obvious. Nor, is the reality that this peculiar proclivity conjures distortions in the news in a variety of ways.

Obviously, the simple over-representation of human and natural violence in our daily allotment of news may, with time, incline us to believe that the world may be a more violent place than, in fact, it is. The question of how much violence is too much and what violent content level in journalism is a realistic one, always will remain a subjective judgement call. But thoughtful efforts have been made to assess the situation, and the conclusions are sobering.

The Ontario Royal Commission on Violence in the Communications Industry, for instance, based its 1977 report largely on data gleaned from twenty-eight commissioned research projects, and from citizens' opinions offered in some 700 written briefs and hundreds more oral presentations at sixty-one public hearings.[20] Among the written briefs, an extensive submission by the Ontario Psychological Association was unequivocal in suggesting that the frequency of media depictions of violence exceeds social reality. Media content, including news and sports content, "contains a higher proportion of violence than is found in the normal daily lives of individuals." Furthermore, "It seems clear that in the eyes of many media people a major function or purpose of the media is for entertainment....Media people also seem to assume that violence is entertaining."[21]

One study of the news content of ten Ontario daily newspapers and nine television stations authorized by the Ontario Royal Commission found that nearly half the news items carried by these media dealt with violence-related subjects. In the language of the study: "News items carried on television and in newspapers focus on violence-related and conflict topics in almost half the news items carried (48.4 per cent for television, 45.3 per cent for newspapers). This figure is probably lower than many would suspect, but still is clearly in excess of the actual experience of most individuals and communities."[22]

Violence takes many forms, and it is useful to keep in mind that some of these can be less obvious than others. As has already been suggested, controversy and confrontation are two of these more subtle forms. They often stand as surrogates for violence. That journalism tends to favour the ingredient of controversy is evident, for instance, in its focus on controversial aspects of politics, such as those heated displays of stylized partisan anger in the daily House of Commons question period.

The potential for violence, and even the memory of past violence, also can trigger the journalistic imagination. This is evident in the coverage given to pockets of neo-Nazis when these occasionally emerge from our darker social corners. Relatively ineffectual individuals for the most part, but newsworthy for the images of Germany of the 1930s that they inevitably conjure; and for all the violent what-ifs of some hopefully improbable future resurgence of Nazism in force.

Pack Journalism and Stereotypes

The news tradition contains other elements with the potential to distort information in publication or broadcast. The urgency of the news process, for instance, rarely leaves journalists with sufficient leisure to examine each new story situation with fresh eyes. Too often, yesterday's story provides an all too convenient structure for today's events. As a result, America's military presence in Central America in the 1980s, for instance, was often paralleled with the completely different circumstances of Vietnam a decade earlier. Similarly, "Watergate" gives birth to "Irangate" and a burgeoning population of governmental embarrassments, in and out of the United States, all lumbered with the common suffix, "gate." In reality, scandal and cant are about the only common ingredients shared with the original episode.

In a related manner, journalism tends to label people stereotypically. In their haste to cover events and report them in their media as quickly as possible, reporters tend to see their news sources not as individual human beings with unique characteristics who, for instance, happen at the moment to be giving speeches on public platforms. Instead, they are "labour leaders" or "student radicals," "feminists," or "politicians." Such labels carry stereotypic attributes and when these prevail, as often they do in journalism's haste, information becomes formula-governed and patterned. The journalist tends to report what he or she anticipates, not what is actually there.

Some observers have suggested that in their haste to produce news and comment according to the the traditional demands of their craft, journalists not only write to formulas and stereotypes, but look over each other's shoulders while doing so. Clive Cocking, a journalist himself, has written an extensive diary chronicling journalistic behaviour during Canada's federal election campaign of 1979. Describing the phenomenon of "herd" or "pack" journalism, Cocking suggests that journalists tend not only to stereotype the people they cover (in this case, political leaders) but to take their lead in doing so from one or two well-regarded members of their own profession. The pack thus takes its form.

Former Progressive Conservative leader Joe Clark was especially savaged by this process in a world tour about a year before the 1979 election that briefly elevated him to Canada's prime ministership. Cocking singles out a well-known columnist with a vitriolic pen as a pack leader in the process:

> Out of it all the media stereotype that has emerged is of Joe Clark as another bumbling Tory leader. The coverage clearly was an example of herd—or pack—journalism. Most of the stories focussed on fumbles: Clark's verbal inanities, wayward luggage, chaotic travel arrangements, a near-disaster with a soldier's bayonet. From this distance it's not possible to tag... Allan Fotheringham as *the* villain, but from reviewing the stories it's clear he was one of the leaders of the pack. He seems to have gone on tour looking for botch-ups.[23]

The American scholar Todd Hunt criticizes what he has called the "event-centred" approach of twentieth-century journalism. He notes that human experience has more to do with continuing processes than with disconnected and isolated dramatic events. This more than anything else may be at the root of the communication problem that seems to exist between modern journalism and its audiences. As Hunt put it: "If a reporter is schooled to understand that he must go out and discover a 'packageable' truth, he is automatically limited in what he can see."[24]

The end result of journalism's continuing insistence on primarily seeking news in dramatic packages, and generally according to the demands of its traditions, has been wonderfully described by the historian and media critic, Daniel Boorstin:

> We need not be theologians to see that we have shifted responsibility for making the world interesting from God to the newspaperman. We used to believe that there were only so many events in the world. If there were not many intriguing or startling occurrences, it was no fault of the reporter. He could not be expected to report what did not exist
>
> Within the last hundred years, however, and especially in the twentieth century, all this has changed. We expect the papers to be full of news. If there is no news visible to the naked eye, or to the average citizen, we still expect it to be there for the enterprising newsman. The successful reporter is one who can find a story, even if there is no earthquake or assassination or civil war. If he cannot find a story, then he must make one—

by the questions he asks of public figures, by the surprising human interest he unfolds from some commonplace event, or by the 'news behind the news'. If all else fails, then he must give us a 'think piece'—an embroidering of well-known facts, or a speculation about startling things to come.[25]

For many people, Daniel Boorstin's gender-bound language of the mid-1970s may ring with already old-fashioned cadences in the modern perception of them, and in a way, this is appropriate. He describes an historic process that developed slowly over the course of a century of evolving news-shaping values. On the other hand, while writing at roughly the same time, Todd Hunt seems more modern and this, too, is appropriate. Hunt's concern is not so much historic in nature, but points to the final state of the thing in a journalism that has become rigidly bound to the formula of the event, framed in an immediacy of time and place, graphic and active in its basic information qualities.

When sudden events are ripped from the course of time, they inevitably and appropriately become the stuff of news. As we have seen, an important part of journalism's work (in Lasswell's metaphor) is to shine its searchlight across the social landscape, seeking out dangers and aberrations. In other words, it is to search for the unexpected, for the isolated event standing in newsworthy readiness for journalistic discovery.

The problem is that most human experience has little to do with events, as such. Mostly as individuals, as institutions, and as nations, our experiences reflect processes more than isolated events. Of course there are the occasional sudden departures of accident, illness, or the winning of a lottery, suggesting that events may punctuate our lives. But we do not live by events; we become whatever we become by process. By and large, our todays are the evolved consequences of our yesterdays.

The pressures on journalism to become ever less oriented to processes, and more to isolated events, are becoming more and more evident in an age of increasingly influential television journalism. It is this, more than anything that explains and describes the distorting influences that the practice of journalism brings to the social mirror it presents to us. The three-day riot in Los Angeles in the spring of 1992 was indeed an event. In fact, it was an event of epic proportions. But it was also the consequence of a complex and evolving process in the life of a great city. To the extent that journalism reported only the event, and ignored the process, it distorted the news we received. It also, thereby, distorted the way we learn to see and understand the world we live in.

NOTES

1. Borden Spears, "The Public Trusts Garbagemen more than Newsmen," *Toronto Star,* 12 July 1975.

2. Andrew M. Osler, "A Descriptive Study of Perceptions and Attitudes Among Journalists in Ontario," Ontario, *Report,* Royal Commission on Violence in the Communications Industry, vol. 3 (Toronto: Queen's Printer for Ontario, 1977), 7.

3. Richard Gwyn, *The Northern Magus* (Toronto: McClelland and Stewart, 1980), 319.

4. Harold Lasswell, "The Structure and Function of Communication in Society," in *The Process and Effects of Mass Communication,* rev. ed., ed. Wilbur Schramm and Donald F. Roberts (Urbana: University of Illinois Press, 1974), 84–99.

5. Canada, *Report,* The Royal Commission on Newspapers, vol. 1 (Ottawa: Supply and Services Canada, 1981), 21.

6. Walter Lippmann, "The Nature of News," in *Mass Media and Communication,* ed. Charles S. Steinberg (New York: Hastings House, 1966), 143.

7. Mitchell V. Charnley, *Reporting* (New York: Holt, Rinehart and Winston, 1979), 44.

8. Phyllis Wilson, "The Nature of News," in *Journalism Communication and the Law,* ed. G. Stuart Adam (Toronto: Prentice-Hall, 1976), 23.

9. Osler, *"A Descriptive Study of Perceptions and Attitudes Among Journalists."*

10. Ibid., 17.

11. J. Herbert Altschull, "What Is News?" *Mass Comm Review,* Dec. 1974, 17–23.

12. Gaye Tuchman, *Making News* (New York: The Free Press, 1978), 5.

13. Canada, *Report,* Task Force on Government Information, vol. 1, "To Know and Be Known" (Ottawa: The Queen's Printer, 1969), 10.

14. Peter Brimelow, "A Sensational Canadian Export," *Financial Post,* 18 March 1978.

15. Curtis D. MacDougall, *Interpretive Reporting,* 6th ed. (New York: The Macmillan Company, 1972), 12.

16. Borden Spears, "Hardening a news story can freeze out the facts," *Toronto Star,* 11 February 1978.

17. "Study finds francophone lacks anglo's passion for work ethic," *Globe and Mail,* 27 February 1979.

18. "Just what was said, from Lise Bissonnette in an editorial in *Le Devoir* of March 1, 1979," *Globe and Mail,* 2 March 1979.

19. "Work ethic reports distorted, Jain says," *Globe and Mail,* 7 March 1979. Professor Harish Jain describes his research (and strongly criticizes the *Globe's* reporting of it in this extensive letter to the editor). Jain conducted the research in collaboration with several colleagues at McMaster and McGill Universities.

20. Ontario, *Report,* The Royal Commission on Violence in the Communications Industry, vol. 1 (Toronto: Queen's Printer for Ontario, 1977), 4.

21. Ibid., 145.

22. B. D. Singer and D. R. Gordon, "Content Analysis of the News Media: Newspapers and Television," in Ontario, *Report*, The Royal Commission on Violence in the Communications Industry, vol. 3 (Toronto: Queen's Printer for Ontario, 1977), 604.

23. Clive Cocking, *Following the Leaders: A Media Watcher's Diary of Campaign '79* (Toronto: Doubleday Canada Ltd., 1980), 106.

24. Todd Hunt, "Beyond the Journalistic Event: The Changing Concept of the News," *Mass Comm Review*, April 1974, 23–30.

25. Daniel J. Boorstin, "From News-Gathering to News-Making: A Flood of Pseudo-Events," in *The Process and Effects of Mass Communication*, rev. ed., ed. Wilbur Schramm and Donald F. Roberts (Urbana: University of Illinois Press, 1974), 117.

Creating
Images:
Journalism
and the
Pseudo-
Environment

C
H
A
P
T
E
R

2

Writing more than sixty years ago, Walter Lippmann suggested that human beings create a "pseudo-environment," that they place between themselves and the overwhelming complexity of human existence. We do this because "the real environment is altogether too big, too complex, and too fleeting for direct acquaintance. We are not equipped to deal with so much subtlety, so much variety, so many permutations and combinations. And although we have to act in that environment, we have to reconstruct it on a simpler model before we can manage with it."[1] In the same passage, Lippmann added that much of our behaviour is in response to stimuli from the pseudo-environment, and "because it is behaviour, the consequences, if they are acts, operate not in the pseudo-environment where the behaviour is stimulated, but in the real environment where action eventuates." If this is true, it has disturbing implications for human well-being in this age of the multimedia.

Recognizing the existence of Lippmann's pseudo-environment standing between ourselves individually and collectively on the one hand, and reality on the other is just a matter of common sense. However, several difficult questions arise from the perspective of communications scholars. First, to what extent do the simplified and perhaps distorted images of the pseudo-environment touch and alter reality? Second, to what extent do the mass media play a role in creating the images of the pseudo-environment and in transmitting them to that real environment "where action eventuates?"

With regard to the question of whether or not there is a pseudo-environment, Lippmann restated the ancient truth that human beings, as individuals, directly experience very little of the world. Yet despite this, most of us have a comfortable, holistic sense of at-homeness in the world. Though few Canadians have been to such places, most will be able to conjure instant and familiar mental images of, for instance, a marketplace in Tehran, a temple in Kathmandu, or the view from Lenin's tomb on May Day in Red Square. By the same token, we all feel we "know" about Quebec nationalists, Irish Catholics, fundamentalist Muslims, American Republicans, feminist activists, the poor and the rich, and thousands of other divisions of the human family, even though we may have little or no direct experience of any but the few groups to which we ourselves belong. Our knowledge and impressions of all the many places and people in the world come to us as second-hand information.

The idea of the pseudo-environment was hardly new to Lippmann. In many ways, he simply restated a concept as old as Plato's allegorical cave where imaginary men "chained by the leg and also by the neck" lived assuming wall shadows cast by firelight were the world's realities.[2] Lippmann himself acknowledged a debt more immediate in time to the turn-of-the-century American philosopher William James. But where Lippmann ploughed new ground was in his recognition of a dangerous potential for the distortion of our perceptions of reality contained within the pseudo-environment.

Lippmann applied the word "stereotyping" to describe the process by which the mind creates pseudo-environment images. While recognizing the necessity of this process if we are to have even a simplistic and illusory comprehension of the world, Lippmann also attributed to it the worst effects of human ignorance, racial and religious prejudice, and hostility to groups and ideas that are strange and unfamiliar.

> There is neither time nor opportunity for intimate acquaintance [with all people, things, and ideas around us]. Instead, we notice a trait which marks a well-known type, and fill in the rest of the picture by means of stereotypes we carry about in our heads. He is an agitator. That much we notice or are told. Well, an agitator is this sort of person, or he is that sort of person. He is an intellectual. He is a plutocrat. He is a foreigner. He is a "South European"...
>
> The subtlest and most pervasive of all influences are those which we create and maintain in the repertory of stereotypes. We are told about the world before we see it. We imagine most things before we experience them. And these preconceptions, unless education has made us acutely aware, govern deeply the whole process of perception.[3]

Lippmann confidently joins a credible philosophic tradition in describing a pseudo-environment that parallels reality, and that reflects its simplified and frequently distorted images back into the real environment. However, he seems less certain of his ground when he tries to explain how images in the pseudo-environment are identified, shaped, described, sorted, and transmitted back to the real world. His uncertainty in this regard raises the most important question in any consideration of the mass news media and their social consequences. Do the news media powerfully shape, prioritize, and perhaps even create the images we receive and take as our realities? Or, as some commentators and many journalists believe, are news people little more than humble observers and chroniclers of the passing scene? Are their newspapers and magazines, radio and television stations nothing more than "media" in the true sense of the word—conveyors of thought and information not of their own making—and with little if any intrinsic social power?

Lippmann viewed the media as playing at least a modest role as shapers of pseudo-environment images, and therefore with powers somewhat beyond those of mere conveyors of fact and opinion. But Lippmann wrote at a time when print was the only medium of consequence, and radio as a public medium was in its infancy.[4] Thus, he saw the news media sharing the function of creating content in the pseudo-environment with many other communicators—lawyers, clergy, politicians, and bureaucrats, among others. Above all, he also saw the process as having an important interpersonal element, being largely the product of people communicating directly with each other in their homes, communities, and organizations.

Ellul and the Idea of Propaganda

Many recent media theorists have tended to make a stronger and more disconcerting case for the idea of inherent media power, however. Jacques Ellul, the French scholar, wrote a full generation later than Lippmann, by which time both radio and television were well established, and the world had experienced the appalling National Socialist and Communist applications of mass-mediated propaganda in Germany and the Soviet Union. Ellul saw the media playing a far greater role, even a dominant one in providing and shaping the content of the pseudo-environment.

An eclectic thinker and teacher, Ellul, who was born in 1912, taught history and sociology in the Faculty of Law at the University of Bordeaux for many years. His political activities included a leadership role in the French Resistance during World War II and service as deputy mayor of Bordeaux during the immediate post-war years. Ellul's early Marxist interpretation of the human condition, touched by a sense of the numinous, evolved during the 1930s into a committed Christian perspective on life. Something of a dialectic seems to have evolved as a result of the blending of these two creative forces, generating a form of technological determinism (the assumption that all things in life are shaped, ultimately, by available technologies) that gave structure to virtually everything he ever wrote.[5]

Ellul expanded the word "propaganda" and used it to describe the content of what Lippmann called the pseudo-environment. For Ellul, propaganda becomes nothing less than the effort by states and institutions in the modern mass society to modify values and behaviour on a culture-wide basis "by reaching and encircling the whole man and all men. Propaganda tries to surround man by all possible routes, in the realm of feelings as well as ideas, by playing on his will or on his needs, through his conscious and his unconscious, assailing him in both his private and his public life. *It furnishes him with a complete system for explaining the world,* and provides immediate incentives for action."[6] The italics are added to the original passage in order to emphasize that Ellul sees much more in propaganda than the traditional perception of propagandists as shabby purveyors of lies and half-truths, cynical manipulators of information on a small or large scale, with their audience being the innocent, passive, and unaware recipients of distorted messages.

Rather, Ellul sees propaganda on a broad scale as being necessary to the successful operation of governments and large private organizations functioning in all mass societies, even when these societies describe themselves as democracies. Moreover, Ellul argues that far from being the innocent and passive recipient, the individual in the mass society (often isolated in the modern world from such traditional value-affirming reference groups as strong families, religious communities, and so forth) who ultimately receives and internalizes propagandized information, actually "craves propaganda from the bottom of his being."[7] This for the simple reason that what Ellul describes as propaganda creates much of the world-defining content of Lippmann's pseudo-environment. As Ellul argued, without the mass media there could be no modern propaganda, and to be effective for the purposes of propaganda, the media need not be under state control, as in Nazi Germany or in the Soviet Union. A state monopoly, or a private monopoly is equally effective and he adds that the trend in the Western democracies to ever-increasing concentration in the private ownership of mass media creates a circumstance increasingly favourable to propaganda.[8]

Lest the reader suppose that Ellul presents an extreme case, it is worth noting that his point of view is not far removed in this context from that of the authors of the 1981 Report of Canada's Royal Commission on Newspapers who argued, in this instance with regard to the private concentration of media ownership: "Freedom of the press is not a property right of owners. It is a right of the people. It is part of the right to their freedom of expression, inseparable from their right to inform themselves. The Commission believes that the key problem...is the limitation of those rights by undue concentration of

ownership and control of the Canadian daily newspaper industry."⁹ It
is further instructive that this federally appointed Royal Commission
proposed as its solution a press law, the Canada Newspaper Act (a
version of which was actually introduced in the House of Commons,
but never passed) that would have placed far-reaching press controls
in the hands of the federal government.¹⁰

Implicitly, Ellul raises the disturbing notion that propaganda, or the
substance of the pseudo-environment, is not only powerfully influential and largely created by and through the mass media, but that we
have little capacity or willingness to determine the degree of accuracy
with which the images of the pseudo-environment reflect the world
of realities lying beyond.

This is true, regardless of one's personal sophistication or level of
formal education. The doctor, the research scientist, and the senior
civil servant usually have direct expert knowledge, professional contacts, and access to data bases and other rich sources of non-mass-
mediated secondary information, only within their own highly specialized areas of expertise. They are no better equipped than the
average person, however, when it comes to apprehending the great
world beyond. Like the average person in the street, the doctor or scientist must pick up the paper or tune in the TV news to find out
what is going on in the world outside the consulting room or laboratory. Beyond an ability to apply sheer intelligence and the skills of
logic and language, the educated sophisticate has no greater ability to
assess the veracity and quality of the mass-mediated images he or she
perceives.

According to Ellul, the modern world is characterized by what he
has called "technique," a concept that his translators have wisely
allowed to enter English in a state of ambiguity. Technique, as James
Holloway has suggested, "does not mean and is not reducible to
machines, technology, or this or that means or method for attaining
an end." Rather, as Ellul himself explained, technique involves all the
methods rationally arrived at and having absolute efficiency in every
field of human activity. According to Holloway, what this means is
the enclosure within the idea of technique of all human activity. "The
political, social scientific and economic world today is defined by its
relation to the world of technique. In a word, what determines our
politics, our economics, our science, our social activities is technique...no human choices determine or direct technique."¹¹ For
Ellul, propaganda is a vital aspect of the workings of technique; without it, in fact, there is no technique.

Innis and McLuhan

Ellul is not alone among modern theorists in ascribing such a powerful social role to the mass media of communication, and doing so from something of a determinist's perspective. His concept of technique sees propaganda (in effect, the content of all public communication, and especially that conveyed by the mass media) as a key element in the relationship between human beings and technique. Others would include the rhythm of the various technologies, and the forces of the economy. The idea that media systems and their technologies might be especially consequential in humankind's society-

Marshall McLuhan was prankster and prophet, often both at once. As the subtitle of his book *Understanding Media* indicates, McLuhan saw the media as physical and mental extensions of ourselves. (Canapress Photo Service)

forming relationship with technique, however, was first given important expression by two remarkable Canadians, Harold Adam Innis
and Marshall McLuhan.

McLuhan and Innis are not often examined in the scholarly literature in common context with Ellul, which seems something of an
oversight. McLuhan's sense of intellectual debt to Innis has been well
documented. In fact, McLuhan somewhat self-deprecatingly referred
to his own major work, *Gutenberg Galaxy* (1962), as a footnote to
Innis.[12] No similar intellectual relationship can be said to exist
between Ellul and either of the Canadians, but clearly Ellul's work
and that of Innis, and especially McLuhan, are of a common genre.
Ellul's subtle but darkening vision of an overwhelming technique
emerging with humankind's flight from rural simplicity to urban-
industrial complexity, compares usefully, for instance, with
McLuhan's more abstracted underlying theme of an equally complicated human migration from urban to electric. Noting that McLuhan
was a remarkably controversial figure in the Canadian university community of a generation ago, a contemporary has summarized his
scholarly contribution in language that could as easily describe the
contributions of Ellul: "It may be because he tried to show to what
extent we might be creatures of our own artifacts that McLuhan
began to appear to some as a liberating force and to others as a
threat."[13]

Another McLuhan scholar, Bruce Gronbeck, has noted that "early"
McLuhan (the McLuhan evident in *The Mechanical Bride,* 1951 and
continuing to *Understanding Media,* 1965) generated a "sensory theory
of mind and a linear theory of social evolution." These made possible
such propositions as: "communication media extend or bias human
perception"; "communication media bias human organizations by
allowing for monopolies of knowledge"; and "media therefore are
messages in the sense that they determine and embody what is to be
considered appropriate social organization at any given time." The
"later" McLuhan in Gronbeck's schema (essentially McLuhan the
essayist of the 1970s) allowed his concepts to evolve into a "relational
or phenomenological theory of communication." Thus in the later
writings, as Gronbeck would have it: "Communication media represent
the ordering of 'experiential perceptions' of individuals and of relations
between humans and [especially] their technological environments."[14]

McLuhan and Ellul thus meet at a place, call it "technique" or
"technological environment," where they seem to have much in
common, and where the mass media, especially the technologies of

the mass media, must be recognized as critically shaping the most fundamental circumstances of human existence. There is no question that in following their separate paths, Ellul and McLuhan have radically altered public perceptions about the nature and importance of the mass media among us. They also have given shape and inspiration to much mass communication research, in whatever paradigm or discipline, during the last four decades of the twentieth century. Despite their extraordinary contributions, it is interesting to speculate as to whether public imagination (not to mention mass communication scholarship) might have been so powerfully inspired by either or both of Ellul or McLuhan had it not been for pioneering pathways first carved in the intellectual landscape by Harold Innis.

> It was at the University of Toronto...that the study of media took a decisive turn with the work of Harold Innis. Nowhere until the publications of *Empire and Communications* (1950) and *The Bias of Communication* (1951), had the detailed history of the structural effects of communications media been given such range or breadth. With Innis'...work a founding theory of communications in socioeconomic and historical terms was finally available.[15]

Born in late Victorian rural Ontario, Innis became an economic historian. He was educated at McMaster University, University of Toronto, and the University of Chicago and taught at the University of Toronto from 1920 until his death in 1952. A stolid Upper Canadian conservatism is reflected in much that he wrote, along with the deterministic world view that was so much a part of the Loyalist mentality central to his heritage. Combined with these characteristics, and living in a stark and sparsely populated land, never far removed from nature's harsher guises, Innis' economic interpretations tended to cut to essentials. His search was always for simple and fundamental patterns in things, patterns imposed on nature by technology, and with profound resulting consequences for human beings. It is all reflected, in essence, in the titles of his works on economic history: *A History of the Canadian Pacific Railway* (1923), *The Fur Trade in Canada* (1930), and *The Cod-Fisheries* (1940), that occupied his scholar's talents for many years before he turned, quite late in his career, to questions involving communications. *Empire and Communications* was not published until 1950; and his famous collection of essays, *The Bias of Communication*, did not appear until 1951, the year before Innis' death.

One of Innis' most respectful critics, Dennis Duffy, has suggested that there are two characterizations of Innis' earlier writings. First, there is "the stimulation afforded by the concluding chapters of books whose subject matter scarcely appears engaging to non-professionals." Second, "Innis' writings abound in a sense of determinism." It is in those brilliant concluding chapters that the reader becomes suddenly confronted with far-ranging questions describing or suggesting societal rhythms that in turn are seen as being derived directly from—and determined by—the detailed economic patterns described in his earlier chapters.[16]

As Duffy has suggested, the idea of a common pattern is presented in *The Fur Trade in Canada,* for instance, where Innis sees the economies of early Canada and of the ante bellum American South (fur and cotton respectively) being deterministically and inexorably drawn toward the continentalist and capitalist centre. Duffy proposes that similar patterns, all with that inevitable deterministic quality of argument, are present in every one of those brilliant final chapters of Innis' earlier works. It is only much later, in *Empire and Communications* and in the essays of *The Bias of Communication,* that Innis shifts his attention from trade and geographic patterns, and proposes instead that everything eventually connects to the processes and technologies of communication. Ultimately, as Duffy again suggests: "For Innis improvements in communications media produced three effects: the progressive dislocation of cultures; the creation of successive knowledge monopolies by sinister interests; and (with the appearance of industrial technology), the increasing use of knowledge for violent purposes."[17] It was Innis' argument that society is shaped, or given its "bias," by innate information-shaping qualities in the communications technologies that it contains. Western history became, for Innis, a process of movement away from patterns of social organization favouring temporal stability (multi-generational stability across time as, for instance, the medieval church tended institutionally to exemplify) toward patterns far less stable across time, but remarkable in their capacity to establish complex order and organization across huge territories (the modern era's complex and ever-changing continentally scaled countries such as the United States, Canada, or China.)

The historic process of movement from one pattern, bias in time, to the other, bias in space, is punctuated for Innis by periodic technological innovations in the field of communication, such as the fifteenth-century emergence of Johannes Gutenberg's printing press.

The characteristics of the new technology determine social change, or as Innis himself has put it:

> We can perhaps assume that the use of a medium of communication over a long period will to some extent determine the character of knowledge to be communicated and suggest that its pervasive influence will eventually create a civilization in which life and flexibility will become exceedingly difficult to maintain and that the advantages of a new medium will become such as to lead to the emergence of a new civilization.[18]

McLuhan says much the same in this expression of his perhaps best-known aphorism: "...in operational and practical fact, the medium is the message."[19] None of this is very far removed from the mass-mediated propaganda of Jacques Ellul's technique that reaches and encircles all humanity.

The Sociological Tradition

It is significant that the weight of social scientific research findings in recent years increasingly supports the notion that the media are, in fact, very powerful players. It is also important to recognize that this is a fairly new development in scholarship. During the middle decades of this century, it was conventional wisdom among sociologists specializing in communications research that the mass media actually possessed little in the way of inherent social power, especially power to directly bring about change in public opinion.

Paul Lazarsfeld and his associates conducted a study examining voter behaviour in a county in Ohio during the presidential election year of 1940, and described what has become known as the "two-step flow of communication." The results gave important early credence to the concept of a relatively powerless mass media. This research recognized that:

> [I]nformal social relationships play a significant part in modifying the manner in which given individuals will act upon a message that comes to their attention via the mass media. In fact, it was discovered that there were many persons whose firsthand exposure to the media was quite limited. Such people obtained most of their information...from other people who *had* gotten it firsthand. Thus the research began to suggest a movement of information through two basic stages. First, information moved from the media to relatively well-informed

individuals who frequently attended to mass communication. Second, it moved from those persons through interpersonal channels to individuals who had less direct exposure to the media and who depended upon others for their information. This communication process was termed the "two-step flow of communication."[20]

Subsequent work by Robert K. Merton and others confirmed the concept that the dynamics of influence in society had more to do with a community's elaborate structure of opinion leaders, "influentials" as Merton chose to describe them, than with mass media content.[21] In keeping with the spirit of the time, Bernard Berelson also argued in 1948 that the more "private" a medium, the greater its capacity to effect opinion change. "The greater the amount of 'personalism' the communication act contains, the more effective it presumably is."[22]

Finally in this regard, it is perhaps Harold Lasswell's sociological view of mass communications that was most influential in the 1950s. In his seminal article, "The Structure and Function of Communication in Society," Lasswell identified three basic functions of social communication: "surveillance of the environment," "correlation of the parts of society in responding to the environment," and "the transmission of the social heritage from one generation to the next."[23]

It is most interesting that Lasswell saw the mass media (the newspapers, magazines, and radio of his day) as playing a relatively modest role in the broad process of social communication, especially with regard to opinion formation. This is evident in the following passage in which Lasswell is specifically concerned with the public communication of international political and diplomatic information and opinion:

> When we examine the process of communication of any state in the world community, we note three categories of specialists. One group surveys the political environment of the state as a whole, another correlates the response of the whole state to the environment, and the third transmits certain patterns of response from old to young. Diplomats, attachés and foreign correspondents are representative of those who specialize on the environment. Editors, journalists and speakers are correlators of the internal response. Educators in family and school transmit the social inheritance.[24]

Lasswell, Lazarsfeld, Berelson, and many other mid-century sociologists, whose work was methodologically linked within the context of the "structural functionalist" paradigm,[25] did much to build the rich accumulation of mass communications research literature, the cognitive map-making exploration that is our legacy. If one were to single out an important error in interpretation common to the majority of contributions to this body of literature, it would be the tendency to underplay the significance of mass media in the formulation of both individual and public opinion.

The Magic Bullet

That this should be so becomes understandable when one recognizes that much of the research in question was done in a psychological environment of negative re-evaulation of the "magic bullet" or "hypodermic needle" theory of media influence that had preceded it. This theory, prevalent at the time of World War I, and for several decades thereafter, postulated that mass-mediated messages, when presented strongly enough, could have instant and direct influence on the audience. "Shoot" the audience with a well-aimed media message, or "stick" the metaphorical media hypodermic needle in the collective social anatomy, and the result would be instant and predictable action or opinion change, according to the inherent potency of the message.[26]

The problem with such a view, is that it is grossly simplistic. It tended to create an equal and opposite reaction in research interpretations from 1940 until about 1965. Of course, there always are voices quietly, even unconsciously, raised against the Zeitgeist of any particular epoch. The "powerless media" theory that prevailed, mainly in sociological circles during the 1940s, 1950s, and into the 1960s, is no exception.

Gatekeepers and Agendas

Much of the so-called "gatekeeper" research of the middle years of the century (and the related "agenda-setting" research that continues to the present day) points to a more direct media influence than most of the dominant functionalist research would have allowed.

The metaphor of the gatekeeper compares editors and other journalists to news shepherds, opening the gate of publication and broadcast to a few select elements of information, and closing it to many others.[27] It was David Manning White who first analyzed news selection processes by examining the behaviour of the anonymous "Mr.

Gates," the wire editor on a mid-sized American morning newspaper, during a mid-winter week in 1949.[28] White's work confirmed that news selection is a subjective process, guided more by tradition and feeling than by any objectively applied standards. It recognized that while journalism may not be directly influential in telling us what to think, it plays a vital part in telling us what to think about. Journalism not only establishes important public agendas, it also prioritizes them. In effect, journalism is not only society's great news "gatekeeper," it also contributes in a major way to establishing and prioritizing society's agendas. Citing important work in the area,[29] Gaye Tuchman, has offered this comment on the importance of journalism's agenda-setting role:

> As studies…have indicated, the news media play an important role in the news consumers' setting of a political agenda. Those topics given the most coverage by the news media are likely to be the topics audiences identify as the most pressing issues of the day. This research on agenda setting tentatively indicates that the priorities in the media's ranked attention to topics may prompt the rankings given those same topics by news consumers.[30]

In the same passage Tuchman also notes the media's considerable power to create and shape "news consumers' opinions on topics about which they are ignorant."

For example, few Canadians, especially inland urban Canadians, had any knowledge or opinion relating to the centuries-old annual hunt of baby harp seals on the springtime ice off the coast of Newfoundland, and in the Gulf of Saint Lawrence. It was only when this ancient sanguine practice was brought aggressively to the attention of the mass media during the 1980s by various outraged environmental pressure groups (notably the International Fund for Animal Welfare) that the issue rose from near obscurity to extraordinary prominence in the agendas of the mass media. The resulting negative public opinion not only in Canada, but in the United States and especially in Europe, led to an effective boycott of Canadian seal pelts in offshore markets. Pressures eventually became such that by the end of 1987, Transport Minister John Crosbie found himself politically obliged to announce a permanent ban on the large-vessel harvesting of harp seal pups.[31]

Clearly, the agenda-setting and gatekeeping roles of the news media give them considerable influence over public opinion, and presumably in the development of personal opinion as well.

New Departures

Modern research is multi-disciplinary, exciting, and unbound to any specific or dominant paradigm. There are many interesting modern approaches, most of which have two themes in common. Generally, they recognize (with the "hypodermic needle" and "magic bullet" theorists) that under certain conditions, the mass media can be enormously influential. They also recognize (with the mid-century functional analysts) that the processes of influence are wondrously complex.

Closest to the sociological tradition, is research in the framework of the "uses and gratifications" paradigm, outlined in a 1972 article by Erik Karl Rosengren.[32] This paradigm can be seen as the logical evolution of earlier functional analysis work, this time using the computer as a tool allowing researchers to design and treat more ambitious and complex hypotheses. Research conducted within this paradigm extends findings of the early functionalists. In the process, it emphasizes that the audiences of the mass media are incredibly active, but that they attend remarkably closely to media content as well. It also points out that individuals in a given media audience use media content for a complex range of social and individual purposes. In addition, it seeks (thus far with no clear successes) to identify patterns that hypothetically exist with regard to audience attendance to specific media for specific need gratification purposes.

More importantly, much of this research reaches to ideas relating to differences in the "grammars" of the various media. This concept relates to the different inherent powers the media possess with regard to their effectiveness as information providers and as sources of social and personal influence. More than the earlier functionalists sought to do, or were able to do, researchers in the uses and gratification paradigm are interested in distinguishing between long-term and short-term media effects.[33]

Uses and gratifications might be regarded as a modern new beginning in mass communications research in the sociological tradition, but despite its worthiness, it is much too rooted in the traditions of an earlier sociological empiricism to be regarded as a truly new departure. Current research spans an extraordinary range of methodological approaches, some with obvious connections to uses and gratifications, and to the mid-century sociological empiricism, others with no connection whatsoever to this traditional mainstream.

In the first category, for instance, in research deriving from the empirical tradition, but creatively utilizing panels and complex survey instruments, George Gerbner and his associates observed important correlations between public perceptions of social reality and images of reality—symbolic reality—as presented in the entertainment content of television. As Gerbner has reported, with appropriate caution:

> Not just the less educated public, but even our professionals, more and more derive some notion of behaviour in certain situations from having seen these [fictional] situations frequently—sometimes once a week, sometimes once a day—on television. This is why we began with the research into [televised] drama…because we feel that is where most people get much of their information about life.[34]

Gerbner's work provides a strong validation for the existence of Lippmann's theoretical pseudo-environment and for the important role played by the mass media in creating (and conjuring back to the public mind in the real world) the images it contains. Though Gerbner's research has dealt primarily with the dramatic entertainment content of a single medium, television, the implications are obvious for all media in their news and public affairs functions.

It is important to recognize that all modern media and types of media content, are closely interlinked. The Canadian communications historian, Paul Rutherford, has observed that we live in an electronic age in which the various and separate media, and their respective content, be it in news, entertainment, or other formats, have converged into a single "multimedia." Noting from the historian's perspective what he sees as the very considerable power of the modern media, Rutherford has written: "Mass communication would not attain a general sway over the public mind, more properly popular culture, until the triumph of the multimedia."[35]

Semiotics and the Language of News

Outside the sociological tradition in communications scholarship, there are a number of intriguing areas of research and theoretical inquiry, each suggesting in its own way the existence of a profound media capacity to influence. While, for the most part, these have entered the arena of media effects discussion in relatively recent times, in many cases their origins date back many years.

There is, for instance, the body of semiotical literature dating to the writings of Ferdinand de Saussure in the early 1900s. It was de Saussure who gave us the idea that human cognition might be described in terms of a basic unit, that he called the *sign*. Consisting of a single word, or small group of words conjuring a single concept, the sign is described by de Saussure as "a two-sided psychological entity."[36]

Each sign has two parts. The first is the *signifier*, or obvious denotative part, which is objectively descriptive. More important in providing the full richness of meaning, however, is the second or connotative part, the *signified*, which is the perceived understanding of the sign, and bound in subtle linkages to culture and personal experience. Mid-century work, especially that of Roland Barthes, has demonstrated that semiology is not limited to the verbal language, but applies as well to the grammars of photography, cinema, and so forth, or to a combination of these with written or verbal messages. Semiotician, John Fiske, has explained the concept this way: "A signifier is the physical existence of the sign, what it actually looks or sounds like. The signified is the mental concept to which it refers and which it stimulates the receiver to produce. This last point is important, the signified is not reality itself, but a concept of that reality."[37] Thus, in semiotic terms, the sign "Coca Cola" contains the *signifier*, denoting a sweet brown-coloured soft drink. But it also contains (thanks to decades of carefully designed advertising, and purposeful associations in films and popular literature) a *signified* or connotative meaning connecting the beverage, and making it one with, all the mythic qualities of the American way of life. For an American, and perhaps disturbingly, for a great many Canadians, drinking a Coke becomes, semiotically, an act of patriotism.

While a substantial literature exists describing semiotic applications in advertising of all kinds, and in aspects of cinema and entertainment television content, little work has been done to describe its presence in the print and electronic content of the journalism of the modern multimedia. Since they are deeply woven into the myth and fabric of the culture, one has to presume that signs are not consciously selected or used in a purposeful, persuasive manner by journalists working through the daily process of choosing and presenting the news. This does not mean that the content of journalism is not rich in unconsciously included signs (Ellul's idea of encircling propaganda), connotatively directing our thoughts as we mentally respond to the information that journalism provides.

The present lack of published reports of research does not mean that research into the language of journalism is not proceeding apace. In Canada, for instance, William Leiss and colleagues at Simon Fraser

University are adapting traditional quantitative content analysis techniques to include a component of semiotics values.[38] And in Montreal, Maurice Charland is similarly seeking to develop a protocol that will permit empirical investigation of the phenomenon of meaning in mass media content, in the specific case of scientific and technological information, within a context of rhetorical theory.[39]

Linguistics

The theme of language and its symbols is more strongly developed, and with explicit implications for journalism, by scholars working in the field of cultural linguistics. English and Australian scholars, members of the so-called Glasgow Group, have been primarily responsible for this development.[40] This collective endeavour builds on the mid-century seminal work of the French structural linguist, Claude Lévi-Strauss, and is influenced by a Marxist historical perspective. It assumes the presence of many powerful connotative and directive properties in the meanings of words, in the grammatical structures in which words are presented, and in the communicative strengths and limitations of the technology used in their presentation. Receivers of mass-mediated messages, and journalists themselves for that matter, seem unaware of these influence-generating qualities at any conscious level. The Glasgow scholars argue, however, that in fact these message qualities can be recognized and codified through research, and that through analysis, a measure of the powerful and direct influence patterns they generate can be taken. In the words of the Glasgow Group, in this instance with reference to television news:

> The code works at all levels: in the notion of "the story" itself, in the selection of stories, in the way material is gathered and prepared for transmission, in the dominant style of language used, in the permitted and limited range of visual presentation, in the overall duration of bulletins, in the duration of items within bulletins, in the real technological limitations placed on the presentation, in the finances of the news services, and above all, in the underpinning processes of professionalism which turn men and women into television journalists.[41]

It is interesting that the Glasgow Group presumes that not only readers and viewers, but most journalists as well, remain unaware of the linguistic and language-related influence patterns that give structure to the messages of the mass media. The danger here, of course, is that one can easily move from an appreciation of the theory, to the presumption that the code it describes might be covertly manipulated to private advantage by unscrupulous governments, or by media owners in some sort of high conspiracy cabal with the forces of capitalism.

It is safer to assume, as Richard Hoggart does in his sympathetic but critical introduction to *Bad News,* that the news, as a cultural artifact prepared and written by members of the society, tends implicitly to affirm established social values and power relationships. This does not mean that information cannot be manipulated on specific and perhaps frequent occasions by groups or individuals with explicit purposes in mind. Nor does this mean that one should feel comfortable with journalism's apparent ignorance and lack of concern with regard to these matters. As Hoggart states:

> One gets the impression of a trade which has hardly ever thought out its own basic premises but continues, come hell or high water, to rest its case on a few unexamined assertions.
>
> Such as the assertion that their news presentation is "objective," a mirror of the reality outside, that they are merely neutral channels for presenting "the facts," the nuggets of each day's hard news. This is so inadequate as an explanation of the complex process in which they are actually involved that you wonder how people in the news business, or their bosses at the top of the major instruments of broadcasting, can go on making it.[42]

Whatever else readers may glean from concepts outlined in this chapter, they will come away with heightened awareness of the fact that the relationship between our society and its journalism is remarkably complex. Most readers will also have come to appreciate that the accumulated research of the twentieth century is heavily weighted in support of the hypothesis that journalism, in its various and pervasive print and electronic forms, profoundly influences society. The research supports, for instance, the proposition that journalism powerfully influences such elemental matters as the very manner in which we define ourselves in relation to others. Journalism gives us our sense of social dynamics; of how issues emerge and how values are shaped in the continuing processes of social definition and redefinition.

To paraphrase Hoggart, the assumption that the media are neutral channels is so remarkably and inaccurately simplistic that one wonders how so many people, including many journalists and others involved in media can go on making it. And yet, this is precisely what very many media people seem to do.

These matters were explored at a conference of Quebec journalists reviewing media coverage of Canada's continuing constitutional crisis in the spring of 1992. In the course of discussion, many of the participating journalists agreed, when pushed to it, that phenomena such as the hardening of news values do occur; and that the violent event typically constitutes the ideal news scenario; and that in the realm of politics—including Canada's constitutional politics—confrontation and controversy (as journalistic surrogates of violence) are greatly valued in the shaping of news scenarios. These are the images of political reality passed along to the voting public, and as one attending journalist put it, with widespread agreement from others in the room: "Surely people know that journalism does these sorts of things, and make allowances for it as they read or view the news?"[43]

Such an assumption is extremely dangerous in a time when as never before citizens must rely on the news media for knowledge of their world. They must do so, not only to acquire basic information about vital matters such as the progress of Canada's constitutional debate, but far more importantly, people must depend on the media for the continuing assessment of values and attitudes that accompanies the presentation of the news of the day. Collectively, the media provide the perceived cultural ambience that gives society its day-to-day sense of place, purpose, and definition.

NOTES

1. Walter Lippmann, *Public Opinion* (New York: Macmillan, 1957), 15.

2. Francis Macdonald Cornford, ed., *The Republic of Plato* (New York: Oxford University Press, 1960), 229–30.

3. Lippmann, *Public Opinion*, 89.

4. Walter Lippmann's *Public Opinion*, from which these concepts are extracted, was originally published in 1922. It is generally agreed that radio station KDKA was the first to begin broadcasting in North America, and it went on-air in Pittsburgh, Pennsylvania, in 1920.

5. James Y. Holloway, "West of Eden," in *Introducing Jacques Ellul*, ed. Holloway (Grand Rapids, MI: William B. Eerdmans Publishing Company, 1970), 7.

6. Jacques Ellul, *Propaganda: The Formation of Men's Attitudes* (New York: Vintage Books, 1973), 11.

7. Ibid., 121.

8. Ibid., 102.

9. Canada, *Report*, The Royal Commission on Newspapers (Ottawa: Ministry of Supply and Services, 1981), 1.

10. Ibid., 250–2.

11. Holloway, *Introducing Jacques Ellul*, 21–3.

12. Marshall McLuhan, in an introduction to Harold Innis, *The Bias of Communication* (Toronto: University of Toronto Press, 1964). McLuhan comments at page ix: "I am pleased to think of my own book *The Gutenberg Galaxy* as a footnote to the observations of Innis on the subject of the psychic and social consequences, first of writing and then of printing." The McLuhan introduction appears in the 1964 and subsequent printings of *Bias*, but not in the original published in 1951.

13. Derrick de Kerckhove, "Understanding McLuhan," *The Canadian Forum*, May 1981.

14. Bruce E. Gronbeck, "McLuhan as Rhetorical Theorist," *Journal of Communication*, Summer 1981.

15. de Kerckhove, "Understanding McLuhan."

16. Dennis Duffy, *Marshall McLuhan* (Toronto: McClelland and Stewart, 1969), 15–16.

17. Ibid., 16.

18. Harold A. Innis, "The Bias of Communication," *The Bias of Communication* (Toronto: University of Toronto Press, 1951), 34.

19. Marshall McLuhan, *Understanding Media: The Extensions of Man*, 2nd. ed. (New York: Mentor, 1964), 23.

20. Melvin DeFleur and Sandra Ball-Rokeach, *Theories of Mass Communication*, 4th ed. (New York: Longmans, 1982), 192. Interested students may also wish to see the original report of this research in Paul F. Lazarsfeld, Bernard Berelson, and Hazel Gaudet, *The People's Choice* (New York: Duell, Sloan and Pearce, 1944).

21. Robert K. Merton, "Patterns of Influence: A Study of Interpersonal Influence and Communication Behaviour in a Local Community," in *Communications Research, 1948-49*, ed. Paul Lazarfeld and Frank Stanton (New York: Harper and Brothers, 1949).

22. Bernard Berelson, "Communications and Public Opinion," in *Mass Communication*, 2nd ed., ed. Wilbur Schramm (Urbana: University of Illinois Press, 1960), 531–2.

23. Harold Lasswell, "The Structure and Function of Communication in Society," in *The Process and Effects of Mass Communication*, rev. ed., ed. Wilbur Schramm and Donald F. Roberts (Urbana: University of Illinois Press, 1974), 85.

24. Ibid., 87.

25. An excellent summary account of "functionalism" and the body of communications research which was produced within this general paradigm, is contained in Charles R. Wright, *Mass Communication: A Sociological Perspective*, 3rd ed. (New York: Random House, 1986), 12–23.

26. Ibid., 78–80.

27. Kurt Lewin, "Channels of Group Life," *Human Relations*, vol. 1, no. 2.

28. David Manning White, "The Gatekeeper: A Case Study in the Selection of News," *Journalism Quarterly*, Fall 1950.

29. Maxwell E. McCombs and Donald L. Shaw, "The Agenda-Setting Function of the Mass Media," *Public Opinion Quarterly*, 1972, 176–87.

30. Gaye Tuchman, *Making News: A Study in the Construction of Reality* (New York: The Free Press, 1978), 2.

31. "Fur trade opponents 'delighted' hunt over," *Globe and Mail*, 1 January 1988.

32. Erik Karl Rosengren, "Uses and Gratification: A Paradigm Outlined," in *Current Perspectives in Mass Communication Research*, ed. F. Gerald Kline and Phillip J. Tichenor (Beverly Hills: Sage Publications, 1972), 269–86.

33. Elihu Katz, Jay G. Blumler and Michael Gurevitch, "Utilization of Mass Communication by the Individual," in Kline and Tichenor, *Current Perspectives in Mass Communications Research*, 19–32. Here functional analysis pioneers Katz and Blumler, with Gurevitch, seek on the theoretical plane to bring the empirical tradition forward into the age of computer possibilities in research design.

34. George Gerbner, edited transcript of remarks, in *Report*, The Royal Commission on Violence in the Communications Industry, vol. 1 (Toronto: Queen's Printer for Ontario, 1976), 82–86.

35. Paul Rutherford, *The Making of the Canadian Media* (Toronto: McGraw-Hill Ryerson, 1978), 76.

36. Ferdinand de Saussure, *Course in General Linguistics*, ed. Charles Bally and Albert Sechahaye, translated and annotated by Roy Harris (London: Gerald Duckworth, 1983), 66.

37. John Fiske, "Semiotics: Its contribution to the study of intercultural communication," *Educational Broadcasting International*, June 1979.

38. William Leiss, Stephen Kline and Sut Jhally, *Social Communication in Advertising* (Toronto: Methuen, 1986), 149–229.

39. Maurice Charland describes aspects of his developing theory in an article, "Technological Nationalism," *Canadian Journal of Political and Social Theory*, 1-2, 1986.

40. Membership in the Glasgow University Media Group has expanded and contracted over the years since it first began publishing in the early 1970s. The key figures over the years, however, have been Howard Davis, John Eldridge and Paul Walton.

41. Glasgow University Media Group, *Bad News* (London: Routledge and Keagan Paul, 1976), 10.

42. Ibid., ix.

43. The exchange described here took place at a conference, "Are the Media Losing Their Grip?" sponsored by the Fédération professionnelle des journalistes du Québec. Montreal, April 26, 1992. The writer participated as a panelist in a session entitled, "Do journalists incite intolerance because of the way they report the news?"

The Press

and its

Freedom:

Evolving

Concepts

I t is now more than 360 years since the first irregularly published newsbooks appeared in London and more than 325 years since the first recognizable English-language newspaper, the *Oxford Gazette*, began publishing twice weekly for members of the court who had fled to Oxford to escape the plague sweeping London in 1665. In passing, it may seem odd to the modern media consumer, so accustomed to daily volumes of war, disease, and other mass-mediated accounts of human disaster, that the *Gazette*, founded in a year of unparalled agony, noted the plague and numbered the victims of a single week in just two poignant lines at the bottom of its first number (undated, but probably printed in early November of the plague year): "The accounts of the weekly Bill at London runs thus: Total, 1359. Plague 1050..."[1]

The *Gazette* moved to London after publishing just twenty-three issues in Oxford, and it survives to this day—not as a newspaper, but as an official vehicle for the "gazetting," or formal publishing, of government announcements. While the *Gazette* is of obvious historic interest, it did not have a particularly influential role in the development of English-language journalism. It was not until after Parliament ended press censorship by allowing the licensing act to lapse in 1694, some thirty years after the arrival of the *Gazette*, that England actually experienced the beginnings of the explosion in innovative daily and periodical journalism that was to become a central part of eighteenth-century public life.

The *Daily Courant*, which began publication in March 1702, is generally recognized as being England's first daily newspaper. Other dailies emerged at about the same time to compete with large numbers of weeklies, biweeklies, and triweeklies, most of unremarkable quality. One observer has described much of the journalism of the era as being generally "in the rough pioneer state—inadequate, poorly written and lacking in any professional standards."[2]

Despite the lapse of licensing in the 1690s, the political and social environment in which early eighteenth-century journalism was practised was not an especially honorable one. Freedom of press, in any modern understanding of the term did not exist. For many years in the eighteenth century, parliament refused to allow popular publication of accounts of its debates. This was not entirely without good reason, given the quality of much of the journalism of the era. The notorious stamp tax, first levied in 1712, added either a halfpenny or a penny to the price of a paper depending on its size. The government saw the tax not so much as a means of raising revenues, but as an "effectual means of suppressing libels."[3] It is interesting to recall that the stamp tax applied not only in England, but in the colonies as well, and ultimately became a major colonial grievance leading to the American Revolution.

Journalists and printers were regularly jailed under one official pretext or another, and as the eighteenth century progressed, the government commonly attempted to bribe newspapers by offering subsidies to them. Harold Herd tells us, for instance, that until the end of the eighteenth century, leading English newspapers of the day such as the *Morning Herald* and the *World* were in receipt of annual government allowances of £600. Even the *Times* is said to have annually accepted £300 in government largesse.[4] This era did, however, produce many individual examples of fine and innovative journalism.

A Growing Enlightenment

Early journalism played a vital role in the humane processes of the developing intellectual and artistic Enlightenment of the eighteenth century. The *Times*, which began publication in 1785, rose to become the standard of excellence in nineteenth-century English-language journalism throughout the world. Many fine publications, most in the form of periodicals published less often than the weekly or more frequent newspapers, were already influential in public affairs in the early decades of the eighteenth century. The *Tatler*, founded by Richard Steele in 1709, is an early example. Joseph Addison later joined in the venture and the two men became innovators in the use of the prototypical magazine-style publication as a vehicle for the work of the essayist. This form of periodical writing had a catalytic effect on the social and political reform in eighteenth-century England. The *Tatler* was one of a number of publications that Addison and Steele (individually or in partnership) were associated with during the first half of the century. Another of their important early ventures was the *Spectator*, a daily launched in 1711, that became a standard of excellence for daily journalism during its eighteen months of publication. Other great editors and essayists of the era included Samuel Johnson, Daniel Defoe, Jonathan Swift, and Henry Fielding, to mention just a few whose names have survived in public memory.

It is important to recognize that even though early English journalism achieved excellence, and its contributions were of great ultimate consequence, it was still a dangerous business for its participants. It became a matter of routine for even the finest early journalists, essayists, and editors to experience personal risks to their life and liberty as a price paid for their involvement in the journalism of public affairs. Steele, for instance, was expelled from the House of Commons of which he was an elected member. Defoe spent time in Newgate prison and was pilloried for journalistic offences in 1703. His experiences were hardly so severe as those of Nathaniel Mist who produced *Mist's Weekly Journal.* Mist's periodic critical outbursts, aimed at various well-placed persons and official policies of his day, landed him in jail and pillory on several occasions, and in 1728, he was forced to flee to France. While there, the press he left behind in England was destroyed by persons unknown.

As Herd has summarized, the painful emergence of journalism was "a development that was watched with unfriendly eyes by kings and Parliaments alike."[5] But journalism in an environment of developing liberty did, inexorably, emerge. As Harold Innis observed many years later, "the advantages of a new medium will become such as to lead to the emergence of a new civilization."[6] One might argue that Innis' observation puts the case of the influence of journalism and the printing press too strongly, perhaps with too much of a deterministic flavour. But there can be no question that the journalism of the early English press had a vital effect on the social change that characterized the English Enlightenment.

The principles established at that time remain at the root of modern journalism's understanding of its role in a democratic society. They also underlined the nature not only of freedom of press and expression as fundamental liberties, but of all the liberties that we enjoy in the modern era.

These principles are often described today as the "libertarian" theory of the press.[7] For all practical purposes, they have their origin in seventeenth-century England, a time of civil war as English society struggled with inexorable change. In effect, England was finally extricating itself from the grasp of medieval feudalism characterized by absolutist monarchical government and rigid hierarchical religious authority. It was moving—ultimately—toward more modern constitutional forms. The printing press with moveable type had been refined since its introduction in England in the 1470s.[8] It had been instrumental in focussing forces for religious change in Germany, especially in the person of Martin Luther. In seventeenth-century England, the printing press and the levels of literacy it helped to generate became the central weapons in a psychological and religious battle for hearts and minds that was possibly more consequential in the course of events than actual military confrontations between the Royalist forces of the Stuart kings, and Oliver Cromwell's Puritans.

John Milton

One of the earliest and finest statements advocating and defining the liberty of the press is John Milton's *Areopagitica*, originally delivered as a speech to the Puritan Parliament of 1644. Milton's perspective was a religious one, more medieval than modern in language and imagery. His argument against press licensing was primarily for the reason that the individual must be free to choose between good and evil as a part of his or her personal struggle for salvation. In Milton's words: "He that can apprehend and consider vice with all her baits and seeming pleasures, and yet abstain, and yet distinguish, and yet prefer that which is truly better, he is the true wayfaring Christian.... Assuredly we bring not innocence into the world, we bring impurity much rather: that which purifies us is trial, and trial is by what is contrary.[9] Later in the same passage, Milton makes it clear that the unhindered circulation of printed material is the key, arguing that even "those books...which are likeliest to taint both life and doctrine cannot be suppressed without the fall of learning, and of all ability in disputation."

Admittedly, Milton drew certain limits that might be expected of the Puritan mindset of his era. While he would extend freedom from licensing to all publications (primarily because he saw no practical way of doing anything less), he also saw no problem with post-publication condemnation of theologically inappropriate works, and presumably of their authors as well. He doubtless had the beleaguered Roman Catholics of his time in mind when he wrote this caveat: "I deny not that it is of greatest concernment in the Church and Commonwealth to have a vigilant eye how books demean themselves as well as men; and thereafter to confine, imprison and do sharpest justice on them as malefactors."[10] His view of the early journalism of the newsbooks was equally jaundiced: "Do we not see—not once or oftener, but weekly—that continued court-libel against Parliament and City...dispersed among us, for all that licensing can do?..."[11]

Milton's primary case in *Areopagitica* therefore was less than democratic in any modern sense of the word, but in the process of arguing it, he laid the foundation for the freedom of the printed word as we now understand the concept.

His first and most practical concern was to wonder where intelligent and literate censors might be found to read (prior to publication) the large volume of printed material being produced in

SPECTATORS at a PRINT-SHOP in St PAUL's CHURCH YARD.

Printed for Carington Bowles, at his Map & Print Warehouse, N° 69 in St Pauls Church Yard, London. Published as the Act directs.

This antique English cartoon print dates to about 1790. Its most likely interpretation is that the print shop owner is being arrested by the figure on the right, possibly for a printer's libel.

England. He also wondered how, in a world of imperfect human beings, any might be found with sufficient virtue to serve as censors, "unless we confer upon them, or they assume to themselves above all others in the land, the grace of infallibility and uncorruptedness."[12]

Milton's main concern was that men and women be allowed to choose between good and evil, for their salvation. It was because of this concern (ironically medieval in its expression), that he espoused, as the central and modern argument in his defence of free expression that despite all inherent dangers, people must be allowed to choose between good or evil in a free marketplace of ideas. "Why should we then effect a rigor contrary to the manner of God and nature, by abridging or scanting those means which books freely permitted are, both to the trial of virtue, and the exercise of truth?..."[13]

Milton gave first expression to the arguments that intellectual vigour and growth are the products of dispute in public debate. Even if a published concept is bad or merely mediocre, it may contain a worthwhile germ of knowledge that should not be snuffed out by any censor's hand. And even where no redeeming virtue is to be found in a printed work, its publication still serves the purpose of arming right-minded people with arguments that will allow considered rejection. As Milton put it, "such books are not temptations, but useful drugs and materials with which to prepare strong medicines."[14]

In summary, then, Milton argued against licensing or censorship in any form, mainly on the grounds that they are too cumbersome to manage, especially in avoiding corrupt practice. He also argues that good and useful concepts can only be identified by testing them in an open marketplace of ideas, where all ideas—good, bad, or indifferent—compete for public attention and acceptance. He then makes the important point that even the fundamentally unsound or bad piece of printed work may contain some useful germ of truth, that society would doubtless lose in the stifled environment of a licensed press. Even writing that is clearly worthless should be protected from the censor's pen, if only because public exposure may strengthen reasonable public opinion against bad concepts. (It would be for this reason, for instance, that one might defend the publication of a work such as *Mein Kampf*, Adolph Hitler's perfidious grand design for the Third Reich.)

Finally, Milton made one more argument in favour of an unlicensed press. It is a vital one, left to this point in this discussion to give it the special emphasis it requires.

Milton's Christian perspective assumed that God took an active and benevolent interest in human affairs, and that God had designed human beings as creatures of reason. Milton argued that truth and good necessarily will prevail, in the long run, over that which is bad and untrue. As he expressed the concept: "who knows not that Truth is strong, next to the Almighty. She needs not policies, nor strata-gems, nor licensings to make her victorious—those are the shifts and the defences that error uses against her power."[15]

Milton introduced a concept that later writers made more explicit. It is the belief that there is a self-righting process at work in the free marketplace of ideas. Most people will usually be inclined to select good and useful ideas from all they read, and reject the ideas that are bad or worthless. Thus, over the long run, the marketplace of ideas may cleanse itself, and no censor or act of licensing is therefore necessary.

John Locke

Given the central role of the printed word in the processes of the English Enlightenment, it is surprising that it received little direct mention in the writings of most of the great social and political philosophers who followed Milton in the seventeeth and eighteenth centuries. This is not to say that the concepts articulated by Milton were not confirmed (if inferentially) by many of these thinkers, most importantly by John Locke. Writing a generation later than Milton, Locke sought to define the individual's place in a society of emerging liberal values, and the Miltonian perception of a free press became refined in the process. There are three themes in Locke's writing that are important here.

First, a strong emphasis on the individual and an equally strong mistrust of collective social structures and mechanisms of state per-meate Locke's thinking. "Personally religious and ethically Christian,"[16] as Sabine has described, Locke seems to have taken it as a prior assumption (to be appreciated by all reasonable people) that God makes individuals, not societies or states. Thus, human rights are primarily the rights of individuals, the gifts of the Creator to the individuals called into being. Some latter-day critics have seen the absence of any detailed discussion of a concept so critical to his politi-cal philosophy as revealing cynicism in Locke. They argued that his primary concern was obsequiously to please his patrons by presenting them with a justification of their own positions of privilege, and thereby advance his own interests in the process. While there can be no doubt that the individualism espoused by Locke, and by most others who followed in the course of the eighteenth century, comforted the privileged classes of the era, it is unfair to presume the presence of cynicism. As Peter Laslett has explained:

> To John Locke this was a proposition of common sense, the initial proposition of a work which appeals to common sense throughout. It is an existentialist proposition, which men have not thought it worth while to question seriously until our own day, and it relies not so much on the proved existence of a Deity as upon the possibility of taking what might be called a synoptic view of the world, more vulgarly, a God's-eye view of what happens among men here on earth. If you admit that it is possible to look down on men from above, then you may be said to grant to Locke this initial position.[17]

No matter how the modern reader views this or any other justification of Locke's individualism, the historic fact is that emphasis on the individual and individual rights remained the centrepiece of liberal political philosophy in the English-speaking world throughout the eighteenth century, and most of the nineteenth as well. For the evolving liberal press philosophy, Locke's individualism meant that freedom of the press, and public perceptions of the purposes of a free press, came to be seen in terms relating to the needs of the individual.

Freedom of press evolved as an individual right, an extension of freedom of expression. From this emerged the libertarian view of a press that allowed individuals to freely establish newspapers or other periodicals, and to write in them, for their own individual reasons. This permitted people to communicate publicly with the relatively small audiences, viewed collectively as groups of indivduals, that the technology of the age allowed. The idea of mass-produced publications for anonymous mass audiences remained two centuries away.

Obviously the concept was already present in Milton's *Areopagitica*. Locke's contribution was to affirm it in the maturing libertarian understanding of the purpose of the press. The same might be said of the second important concept in Locke's political thought. While Milton saw human beings choosing between good and evil in a free marketplace of ideas as part of seeking salvation, Locke developed the concept (making it amenable to a more secular point of view), by suggesting that individuals are endowed at their birth with three fundamental rights—to life, liberty, and property. "Instead of a law enjoining the common good of a society, Locke set up a body of innate, indefeasible, individual rights which limit the competence of the community and stand as bars to prevent interference with the liberty and property of private persons."[18] Thus for the purposes of the developing libertarian press philosophy, freedom of press as an extension of individual freedom of expression becomes a matter of God-given—or natural—right. Similarly, Locke's elaborately constructed thesis on private property states that a natural right to private ownership follows whenever a person applies "the labour of his body and the work of his hands"[19] to the common pool of resources placed in the world by its Creator. Once again, by logical extension, ownership of a newspaper or other periodical becomes a matter of naturally endowed private right, and this Lockeian concept adds to the libertarian understanding of the press, its place, definition and purpose.

Finally, an important libertarian tradition grafted from Lockeian concepts to Milton's original statement has to do with the press as the necessary watchdog set to guard against inappropriate government ambition. Therefore the press must be free from government regulation or other interference.

Locke almost grudgingly allows that individuals must organize themselves if they are to have the full enjoyment of their endowed rights. He thus borrows the idea of the social contract from Thomas Hobbes and other writers, and permits government a legitimate though limited place as guarantor of individual rights. As Sabine has expressed, quoting in part directly from Locke:

> [C]ivil power can have no right except as this is derived from the individual right of each man to protect himself and his property. The legislative and executive power of government to protect property is nothing except the natural power of each man resigned "into the hands of the community," or "resigned to the public," and it is justified merely because it is a better way of protecting natural rights than the self-help to which each man is naturally entitled.[20]

As in other places in his work, Locke is vague in many aspects of his consideration of the social contract, this includes his uncertainty as to an appropriate form government should take. For the purposes of this discussion of press traditions and philosophies, it is sufficient to note that Locke's social contract notions were incorporated into the libertarian understanding of the press and importantly established the press as the public watchdog set against inappropriately ambitious governments. This point is perhaps most explicitly made in the Jeffersonian language, largely borrowed from Locke, of the first amendment to the constitution of the United States.

Thus with Locke's notions of individual and natural rights in person and property, and the social contract, added to Milton's earlier defence of an unlicensed and self-righting press, the basic ingredients of the libertarian understanding of press freedom and press purpose fell into place.

Fox's Libel Act

Edmund Burke, the great conservative eighteenth-century constitutionalist, affirmed the model as Locke left it, and the libertarian view of the press gradually received enshrinement in law as the era of the Enlightenment passed into the nineteenth century. As we have seen, Milton's opposition to press licensing eventually received recognition in law when Parliament allowed the licensing act to lapse in 1694. Perhaps no less could be done, as the principle of freedom of expression in Parliament had been formally recognized a few years earlier in the Bill of Rights of 1689. As we have seen, however, such moves in no way liberalized official behaviour toward the press, and it was only by a process of gradual erosion during the eighteenth and nineteeth centuries that liberal journalism gained a secure place before the law.

Burke, working with Charles James Fox, Lord Erskine, and others, brought about the first important move toward reform of English libel law in 1792.[21] Fox's Libel Act, as it became known, placed the determination of whether or not a controversial published work was libelous, in the hands of a jury. Such matters previously had been determined by a judge alone, but as Kesterton has pointed out, the courts continued for a number of years to find for the establishment in such cases.

Nevertheless, reform had become an irresistible force for the long run. Public opinion, as serviced by a maturing press, placed government in a position where it was more or less politically obliged by 1803 to open Parliament to routine and orderly processes of journalistic coverage. Places were set aside that year for reporters in the public gallery. Finally, the Libel Act of 1843 made truth without malice a defence in libel proceedings, thus creating the basis for a secure legal environment for liberal journalism, and making it possible to begin a process that continues today to define journalism's reasonable limits under the law.[22]

John Stuart Mill

Practical processes of the law and politics aside, it is surprising that after Locke there were few developments of consequence in the political philosophic literature relating to libertarian press concepts until the appearance of John Stuart Mill's utilitarian essays toward the middle of the nineteenth century.

In many ways, Mill's arguments are as concerned with the rights of the individual as those of his predecessors. He notes in the early pages of *On Liberty*, for instance, that the individual's appropriate mistrust of government extends to the collective force of society itself that "can and does execute its own mandates: and if it issues wrong mandates instead of right, or any mandates at all in things with which it ought not to meddle, it practises a social tyranny more formidable than many kinds of political oppression."[23] If there were any doubt as to his position with regard to the individual, Mill placed himself firmly within the tradition when he suggested that "the sole end for which mankind are warranted, individually or collectively, in interfering with the liberty of action of any of their number, is self-protection."[24]

The important difference in Mill's approach lies in the utilitarian philosophy that he inherited from his father, James Mill, and his father's friend and associate, Jeremy Bentham. At its simplest reduction, the utilitarian view maintains that to always seek the greatest happiness for the greatest number of people is the only way that society (and more particularly, its governments) can ensure that mandates do not become tyrannical. Adherence to this utilitarian "greatest happiness principle" obliges Mill to go beyond the individualists of the Enlightenment and to consider that while human beings may be individuals, they are social beings also. Freedom of expression thus becomes not merely an individual right, but a social duty.

> [T]he peculiar evil of silencing the expression of an opinion is, that it is robbing the human race: posterity as well as the existing generation; those who dissent from the opinion still more than those who hold it. If the opinion is right, they are deprived of the opportunity of exchanging error for truth: if wrong, they lose, what is almost as great a benefit, the clearer perception and livelier impression of truth, produced by its collision with error.[25]

Mill affirms the libertarian tradition, completing it with his utilitarian insistence on the social as well as the individual nature of the human condition, with these four summary observations on the purpose of liberty of expression.

1.   A silenced opinion may be true, and to deny this possibility is "to assume our own infallibility."

2.   While a silenced opinion may be in fundamental error, it may contain some element of truth, "and since the general or prevailing opinion on any subject is rarely or never the whole truth, it is only by collision of adverse opinions that the remainder of the truth has any chance of being supplied."

3.   Even when a prevailing opinion is the whole truth, if it is never contested, it will be "held in the manner of a prejudice, with little comprehension or feeling of its rational grounds."

4.   The very meaning and purpose of a good and widely held doctrine [a system of values relating to religion or to a benign political process] will fall into the "danger of being lost, or enfeebled, and deprived of its vital effect on the character and conduct: the dogma becoming a mere formal profession, inefficacious for good, but cumbering the ground, and preventing the growth of any real and heartfelt conviction, from reason or personal experience."[26]

The libertarian press philosophy thus becomes complete with Mill. Milton's individualism is affirmed and expanded by Locke's more secularized concept of the individual's natural rights to life, liberty, and property. Locke's perception of a social contract adds the notion that a free press is not only as Milton believed, an endowed personal right, but also a practical necessity to serve as a watchdog set on the ambitions of those who govern.

Especially in Milton, but also inferred in Locke's description of the social contract, is the optimistic notion of a self-righting process eliminating any need for censorship or other controls. To this, Mill at last adds the utilitarian's sense of the social need balancing the individual right. In doing so, it is somewhat ironic that Mill also warns against what he correctly saw as a growing emphasis on the social, as opposed to the individual, value in these matters.

In his introduction to *On Liberty*, he implied that this concern motivated him to write this essay in the first place:

There is...in the world at large an increasing inclination to stretch unduly the powers of society over the individual, both by force of opinion, and even by that of legislation; and as the tendency of all the changes taking place in the world is to strengthen society, and diminish the power of the individual, this encroachment is not one of the evils which tend spontaneously to disappear, but on the contrary to grow more and more formidable.[27]

The New Collectivity

Whether or not one shares with Mill the notion that the developing nineteenth-century emphasis on social values constituted an evil encroachment on individualism, such a process was clearly under way, and has continued to work its effect down to our own time. Mill was a contemporary of Karl Marx, whose remarkable theories of historic and economic necessity made powerful moral statements with close and profound humane parallels to traditional Christian social principles. Ironically, these theories have been influential in creating a major force of political totalitarianism in much of our own century, with its coincidental reduction of the human individual to the level of cipher wherever it held sway.

Marx was a product of his time—a time of exploding population growth, and with it the emergence of the modern urban mass, with many of its anonymous members living in conditions of extraordinary poverty and deprivation. This was also a time of ascendant secularism and materialistic notions of human progress; of the emergence of titanic empires, with equally titanic governments to administer them. There can be little wonder that Marx's revolutionary philosophy, and the gentler democratic socialism to which it also gave birth, were essentially pessimistic and primarily saw only in the collectivity what little hope there might be for humanity.

The twentieth century has seen the sources of pessimism become more numerous and more complex. Economic depression and the horrors of mechanized warfare provide alternating scenarios of human hopelessness on a global scale. Marxist theory was corrupted into Soviet totalitarian reality, and at the other end of the political spectrum, Fascist and National Socialist alter egos emerged. Even in the democracies during this time and by the 1930s, a forlorn Charlie Chaplin and a fragile Mickey Mouse seemed to stand apart as the last representations of human individuality. The helpless characters created by Émile Zola in the last century, and by Albert Camus, Thomas Mann, and many other great literary minds of the twentieth century, came even closer to pessimistic modern perceptions of ordinary individual reality.

The nineteenth century also gave birth to the objectifying academic disciplines of psychology and sociology, the latter receiving its initial structure in the seminal writings of Émile Durkheim, especially in his major opus, *The Division of Labor in Society*, first published in 1893. Durkheim proposed that urban growth and the complexities of industrialization combined to rearrange human relationships in society. Becoming less important, if not disappearing entirely, was an older and more homogeneous form Durkheim called mechanical solidarity, in which the similarities joining people were more marked than the differences separating them and in which all shared in a common structure of beliefs, values, and traditions.

Replacing these older patterns in Durkheim's scheme, was a new organic solidarity in which the complex work relationships of maturing urban industrialism produced, in theory at least, a population of increasingly specialized individuals. These people would be specialized not only in their relationships within the workplace, but in their social relationships as well. In other words, an age of true individualism, of social heterogeneity, emerges with the paradoxical effect of isolating the individual and greatly reducing his or her consequence in the huge social collectivity that is the modern division of labour.[28] It is especially interesting to the student of mass communications that Durkheim saw pathological possibilities in the shift from the mechanical to the organic form of social solidarity. It is possible, he proposed, that individuals might become so isolated, in some circumstances, as to be unable to relate to one another or to society in any meaningful way. At the personal level, suicide and other forms of personal self-destructive behaviour would be symptomatic of this "anomie," as Durkheim labeled it. Perhaps by extension, violent social behaviour, street crime, and so forth would be collective manifestations. Be that as it may, Durkheim warned: "Collective sentiment becomes more and more impotent in holding together the centrifugal tendencies that the division of labor is said to engender, for these tendencies increase as labor is more divided, and, at the same time, collective sentiments are weakened."[29]

In a time of great change, Durkheim's sociology influenced the developing body of social theory of mass communication. Early twentieth-century ideas about powerful "magic bullet" or "hypodermic needle" media (discussed in chapter 2) were based in Durkheim's images of isolated, anomie-stricken individuals, desperately seeking some form of meaningful bonding with others. They found the bond, at least in theory, in the common ground of mass media content. In the mid-century era of the popular "powerless media" research presumption, Durkheim's ideas were still at work describing the huge, passive, and anonymous mass audience, that most of the social research of the time took for granted. Durkheim's fundamental concepts arguably are still influencing current communications research, which continues to assume a mass and heterogeneous audience of anonymous and isolated individuals that actively use the content of the multimedia for their individual purposes, but at the same time share in a common media-conjured world view.

Whether one sees the mass media as cultural artifacts of place and time, or as catalysts in the chemistry of social change, or as the actual instruments of change, one observation will hold true across the range of possibilities: The values and attitudes held within a society toward its institutions also will apply to its media institutions. Thus, as we have seen, the libertarian press philosophy was a natural companion piece to the optimistic individualism of the Enlightenment that prevailed, to the benefit of at least society's more fortunate members, well into the nineteenth century. But as the world moved into the modern age of the mass society[30] with its relative pessimism, its secularism, and above all, its emphasis on the perceived collective social good, as opposed to the perceived good of the individual—changes in attitudes toward the media also were inevitable.

Criticisms of the libertarian press philosophy were being expressed in various quarters before the ink was dry on Mill's *On Liberty*, but it was not until the late 1940s that articulate theoretical alternatives began to emerge. Britain's first Royal Commission on the Press made an important contribution when it reported in 1949 with its recommendations relating to a national press council.[31] In Canada there has been a rich series of Royal Commission reports and other government studies, beginning with the Report of the Royal Commission on National Development in the Arts, Letters and Sciences in Canada in 1950 (The Massey Report) and concluding—for the time being, at least—with the 1986 Report of the Task Force on Broadcasting Policy (the Caplan-Sauvageau Report).

Among the more influential documents, however, was a major report produced at the University of Chicago in 1947 by the Commission on the Freedom of the Press.[32] Funded by Time Inc. and Encyclopedia Britannica, this commission deliberated for five years between 1942 and 1947 under the leadership of Robert M. Hutchins, then chancellor of the University of Chicago. The Hutchins Report by no means stands as the most scholarly or insightful study, but as the first modern American offering of consequence, it may have been the most influential. The Hutchins group gave a lasting structure to libertarianism's collective alternative. It also gave it a name: the Social Responsibility Theory of the Press.

Social Responsibility

Many apologists for the social responsibility theory have suggested that it extends principles already well established in libertarian thought. In fact, the newer position constitutes a radical departure, as is indicated in these words from the Hutchins Report:

> The notion of rights, costless, unconditional, conferred by the Creator at birth, was a marvelous fighting principle against arbitrary governments and had its historical work to do. But in the context of an achieved political freedom the need of limitation becomes evident. The unworkable and invalid conception of birthrights, wholly divorced from the condition of duty, has tended to beget an arrogant type of individualism which makes a mockery of every free institution, including the press.[33]

In this single paragraph, the Hutchins group effectively provided the tone of much of the criticism of the libertarian viewpoint that had emerged since the end of the nineteenth century. The key is in the gradual distancing, ironically a process which began early in the years of the Enlightenment, that developed between Western society and the idea of a concerned, benevolent, and immediately involved deity—the God envisaged by Milton.

To an increasingly secular society, and to its philosophers, authors, and artists, it became increasingly difficult to support the optimistic individualism of both Milton and Locke based on the prior assumption of endowment at birth with inalienable rights to life, liberty, and property. It became equally difficult to accept related notions, all vital to the libertarian world view, such as the individual as the Creator's special masterwork, inclined by nature to be reasonable and to choose the good. With the removal of these basic foundation blocks, the whole idea of a self-righting process lost any validity it might have had, and libertarianism lost its basis in logic.

For good or ill, a much more pessimistic view of humankind and of uncontained journalism emerged. This notion is again evident in the words of the Hutchins Commission: "Freedom of the press to appeal to reason is liable to be taken as freedom to appeal to public passion, ignorance, prejudice, and mental inertia."[34] It is not always recognized in scholarly comment on the Hutchins report that the social responsibility theory was no mere extension of the libertarian tradition as Theodore Peterson argues when he suggests that social responsibility "is largely a grafting of new ideas onto traditional theory."[35] In fact, radical departures from tradition are proposed in at least three areas.

First, the Hutchins report argues that it is not sufficient to define freedom negatively, as is done primarily by implication in the libertarian tradition. Rather, freedom must be defined positively. In other words, the negative concept of *freedom from* (total freedom with a few specific and clearly stated legal limitations) must be replaced by *freedom for* (freedom perceived as having a positive purpose or purposes, a freedom that will actively guide people toward self-improvement and desirable social goals). The commissioners were cautious in developing this concept, stating that "a free press is free for the expression of opinion in all phases."[36]

In another context, they added considerable substance to their perception of a positively free media system when they noted that the media collectively constitute an educational instrument in society, and must act like educators by stating and clarifying the ideals toward which the community should aim.[37]

Second, in a reversal of the traditional libertarian position, the Hutchins group pointed to a need for government involvement in guaranteeing a socially responsible press. While the report admits that "any power capable of protecting freedom is also capable of infringing freedom,"[38] it also argues that the main question is whether press performance can any longer be left unregulated.[39]

The commissioners saw government legitimately acting in three possible capacities. First, as an enabler and without interfering in press activities, government may act to improve conditions under which they occur. Second, as a provider of media content, and perhaps of media systems, government may and should be involved in press comment and news supply, "not as displacing private enterprise, but as a supplementary source. In doing so, it may provide standards for private emulation." Third, and most draconian, new legal processes and preventions could be used as aids to checking the more obvious abuses of the press.[40] In the same passage, and in defence of these proposals, the commissioners suggest, "Such legal measures are not in their nature subtractions from freedom but, like laws which help clear the highways of drunk drivers, are means of increasing freedom, through removing impediments to the practice and repute of the honest press."

Third, the Hutchins group helped to reshape opinion about the very purpose of press freedom. For the libertarian, press freedom was oriented to the individual, and seen as a two-way process involving the paired rights to express ideas freely and to freely receive available information and opinion. Social responsibility predictably moves toward the collective value and emphasizes the relatively passive right of society to be informed on matters of consequence. Freedom of individual expression loses much of the importance placed upon it in libertarian thought; the concept of a two-way flow of information and opinion from individual to society and back again through the media is significantly devalued.

W.E. Hocking, a member of the Chicago commission, provided a sense of all of this when he wrote: "The phrase 'freedom of the press' must now cover two sets of rights....With the rights of editors and publishers to express themselves there must be associated a right of the public to be served with a substantial and honest basis of facts for its judgement of public affairs. Of these two, it is the latter which today takes precedence in importance."[41] The more recent concept of a passive public right to know thus was granted supremacy over individual free expression as the primary raison d'être of free news media.

The Five Tenets

Along with the three major changes that social responsibility sought to impose upon libertarianism, there are the well-known tenets of a socially responsible press. These five tenets have influenced public debate on the proper nature and purpose of a free press in the Western democracies in the four decades since their original publication.[42]

First, the news system has a responsibility to provide "a truthful, comprehensive and intelligent account of the day's events in a context which gives them meaning." There is no great departure from the libertarian ideal here. This first tenet simply stands as a plea for sound journalism that links the events of the day into a meaningful package, presented in a manner the ordinary reader will understand. There is an implied and somewhat pessimistic assumption here that the libertarians did not share. It is that the average reader needs to have his or her information carefully prepared and predigested, in the first place. As the commissioners explained, "It is no longer enough to report the fact truthfully. It is now necessary to report the truth about the fact."

Second, the news media must provide "a forum for the exchange of comment and criticism." Here the commissioners argued that in an age of very large media where chain and group situations tend to concentrate media ownership in uncomfortably few hands, it is vital that the media strive to present a broad range of information, and especially to represent many points of view. It is important to note, however, that the commissioners were not proposing a complete opening of news and comment pages or broadcast time to all comers. This caution is offered, in keeping with the social responsibility theorist's perception of a relatively passive audience and its right to know. "The press cannot and should not be expected to print everybody's idea. But the giant units [news media] can and should assume the duty of publishing significant ideas contrary to their own."

Third, the news media have a responsibility to project a representative picture of the constituent groups in society. In a world where a few large media organizations serve big populations, it becomes vitally important to ensure that the needs, interests, and opinions of all ethnic, religious, economic, and other significant groups in the community are reasonably and accurately reflected in media content.

Fourth, the news media have a responsibility with regard to the "presentation and clarification of the goals and values of society." This key tenet emphasizes the collective as opposed to the individual need and reflects twentieth century pessimism about the willingness or capacity of individuals to think for themselves. Here, the social responsibility theory departs most significantly from the libertarian tradition. This tenet proposes that "the agencies of mass communication are an educational instrument, perhaps the most powerful there is; and they must assume a responsibility like that of educators in stating and clarifying the ideals toward which the community should strive."

Fifth, for the media to perform effectively, they must have "full access to the day's intelligence." This assertion is reasonable in the eyes of both the libertarian and the modernist.

Apart from the obvious changes in philosophy that social responsibility implies, the five tenets also suggest a considerable extension of the news media's responsibility to their readers, listeners, and viewers. No longer is it enough for free media simply to exist as brokers in the exchange of information and opinion among the individuals in society. Instead, if the arguments of the social responsibility theorists are to be accepted, journalism must be seen as a source of influence and consequence in itself. It also becomes socially accountable for its actions to society's agent in the form of government, if necessary.

Most importantly, news media are no longer merely conveyors of information and opinion, but as educational agencies, the media have important responsibilities relating to the preparation and ordering of public information, and in guiding the development of sound public opinion.

The social responsibility theory articulated by the Chicago group in the 1940s, has strongly influenced the content of many subsequent government and privately sponsored media studies in the United States, Canada, and other Western jurisdictions. Social responsibility has thus greatly influenced the shaping of public policy during the past four decades. As we shall see, however, it is not at all certain that social responsibility theory has replaced libertarian values in the hearts of journalists.

NOTES

1. Harold Herd, *The March of Journalism* (Westport, CT: Greenwood Press, 1973), 32-4.

2. Ibid., 37.

3. Ibid., 43.

4. Ibid., 64.

5. Ibid., 11.

6. Harold A. Innis, "The Bias of Communication," *The Bias of Communication* (Toronto: University of Toronto Press, 1951), 34.

7. Fred S. Siebert, "The Libertarian Theory of the Press," in Fred S. Siebert, Theodore Peterson, and Wilbur Schramm, *Four Theories of the Press* (Urbana: University of Illinois Press, 1956), 39-71. (The eighth printing, 1973, is quoted here. Though essentially a criticism, Siebert's discussion of the system of press values which emerged between the time of Milton and the dawning of the twentieth century is one of the best concise essays on the subject.)

8. The printing press with moveable type was invented by Johannes Gutenberg and introduced in Germany in the mid-fifteenth century. William Caxton adapted it for the English language in 1476.

9. John Milton, "Areopagitica," in *Milton*, ed. Maynard Mack (Englewood Cliffs: Prentice-Hall, 1956), 81.

10. Ibid., 78.

11. Ibid., 85.

12. Ibid., 82.

13. Ibid., 84.

14. Ibid., 82.

15. Ibid., 97.

16. G. H. Sabine, *A History of Political Theory*, 3rd ed. (New York: Holt Rinehart and

Winston, 1966), 518.

17. John Locke, *Two Treatises of Government*, ed. Peter Laslett (Toronto: Mentor Books, 1965), 106.

18. Sabine, *A History of Political Theory*, 529.

19. Locke, *Two Treatises of Government*, 329.

20. Sabine, *A History of Political Theory*, 532.

21. Herd, *The March of Journalism*, 75–6.

22. Wilfred H. Kesterton, *Law and the Press in Canada* (Toronto: McClelland and Stewart, 1976), 5.

23. John Stuart Mill, *On Liberty*, ed. Russell Kirk (Chicago: Gateway Editions, 1953), 5.

24. Ibid., 11.

25. Ibid., 21.

26. Ibid., 65–6.

27. Ibid., 17.

28. Émile Durkeim, *The Division of Labor in Society*, trans. George Simpson (New York: The Free Press, 1964). Originally published in French in 1893. An excellent summary of Durkheim's concepts, as bearing upon communication theory, is in Melvin L. DeFleur, and Sandra Ball-Rokeach, *Theories of Mass Communication* (New York: Longman, 1982), 153–6.

29. As quoted in DeFleur and Ball-Rokeach, *Theories of Mass Communication*, 156.

30. The concept of a "mass society" has its origins as early as Durkheim, and has been described by Harold Lasswell, Leonard Broom, and Philip Selznik, among others. It has less to do with actual population size, than with social complexity. As DeFleur and Ball-Rokeach, *Theories of Mass Communication*, 157, have described the concept: "Mass Society refers to the relationship that exists between individuals and the social order around them. In a mass society…(1) individuals are presumed to be in a situation of psychological isolation from others; (2) impersonality is said to prevail in their interactions with others, and (3) they are said to be relatively free from the demands of binding informal social obligations."

31. United Kingdom. Parliament. Report of the Royal Commission on the Press (London: His Majesty's Stationery Office, 1949).

32. Commission on the Freedom of the Press, *A Free and Responsible Press* (Chicago: University of Chicago Press, 1947).

33. Ibid., 121.

34. Ibid., 115.

35. Theodore Peterson, "The Social Responsibility Theory of the Press," in Siebert, et al., *Four Theories of the Press*, 75.

36. Commission on the Freedom of the Press, *A Free and Responsible Press*, 129.

37. Ibid., 27–8.

38. Ibid., 115.

39. Ibid., 125.

40. Ibid., 127.

41. William Ernest Hocking, *Freedom of the Press: A Framework of Principle. A Report from the Commission on Freedom of the Press* (Chicago: University of Chicago Press, 1947), 169.

42. Hocking, *Commission on the Freedom of the Press*, 21–9.

The Quality

Conundrum:

Toward a

Free but

Accountable

Journalism

C
H
A
P
T
E
R

4

T he importance of good and responsible journalism to the health of society is receiving increased recognition, along with the notion that it is far too important a business to leave entirely to the journalists and to the media industries that employ them. A variety of proposals relating to this quality conundrum have been suggested, and in some cases put into practice. It has been argued in some quarters, for instance, that the craft of journalism should be encouraged to acquire the self-governing mechanisms of a profession, like those of medicine or the law. Meanwhile in actual practice, the ombudsman movement has enjoyed increasing popularity in the the United States and Canada in recent years. The concept of the voluntary press council, which has been applied in several Western democracies, most notably for nearly four decades in Britain, is seeing extensive development now in Canada.

Regulation by government has not only been proposed, but widely applied in the case of broadcasting (though usually with protections that seek to keep news and public affairs broadcasting at arms length from the regulators). Amid much controversy in Canada, the 1981 report of the Royal Commission on Newspapers recommended a comparable regulatory environment for the daily press. Draft legislation to establish such a system was announced in 1982, and actually reached the floor of House of Commons. It eventually died on the Order Paper, however, with no attempt made since to revive it.[1]

The provision of sound and ethical journalism is as important in modern democratic society as the provision of sound and ethical medical and legal practice. The problem is how to achieve high ethical standards and still guarantee the essential freedom necessary for democratic journalism. There are no easy solutions.

Journalists themselves are perhaps the most befuddled of all when it comes to considering these matters, and one can sympathize with them in their predicament. As we have seen, there is no clear consensus among them about such basic matters as the definition of news itself. Similarly, there are as many points of view as to what constitutes an appropriate collective ethic (including the possibility that it might not be ethical to propose one at all) as there are journalists.

An Uncertain Philosophy

Most journalists are caught somewhere between the libertarian tradition and the latter-day tenets of social responsibility that represent a more radical departure from tradition than most journalists, government policy makers, and academic critics appear to realize. At heart, most North American news people remain fundamentally libertarian in that they think of themselves as individuals set apart. They abhor the prospect of state interference with an absolute freedom of the press, and mistrust proposals for outside intervention. A substantial minority continues to oppose even such clearly benign and non-governmental interventions as the establishing of voluntary press councils. On the other hand, the concepts of social responsibility inadvertently play to human vanity by granting the journalist considerable social importance as educator, provider of a "truthful, comprehensive and intelligent account of the day's events," and as the great "clarifier of social goals." News people often want to have it both ways, as is made clear in the *Toronto Star's* formal submission to the 1970 Special Senate Committee on the Mass Media. The *Star's* interpretation of journalism's purpose was pure social responsibility, as evident in these words from the brief: "newspapers are no longer in the transmitting but the education business….[I]t is no longer always possible to arrange facts into logical sequences; to simply report events and hope the reader can judge what to accept. Newspapers must examine appearances as well as reality, experience as well as facts."[2] Despite these ambitious sentiments, when it came to the social responsibility requirement that there be meaningful public accountability, perhaps even by the agency of government, the *Star* reverted to a purely libertarian stance, allowing only that some form of voluntary press council system might be permissible.

The American media scholars John Merrill and Ralph Lowenstein have observed that philosophic uncertainty is considerably more complicated than a simple schism between social responsibility values and those of the libertarian tradition. There are divisions within the separate camps as well, as the following passage suggests:

> [J]ournalists…are not really agreed on a basic press concept. Some might say that the basic function would be free expression; others might say profit or incentive to the total economy; others might say political guidance; others might say support of the social and political status quo; others might say social change.
>
> In other words, there is probably no one concept….Or if there is, we know of no student of the press who has isolated it.[3]

Historic Divisions

The confusion of purpose and ethic is not purely philosophic in nature. It stems in part from important historic differences in the entire approach to the practice of journalism, leaving us in modern times with at least two basic divisions. On the one hand, there is what has been called elite journalism, as exemplified by such newspapers as the *Times* of London and the *New York Times*, and perhaps in a paler light in Canada, by the *Globe and Mail* and *Le Devoir*. In radio and television, elite journalism is narrowly restricted to some news and public affairs components of such state-owned or sponsored organizations as the Canadian Broadcasting Corporation, the provincial educational television authorities, the British Broadcasting Corporation, and the Public Broadcasting System in the United States. The other basic category of journalism, which might be described as popular egalitarian, is much more widespread. It includes most of North America's metropolitan evening dailies and morning tabloids, most provincial dailies, and the news and public affairs content of virtually all privately owned broadcasting organizations.

The historic schism was not evident until the nineteenth century, and influenced the course of American journalism for a number of decades before the impact was fully felt in Britain. Though there were many technological developments, including the installation of a steam-driven press at the *Times* in 1814, and the first rotary press in 1847,[4] also at the *Times*, the century was not especially innovative in Britain in terms of journalistic approaches. Rather, the era was marked by the development of excellence within a well-established framework of journalistic practice, notably at the *Times*, but at a number of its competitors as well, especially, its long-running rival, the *Standard*.

Published through the century by the three famous John Walters, (father, son, and grandson) and guided by brilliant editors, notably Thomas Barnes in the first half of the century, and John Delane who dominated the second half, the *Times* established itself as an independent British institution. It became equally feared and respected for the quality of its impartial analysis and comment on social and political issues of the day, and for the accuracy and detail of its coverage, notably its legendary foreign dispatches. From the early 1800s and through the century, the *Times* often had detailed information relating to vital foreign developments in the hands of its readers before official dispatches had reached Whitehall.

Yet, the *Times* of the mid-nineteenth century bears little resemblance to most modern newspapers. Its coverage was generally limited to political and economic information and notes from the court. Its writing was verbose, often consisting of verbatim reports of speeches given in Parliament and elsewhere. Objectivity was not a consideration. Little distinction was made between fact and value and little was provided to the reader in the way of interpretation of events. The overall appearance of the *Times*, and that of most of its competitors, was one of unrelieved grayness. There were few drawings and little in the way of headlines or other typographic devices to make the pages readable. Moreover, the *Times*, like most of its competitors, was expensive, costing in the range of four to five pence the copy throughout most of the century, and was generally available only by subscription.

In a word, British journalism of the era was *elite*, prepared for the more privileged segments of society, and purely libertarian in its philosophy.

> The newspaper reader was flatteringly pictured as a serious-minded person whose interests were confined to politics, the law courts and the Stock Exchange and who did not need any help in absorbing the news beyond good eyesight and abundant leisure: the latter was obviously essential....
>
> What most characterized end-of-the-century journalism was its dignity, its high sense of public responsibility, its tradition of giving its readers good substantial fare in the sure confidence that as intelligent men (few women read newspapers then) they required no aids to digestion, for as a matter of personal interest and duty they would want to read the whole paper to keep themselves well informed.[5]

But as the century entered its last decades in Britain, important changes lay ahead, changes that were already very much in progress in the journalism of the United States.

The Penny Press

Until the 1830s, most newspapers in this new republic were cut from much the same elite libertarian cloth as their English counterparts. The same verbose grayness prevailed, and the same self-motivated audience of privileged readers was assumed. But America of the 1830s was a place of considerable social change. This was the era of Andrew Jackson's White House, and a refreshing breeze of frontier egalitarianism was sweeping the land in this age of Jacksonian democracy. The effect was felt in journalism in the form of the penny press that was beginning successfully to challenge the established papers of New York, Philadelphia, Boston, and other growing cities up and down the Atlantic seaboard.

The first of these new papers was the *New York Sun* that began publication in September, 1833. It sold in the streets instead of by subscription, and cost just a penny a copy instead of the typical six cents of the traditional press. Within a few months, it was selling some 5000 copies daily, more than any other New York paper of the era. Within two years, its daily circulation had climbed to a phenomenal 15 000.[6] The rise of the *Sun* was quickly followed by many others, among them James Gordon Bennett's *New York Herald* in 1835, and Horace Greeley's *New York Tribune*, founded in 1841. Ironically, in view of its later prestige and evolution into what is now regarded as a modern elite newspaper, the *New York Times* was established as a penny paper by Henry Raymond in 1851.

Often condemned and even feared in polite society (and certainly in the editorials of the established press) the new penny papers represented a whole new phase in the evolution of journalism. Their financial success depended upon a combination of their cheap price per copy, convenient street sales, and above all, their willingness to accept almost any advertising. The new papers were especially criticized for this practice, as the established press traditionally rejected advertisements for lotteries, theatres, businesses that opened on Sundays, patent medicines of dubious virtue, and others it found objectionable. The penny press *Boston Daily Times* responded: "To this complaint [especially with regard to patent medicine ads] we can only reply that it is for our interest to insert such advertisements as are not indecent or improper in their language, without inquiry whether the articles advertised are what they purport to be."[7]

Editorially, the penny press was even more innovative. The idea of news was extended to include police news, news of the streets, criminal court proceedings, along with other local news and human interest stories. The traditional volumes of verbatim political coverage gave way to greatly reduced summary reports—in some instances, political news disappeared from the pages of the early penny press— and the technique of the journalistic interview was invented. The use of descriptive headlines, graphics, and other typographic design items to brighten the printed page and make it more readable, became standard fare. The emergence of the American penny press marked the birth of the modern *egalitarian* newspaper.

British journalism changed more slowly, but it was eventually and reluctantly influenced in the closing decades of the nineteenth century by forces similar to those that produced the American penny press. As Harold Herd has described the turn-of-the-century situation in England: "When innovators came along in the 'eighties and 'nineties who strongly urged that the primary task of a newspaper was to get itself read, and that there was a whole range of human interests that found no reflection in the columns of existing journals, the reaction of the majority of journalists was violently unfavorable."[8]

As in America, the "new journalism" as it was called in Britain, prevailed in the pioneering hands of such editors as W. T. Stead, and later with publishers of the early twentieth century such as Lord Northcliffe. By World War I, America's penny press and Britain's new journalism had transformed English-language daily journalism. The concept of news was given its modern scale as covering a broad range of human interests and activities. Emotion and entertainment values were now seen as having their appropriate place in print, and the importance of using headlines, drawings, and other graphic devices to make the newspaper readable and visually appealing was recognized. Most important of all, priced at a penny and hawked in the streets, the daily press in its new egalitarian guise, became truly accessible at all social levels.

Yellow Journalism

The discussion of the development of the penny press is not complete without some reference to the competitive excesses of the New York publishers Joseph Pulitzer and William Randolph Hearst in the 1880s and 1890s. This brief phase in American newspaper development is something of an historic anomaly, for it both positively and negatively influenced the extension of penny press egalitarianism into the journalism of the twentieth century.

Pulitzer, who published the *New York World*, is in many ways very interesting. An Austrian Jewish immigrant, he was acutely aware of the needs and problems of the immigrant population that flooded turn-of-the-century New York, and he saw these people as the base of his readership. In return for their loyalty, he used his paper not only to provide them with news and entertainment, but to educate them, and to protect their interests in this strange new country where some scoundrel—official or otherwise—was always ready to take advantage of their poverty and their unfamiliarity with language and custom.

Alternatively, William Randolph Hearst, publisher of the *New York Journal*, is not remembered for any redeeming altruism. His ruthlessness is evident in many anecdotes, one of the most descriptive having to do with his approach to coverage of the 1896 Cuban rebellion against the colonial Spanish authorities. Hearst had dispatched writer Richard Harding Davis and artist Frederic Remington to Havana, and as this apocryphal tale reveals, Remington found little action worthy of his artistic talents. He wired Hearst in New York: "Everything is quiet. There is no trouble here. There will be no war. Wish to return." To this, Hearst allegedly replied: "Please remain. You furnish the pictures, and I'll furnish the war." Indeed he did, or at least he brought enormous public pressure to bear upon the politicians who, then as now, had the actual power to furnish small wars and other such items of journalistic delight.[9]

Admitted innovators in their intense circulation wars, Hearst and Pulitzer went to great lengths to develop newspaper typography and graphics into flamboyant art forms. While this created new levels of sensationalism in journalism (an unfortunate influence that lingers in some elements of the press to the present day), it also encouraged a more extensive and creative use of art than had previously appeared in daily journalism. The Hearst and Pulitzer papers of the late nineteenth century have been credited with providing "the first great era of illustrated journalism." Much of this work involved the painstaking creation of intricate line drawing copies of photographs that were converted to copperplate etchings for newspaper reproduction purposes.[10] (No doubt this activity encouraged the eventual development of the half-tone zinc plate process that at last allowed the direct transfer of photographic images to newsprint. This process was first used in England in 1907, and became widespread in daily journalism in the years following World War I.)

Hearst and Pulitzer also developed typographical innovations that have had a lasting effect. Larger body type was introduced, along with boldface type up eighteen points in size for lead paragraphs on major stories. Banner front page lines originated in the *World* and the *Journal*, along with an unprecedented flamboyance in the application of a variety of typefaces and type sizes in other headlines.[11]

Not least among the innovations of the Hearst and Pulitzer presses was the comic strip. Pulitzer hired cartoonist Richard Outcault whose strip drawings of the "Yellow Kid" first appeared in the *World* in February, 1896. This instantly popular feature also saw the introduction of the first use of coloured ink in daily journalism—yellow. Thus the sobriquet "yellow journalism" was born, initially to disparagingly describe the warring Hearst and Pulitzer papers, but later to describe any journalism coloured in unduly sensational hues.[12]

In their writing, journalists of the yellow press gave birth to the intense, brief, sensationalized "lead" paragraph in news stories, and to the concept of campaign journalism. This concept refers to day after day of focussed, sensational attention on a given perceived social injustice, axe murder, small war, and so on. To entertain (often at the expense of fact and accuracy) became the focal purpose in the news selection and presentation of the yellow press.

Ethics and journalistic quality to one side, the fact that the yellow journalism extension of the penny press was an enormous commercial success is plain to read in the circulation figures. Pulitzer's *World*, climbed from 15 000 when he bought it in 1883 to 600 000 in its combined morning and evening editions by 1896. Hearst's *Journal*, with a circulation of about 450 000 in the same year seems a doubtful second until one compares it with other well-known New York papers of the era whose publishers refused to join the yellow press circulation wars. The *New York Herald* had a circulation of 140 000, in 1896, while the *Tribune* had 16 000, and the *Times* a mere 9000.[13]

As a phenomenon, yellow journalism was short-lived. The *World* and the *Journal* faded from circulation pre-eminence with the turn of the century, and journalism on both sides of the Atlantic entered a brief period of relative calm. But the bright makeup, and lively broad-spectrum reporting of America's penny press and Britain's new journalism remained to characterize the twentieth-century newspaper. The flamboyance of the yellow press did not disappear entirely. Its banner lines and sensationalized reporting enjoyed something of a diffused revival in many newspapers during World War I and the years that followed. That its influence remains with us is clear to anyone familiar with London's increasingly popular tabloids, or with the New York dailies. Even Canada's *Toronto Sun* with its offshoots in Ottawa, Calgary, and Edmonton, the *Winnipeg Sun* (which is not part of the same chain) and the francophone *Journal de Montréal* and *Journal de Québec*, reflect the tradition. As late as the 1960s, the now-defunct *Toronto Telegram* and its arch-rival, the *Toronto Star* were still fighting circulation battles reminiscent of New York's yellow press wars of the 1890s.

A Blending of Traditions

English-language journalism of the modern era has been defined by historic influences that are both elite and egalitarian in nature. The dignified elite libertarian traditions of the established American press that prevailed prior to the arrival of the penny press in the 1830s and 1840s never entirely disappeared. Some papers that began life as penny press offerings actually sought, with time, to assume the virtues of the established tradition, while retaining some of the brightness of makeup and universal approach to news coverage of the penny press. The *New York Times* stands as the great American example. When Adolph Ochs acquired the failing *Times* in 1896, he was determined to retain it as a modern newspaper, and claimed "if a sincere desire to conduct a high standard newspaper, clean, dignified and trustworthy, requires honesty, watchfulness, industry and practical applied common sense, I entertain the hope that I can succeed."[14]

In Britain, a reverse process occurred. There, the *Times* of London, provides the fine example of a great traditional elite newspaper taking on the style of the new journalism and adapting to the egalitarian demands of the new age. The *Times* retained want ads on its front page until World War II, but the real changes occurred when Lord Northcliffe, a great proponent of newspaper reform in the era of England's new journalism, acquired the *Times* early in the twentieth century. "He gave the newspaper a fresh and creative impulse at a time when several famous journals were staggering toward bankruptcy through blind loyalty to an outmoded technique; he restored the prosperity of the *Times* and made the great days live again."[15]

On the other hand, the egalitarian journalistic values of the penny press, and moderately those of the yellow press remain very much in evidence as the dominant philosophy of a majority of modern newspapers. One might suggest that there are two poles, two traditions: those of the older elite libertarian philosophy; and those oriented to the egalitarianism first formulated a century and a half ago in the American penny press. Few newspapers today—perhaps none—fall purely into one camp or the other. The traditions conflict on many points, and contribute to the modern journalist's confusion regarding sense of purpose. For the most part, the older elite tradition pulls journalists toward the individualistic values of libertarianism, while the egalitarian spirit of the American penny press and later, of Britain's "new journalism", attract them toward the collective and egalitarian values expressed in the social responsibility theory.

The Canadian Connection

Patterns in the development of Canadian journalism are similar in most respects to those of Britain and the United States. However, there are differences in historic circumstance that make it both interesting and useful to consider the Canadian experience apart from the others. Britain developed an urbane journalism during the eighteenth century, and the United States (in both its late colonial and early republican phases) had developed a journalism of comparable maturity by the latter decades of that century. The same could hardly be said of early colonial Canada. The few rough and isolated pockets of population that eventually coalesced to form the Confederation, simply were not able to sustain a significantly patterned journalism of any sort; not before the Loyalist migration, certainly, and not for many years thereafter.

There was no press of consequence at all prior to the British conquest of the 1750s. Few important voices were raised in support of a colonial printing industry until 1791 when John Graves Simcoe, the first lieutenant governor of Upper Canada suggested that a printer should be considered "indispensably necessary" to the newly organized colony. Despite this sentiment, anything resembling a mature press remained decades away: "as late as 1800 there were just nine active printing establishments across the length and breadth of British America."[16]

Joseph Howe and his *Novascotian* brought reforms leading to responsible government in Nova Scotia in the mid-1840s. Later in his life, this brilliant early Canadian editor and journalist reluctantly assumed a leadership role in guiding his province into the Confederation of 1867. (Photograph Collection, Public Archives of Nova Scotia)

It is interesting to note in passing, that Marshall McLuhan once suggested that there might have been something of a hidden virtue in Canada's late acquisition of homegrown printing and publishing. He felt it was precisely in not having a pre-telegraphic press with all its centralizing technological imperatives as he understood them, that Canada acquired a flexibility that left it better prepared than most countries for all those troublesome border-diffusing realities of the electronic age. "Canadians never got 'delivery' on their first national identity image…and we are the people who learned how to live without the bold accents of the national ego-trippers of other lands."[17] Perhaps, but be that as it may, Canadians tried to make up for lost time once printing arrived in strength during the 1830s and 1840s. A sort of telescoping of historic processes prevailed and contributed to the circumstance that gave Canada's early nineteenth century journalism its special flavour.

It worked this way: when newspapers finally began to appear in Canada well into the nineteenth century, they were mainly imitative of the egalitarian American penny press, and the emerging "new journalism" in Britain. In Canada's case, however, the kinds of dangers experienced by printers in Britain and America generations earlier lingered to plague pre-Confederation colonial newspapers for a few brief decades, and to provide their editors with a certain spice by now uniquely anachronistic in the English-speaking world.

The consequences of this historic telescoping were evident, for instance, in the public lives of both Joseph Howe in Halifax, and William Lyon Mackenzie in Upper Canada. Arguably, these men were the first to bring a popular and influential journalism to the British North American colonies, and both did so at some considerable personal risk.

With a radical journalistic thrust similar to the developments at the time in the American penny press, Joseph Howe used his *Novascotian* in 1835 to tackle the appointed magistrates who effectively ruled colonial Halifax. At that time, the British North American colonies were run by Crown-appointed lieutenant governors, with the assistance of executive councils generally drawn from local elites. The appointed magistrates of Halifax were simply an aspect of the prevailing colonial coziness among the privileged.

In their effort to silence Howe's editorials against them, the magistrates made a grave tactical error. They resigned as a group, demanding that Howe be charged with libel. He was duly indicted by a grand jury, and tried for "wickedly, maliciously and seditiously

Despite its gray appearance to the modern eye, Joseph Howe's pioneering newspaper, *The Novascotian*, was instrumental in forcing reforms that led to responsible government in colonial Nova Scotia. (Photograph Collection, Public Archives of Nova Scotia)

THE COLONIAL ADVOCATE.

YORK, THURSDAY, DECEMBER 6, 1827.

PRINTED AND PUBLISHED BY W. L. MACKENZIE, PRINTER TO THE HONOURABLE THE HOUSE OF ASSEMBLY OF UPPER CANADA.

Firebrand journalism also poured from the pages of William Lyon Mackenzie's *Colonial Advocate,* a great early reform newspaper published in "Muddy York," the little community in colonial Upper Canada that was to become Toronto. (Metropolitan Toronto Reference Library)

contriving, devising and intending to stir up and excite discontent among His Majesty's subjects."

Despite the trial judge's charge to the jury that the paper was libelous and that Howe should be found guilty, it took the jury all of ten minutes to find him not guilty. And as C.E. Wilson has described the resulting popular outburst in Halifax: "Howe was carried from the courthouse to his home on the shoulders of the throng. Bands paraded in the streets all night, and Howe was forced by the cheers and shouts to make a speech from a window in his house."[18]

Howe's campaign in the *Novascotian*, and his subsequent trial, effectively ended the use of libel as a protection for the privileged, not just in Nova Scotia but throughout British North America. This precedent more or less duplicated a similar reform provided more than forty years earlier in Britain with the passing of Fox's Libel Act in 1792. It also demonstrates the historic telescoping process as it worked its effects in the evolution of nineteenth-century Canadian colonial journalism.

Howe's journalistic activities led him on to a remarkable political career. His Reform Party effectively brought responsible government to Nova Scotia in the 1840s, and many years later he played an important role—albeit a reluctant one—in bringing his province into the Confederation of 1867.

The efforts of William Lyon Mackenzie were equally important to the evolution of Canadian journalism, though far less successful personally. An eccentric in most aspects of his being, Mackenzie was an instantly recognizable figure on the streets of "Muddy York", the Lake Ontario settlement of the 1830s that was to become Toronto. He is best known as publisher and editor of the *Colonial Advocate* and later of the *Constitution,* journalistic vehicles that carried his radical notions of political reform and that led him to a leadership role in the Upper Canada rebellion of 1837. Despite the failure of the rebellion, Mackenzie's legitimacy as a journalistic radical and reformer is beyond question. Altogether, he started six newspapers during his lifetime. Twice his printing offices were wrecked by angry mobs, and five times he was ejected from the Upper Canada assembly (to which he had been duly elected) for alleged libels printed in his papers. He was obliged to spend a time in exile in the United States where he continued his attack (from a relatively safe distance) on the colonial authorities of Upper Canada. His overriding credibility prevailed during the mid-1840s, when he served as a political correspondent for Horace Greeley's New York *Tribune*, arguably the finest of the penny papers of the era. Mackenzie died in penury in 1861.[19]

The brilliant Howe and the equally but tragically brilliant Mackenzie stand, with just a few others, as editors representing the unique Canadian era of a journalism of telescoped historic circumstance. This was a time during which the British North American colonies played a form of catch up with the rest of the English-speaking world. Their reforming penny press papers were shaped by the battles that they fought for basic freedoms long since achieved elsewhere. But by the 1840s and 1850s the catch up was more or less complete, and British North American journalism settled into patterns already well established elsewhere. George Brown's *Globe*, founded in 1844, for instance, experienced a safe and settled existence more reminiscent of journalism in the United States at that time, than of Upper Canada a decade or two earlier. Like its New York contemporaries—the *Times*, for instance, or Greeley's *Tribune*—the *Globe* was a successful commercial and journalistic venture. Its circulation climbed from 18 000 to 45 000 between 1856 and 1872.[20]

Many other papers of the era experienced similar operating conditions. This was the birth of Canada's modern journalism. The Montreal *Star* came into existence in 1869, followed by the the Toronto *Telegram* in 1876, *La Presse* in 1884, and the Ottawa *Journal* in 1885. All of these papers, and others that emerged during the era of the confederation, fell into popular but conforming models. Though these were Canadian papers, they also were typical of those being published throughout the modern world beyond Canada, particularly in the United States and Britain. The process perhaps reached its completion when Joseph E. Atkinson acquired the *Toronto Star* from a group of striking printers in the late 1890s. Though the *Star* has become more respectable in the modern era, it clearly began life with the infusion of Atkinson's journalistic philosophy, imported in whole cloth from the yellow press of New York.

The Canon of Objectivity

Apart from the differences arising from elite and egalitarian traditions, a further source of confusion originated in the nineteenth century, and became dominant as an assumed canon of virtuous journalism in the twentieth century. It is the notion that fact and value somehow must be rigidly separated in the printed page and in news broadcast. Values and opinions must be restricted to editorials, clearly identified columns, and other commentary situations, while all information contained in news columns and newscasts must be purely objective in its presentation.

The ideal of journalistic objectivity is simple enough. It assumes that readers or listeners or viewers of news are sufficiently intelligent, informed, and motivated to interpret the meanings of facts for themselves. It is their duty as citizens of a democracy to do this, to decide for themselves, and to formulate their own opinions, on the issues at hand. According to this view of information flow, the journalist's function is purely and simply to present facts. Any garnishing of the facts with personal opinion or bias becomes a violation of the journalist's ethical obligation to observe and report, but never to colour. This impossible ideal was held as an unquestioned canon of good journalistic practice through the first half of this century, and was enshrined by the American Society of Newspaper Editors in the code of ethics that it developed in 1923. In the words of the code, anything less than the objective account becomes "subversive of a fundamental principle of the profession."[21]

It is an ironic twist of historic realities that the concept of journalistic objectivity seems to stem naturally from traditional libertarian values. It is often argued by its defenders that objectivity simply demonstrates the natural respect that the libertarian journalist holds for his or her audience. The intelligent, self-motivated audience member wants and needs only the facts, and should be left to develop his or her own opinions, as the argument goes. Thus, the proper role of the reporter must be to serve as an extension of the audience member's sensory organs—to see and hear, and then report.

Such a perception of journalism never was a part of the libertarian tradition. In fact, throughout the Enlightenment, and into the late nineteenth century, fact and value were freely mixed in the news columns of most newspapers. Quality in journalism was measured by such features as literary style, wit, accuracy, and detail, not by the inherent "objectivity" of reports.

Some sense of journalism's joyful disregard for objectivity throughout most of its history is suggested in historian Paul Rutherford's observation that as late as 1900, seventy-seven Canadian daily newspapers representing some fifty-three per cent of daily circulation at the time, were partisan in their orientation. As Rutherford put it: "the typical publisher or editor remained addicted to playing politics, for him a grand sport that added spice to life and gave significance to his calling."[22]

The historic reality is that objectivity as a canon of journalism had origins based more in the demands of technology and economics than in social philosophy. America's penny press and England's new journalism propelled newspapers into the modern era, and the volume of advertising revenue became more and more directly linked to circulation figures. Publishers began to recognize the economic fact that bias in news columns, especially relating political bias, drove away as many readers as it retained. Thus was born what Westley called the "enterprise" press. This press saw itself as the honourably objective observer, its perception of its role changed "from being a mouthpiece of a regime or its loyal opposition to an independent check on all branches of government responsible to its readers alone."[23]

The great wire services, which evolved with the telegraph in the last half of the nineteenth century, also found objectivity a necessary principle. It was essential if they were to have any hope of providing usable information to their many newspaper clients and members representing a wide range of political and social bias. The need for haste in the increasingly competitive business of news dissemination, and the inherent unreliability of early telegraphic transmission systems, combined to create a need for brief, to-the-point (and, by definition, objective) accounts of events in wire service news budgets.

Thus the objectivity principle, linked to the libertarian tradition in twentieth-century journalistic myth, became a canon of the craft that went largely unchallenged until the post-World War II era. Criticism began to emerge with the hearings of the post-war press commissions in the United States and Britain. When the American Commission on the Freedom of the Press called in 1947 for the expansion of the objective reporting of facts to the provision of "a truthful, comprehensive and intelligent account of the day's events," Theodore Peterson was moved to remark: "Here then is a suggestion that the press has developed a curious sort of objectivity—a spurious objectivity which results in half-truths, incompleteness and incomprehensibility."[24]

Peterson and others essentially argued that the objectivity principle tended to corrupt reporting in a number of ways. It discouraged journalists from explaining and providing background to the facts they offered; it encouraged them to accept information from their sources at face value, without due consideration given to the veracity and reliability of the source; and—perhaps most dangerously—it encouraged journalists to regard themselves as merely disinterested observers who reported what they saw, and in no significant way influenced the events they chronicled.

The McCarthy Hearings

The classic example of the consequences of this narrow objectivity remains the media coverage in the early 1950s of the vitriolic public hearings in the United States of Joseph McCarthy's Senate investigations sub-committee. The senator had turned the affair into a communist witch hunt damaging hundreds, if not thousands, of innocent reputations in the process. McCarthy was eventually exposed by Edward R. Murrow in a March 1954, segment of his pioneering CBS network documentary, *See It Now*. Murrow, and his co-producer, Fred W. Friendly, carried out good interpretive journalism by showing up McCarthy's obsessive anger, the shallowness of his allegations, and his unfair method of questioning witnesses.[25] The Murrow show turned the tide of public opinion against the excesses of McCarthyism. The post-mortem in the courts of public opinion that followed the McCarthy era included widespread recognition of the problems of narrow journalistic objectivity. A journalism that failed to check the validity and motivation of sources, and that simply regurgitated "facts" as they emerged from the hearings, had passively and greatly contributed to the growth of the issue to democracy-threatening proportions.

The reaction to McCarthyism, bolstered by the theoretical proposals of the Hutchins commission, tended to move American journalism away from the narrowness of pure objectivity, toward the interpretive approaches suggested by the social responsibility model. The "investigative journalism" of the Watergate years was another outgrowth. The most radical departure from tradition however, emerged from the underground press of the 1960s and 1970s in the form of the hippie era's version of new journalism (not to be confused with turn-of-the-century British developments of the same name, despite certain similarities in purpose).

Radicals of the 1960s

Traditionalists of the established media too easily dismissed the latter-day new journalism as youthful rebelliousness without lasting substance. They believed these were kids out to shock the grown-ups by spilling outrageous emotions and dirty words across the pages of pretend newspapers with odd names like the *East Village Other* in New York, or the *Georgia Straight* in Vancouver. While some of the new journalism of the 1960s was, in actual fact, little more than an outpouring of rebellious immaturity, a great amount of it constituted a serious attempt at reform. It especially tried to throw off the restraints of the old objectivity and the creative limitations of what had become conventional in the journalism of the twentieth century. As one chronicler of the era's underground press, has explained: "the principal distinguishing mark of New Journalistic style is the writer's attempt to be personalistic, involved, and creative in relation to the events he reports and comments upon." This journalism, in general, does not pretend to be objective, but clearly reflects the writer's commitment and personality.[26]

Whatever the intentions of its creators may have been, the new journalism of Tom Wolfe, Norman Mailer, Truman Capote, Rex Reed, Hunter S. Thompson, and all the others, left its lasting mark on the media mainstream. Most notably for our immediate purposes, the new journalists cast permanent doubt upon the merits of traditional objectivity in journalism. Debate continues today on the relative merits of an objective frame of mind, on the one hand, even if journalistic objectivity in the abstract is an admitted human impossibility, as opposed to the subjective journalism of personal involvement on the other.

A Question of Ethics

The debate on objectivity has left modern democratic journalism with three principal approaches to ethics, with many variations on each theme.

Within what might loosely be described as the traditional/libertarian/objective camp, a *legalistic* approach prevails. For the legalist, ethics is an unbreakable system of rules to be applied in all circumstances, regardless of consequences. Formal law, and the moral structures of most organized religions and social ideologies are derived from this sort of "rule book" approach to proper and improper behaviour. For the most part, journalists holding such a view see their task as reporting the facts as they are found. They must be as accurate, impartial, and objective as humanly possible in the presentation of discovered facts and accept no responsibility for the consequences of publication. Most formal codes of journalistic ethics are based upon a legalistic perception of ethics.

Critics have pointed out that such a posture can, and does, result in a certain detachment that may reach a point of destructive indifference on the part of the journalist. Despite its strict impartiality and outward appearance of fairness, this detachment can do great and inappropriate damage to individuals and institutions in the news. In the extreme case, in the hands of the profound cynics of the gutter press, legalism can become a form of justification for the worst sorts of excesses. Even in more honourable hands, it can lead journalists to refuse to recognize the existence (let alone the consequences) of such broad media-related issues as the potential effects of violent media content in society; or of the controversy-structured presentation of political information. The possibility that something might be fundamentally wrong with the basic journalistic understanding of the concept of news itself has no place in the world view of the ethical legalist.

Ethical legalism is predictable, however. Where it is honorably applied, the approach is orderly and logical, and the gathering and presentation of news information becomes a matter of established routine. In a society of great complexity, change, and unpredictability, there is merit in such an approach, despite its evident drawbacks. Far better the ethical legalist, than the opposite number, the practitioner of the *antinomian* ethic, literally, the non-ethic. Merrill and Lowenstein have described this individual as making ethical decisions without even being aware of making them. "Rather, they are just feelings, instincts, inclinations, intuitions. This ethical (or nonethical) system might simply be referred to as 'whim ethics.'"[27]

Oddly, the antinomian case cannot be dismissed out of hand. It can be argued that here is the ethic of the free spirit, the free journalist functioning in a social environment where absolute freedom of expression is a respected and fundamental philosophic principle. Such an argument ignores the fact that every freedom has its concomitant responsibilities. This has been recognized by virtually every important social thinker who has considered the nature and purpose of press freedom from the time of Milton forward. Nonetheless, there remains a certain logic to the essentially antinomian argument that, by definition, ethical rule books compromise freedom. It is a concept that has many adherents among the ranks of working journalists.

Finally, there is the middle ground of *situation ethics*. It tends primarily to be proposed in modern times as a concept in theology seeking to ease the coldness of formal moral legalism with the leaven of human compassion. Situationism has also caught the imagination of many journalists searching for a decent middle ground. Applied in the context of journalism, this ethical approach takes on a somewhat utilitarian flavour. It recognizes formal rules and obeys them most of the time. But it also is prepared to set these rules aside when good reason is perceived for doing so. Merrill and Lowenstein have described the journalistic situationist as the person who believes it is acceptable to misrepresent a story, or even to lie, in a case where he or she feels telling the truth might bring harm to the newspaper or the country. "There are times when it is *right* to play down—or leave out completely—certain stories or pictures; there are other times when it would be *wrong*. But the important thing here is that the journalist thinks before he takes a certain action." Journalists must have reasons for their actions. They do not act only on instinct or intuition.[28]

Situationism has obvious appeal to many who categorize themselves as journalistic practitioners in the social responsibility mold and certainly for those who would define themselves as new journalists. It allows for the writer's personal and emotional involvement with the subject matter at hand. It is appealing on humane grounds, but just as legalism has its associated problems, so too, does situationism. In its originating Christian context, situationism is protected from sliding away into antinomian chaos by what can be called the "absolute element," the overriding and guiding love God has for Creation and to which the Christian situationist must make constant reference.[29]

In an effort to avoid slipping into pragmatic relativism, secular journalists have struggled to develop notions of ethical accountability beyond such Christian beliefs. John Merrill, for instance, argues an interesting case for what he defines as the ethic of an existential journalism. He applies the existentialist's argument that responsibility is "freedom's anchorage." Thus, the existential journalist will recognize, and be governed by, the reality that "each person must act freely and accept responsibility for his own actions."[30] Thus, the journalist of the situation ethic who cannot see the way to courageous virtue in religious faith, perhaps can find it in the existentialist's primal anguish.

Journalism and Professionalism

Of the various proposals regarding the quality of journalism listed at the beginning of this chapter, the least workable at this time would be the creation of a formal professional environment. If journalism were to seek to imitate the legal or medical professions and become formally professional, as the concept is traditionally understood, a number of elements would have to be agreed upon and put in place.

    a) *Education and admission standards.* Traditional professions have well-established educational programs and examination procedures by which newly minted practitioners are licensed and admitted. In the case of journalism at the moment, educational requirements depend largely upon the demands of the marketplace. High school graduation (or less) remains an adequate standard for many Canadian weekly newspapers, some small dailies, and a majority of radio stations. On the other hand, a university degree, and increasingly two of them (often in journalism nowadays, but not necessarily), is the conventional requirement for journalists employed with a metropolitan Canadian daily, or in a major television or wire service newsroom. No one (to this writer's knowledge) has given much thought to any form of standardized admission or licensing procedure.

Moreover, in the unlikely event that at some future point minimum educational requirements are formally established, and a professional admissions procedure created, there would be serious ramifications for spontaneous freedom of expression—the essence of democratic journalism. By its very nature, journalism must be open to the occasional writer, the freelancer, outraged writers of letters to the editor, and articulate curmudgeons of all sorts. Medicine and the law (if these are to be our hypothetical models) have no comparable concern with a democratic imperative to license the amateur.

b) *Enabling legislation.* Medicine and the law, as these are practised in Canada, are governed by the provisions contained in provincial statutes enacted for the purpose. If there is one thing upon which most journalists are agreed, it is the notion that their craft should not be touched by legislation.

c) *Disciplinary Procedure.* The enabling legislation of the established professions provides for procedures, by which, a committee of senior and respected professionals monitor the conduct of their colleagues, based on the provisions of an elaborately developed statement of professional ethics.

It goes without saying that journalism, as it is presently practised, is ready for none of this. Yet there remains a considerable and growing public demand for professionalism in journalism, even though conditions in the craft make the establishment of a formal profession entirely improbable for the future. Fortunately, there are alternatives.

The Ombudsman

Many media organizations in the United States, and some in Canada, have appointed a well-regarded individual (often a senior editor) as ombudsman. The concept originated in Sweden, where the first

ombudsman was established about a century ago to serve as a media-
tor between government and citizen. In its modern use in daily newspapers, the ombudsman usually is seen as the defender of the reader's
interests. In Canada, the concept was pioneered at the *Toronto Star*
where the late Borden Spears (a member of the Royal Commission on
Newspapers) served as ombudsman for a number of years. It is interesting to note in passing that neither the ombudsman concept, nor
that of the press council discussed below, has been used to any great
extent in the electronic media. These seem to be print phenomena.

The duties of the ombudsman in modern newspapers are essentially
these: to deal with all readers' concerns and complaints; and to comment on the quality of journalism produced in his or her newsroom
and, when necessary, to make recommendations regarding improvements. In most cases, the ombudsman also writes a periodic column
on matters relating to reader concerns, or to the state of the journalistic art in general. Where the ombudsman is both a good journalist
and a courageous individual, the concept serves usefully. But it has its
problems.

Obviously, the ombudsman is always an employee of the newspaper, the source of his or her salary, related benefits, and future pen-
sion. Where his or her personal courage is not strong, or the employer
is unprepared to give more than lip service to the potentially embar-
rassing public musings of a resident critic, the ombudsman's output
will be shallow and of little consequence. Second, even where the
concept works at its finest, the ombudsman remains one individual
working alone in a given newsroom. He or she will be subject to constant and understandable peer pressure not to embarrass colleagues.
And finally, while the ombudsman may influence the quality of a
given newspaper, it is not a concept that can be expected to work
direct improvements in the overall industry.

The Press Council

Of all the approaches that have been proposed or implemented relating to the long-term improvement of the press, the best hope (short
of government intervention, that raises all sorts of other problems)
lies in the concept of the voluntary press council. Such councils have
operated in a number of democratic jurisdictions for many years,
but the best working example remains the British Press Council,
established in 1953.

After thirty-five years in the business of monitoring and commenting upon Britain's newspapers, great and small, the performance of the council remains an uncertain success. Viewed at its inception as a mere "proprietorial concession to parliamentary pressure,"[31] the council is still dismissed a full generation later in many quarters as being ineffectual in bringing any real improvement to the quality of British journalism. In 1980, the National Union of Journalists (a trade union representing some 23 000 news people in Britain) withdrew from membership on the grounds that despite the input of three royal commissions (the initiating commission in 1947, and subsequent commissions that reported in 1962 and 1977) and three and a half decades of experience, the council remained "incapable of reform."[32]

Criticism usually has been along the lines that the council remains essentially a publishers' organization, public relations window-dressing to stave off periodic threats of direct government intervention. There is some substance to this point of view, especially given the fact that the council has no power to enforce its decisions and is often abysmally slow in rendering them. Historically, the council has rarely taken initiative in identifying and commenting upon press-related problems outside the context of its after-the-fact adjudication process. But despite these difficulties, the council does not deserve outright dismissal. As we shall see, there is an important positive side.

In its present form, the British Council consists of thirty-six members, drawn equally from the lay public and from the eight publishers' and journalists' organizations that support and fund it. In addition, there is a chair (usually a nationally respected member of the legal profession) and a staff of eleven. In 1983, its Complaints Committee received 979 complaints relating to the performance of dailies, weeklies, and other periodicals from individuals and organizations in the general public. It formally adjudicated 124 of these, finding for the complainant in sixty-two cases.[33]

Whatever its merits or demerits, the British Press Council has been imitated in many other jurisdictions, most notably in Canada where a number of regional councils have adopted it as a basic model. Voluntary press councils have existed in Canada since the early 1970s when they were set up in Ontario, Quebec, and Alberta. This in response to a call for their establishment contained in the recommendations of the 1970 report of the Special Senate Committee on the Mass Media.[34] Councils also have been established in more recent years in most other regions of Canada. These include: the British Columbia Press Council, and the Atlantic Press Council, with jurisdiction in the four Maritime provinces.

In some ways the Conseil de presse du Québec has been the most interesting, monitoring the content of the electronic as well as the print media. Unlike other Canadian councils, which receive their revenues entirely from member newspapers, the Quebec council receives some of its funding through a foundation established for the purpose and has considered seeking provincial government support. Also, unlike its other Canadian counterparts and the British original, the Quebec council purposefully weights its membership against the ownership and senior management groups. Of the current council's nineteen members, seven (including the chair) are drawn from the public at large, while another six are from the Fédération professionnelle des journalistes du Québec, and just six from the ranks of media ownership and management.[35]

The other Canadian councils follow the British model precisely in most matters, with the Ontario Press Council being the oldest and largest example. Established in 1972, the OPC functioned for many years with just eight of the province's daily newspapers as members, five in the Southam group, along with three independent newspapers, *The London Free Press,* the *Kitchener-Waterloo Record* (which became a Southam paper in 1989) and the *Toronto Star.* Two other Southam papers, the North Bay *Nugget,* and the Owen Sound *Sun Times,* joined the council in 1975.

While a number of weeklies joined during the 1970s and early 1980s, the great majority of Ontario dailies ignored the council until draft legislation based on the recommendations of the 1981 Report of the Royal Commission on Newspapers was announced in May, 1982, and later introduced in the House of Commons. This legislation (never passed into law) called for mandatory membership of most daily newspapers in a national press council to be established and funded by the federal government, the proposed Canadian Daily Newspaper Advisory Board. Exceptions were to be made for dailies already belonging to viable voluntary press councils wherever these existed in Canada.[36] The result was a flood of applications for membership in the existing councils, and a flurry of activity relating to the establishment of new ones. The OPC was able to boast a roster of forty-two dailies, virtually all the dailies published in the province, in its annual report for 1985.[37]

The OPC has a governing council of twenty-one individuals, consisting of the chair, ten journalist members, and ten public members. Their main work is through the council's adjudications committee that in 1985 received 168 complaints. Of these, thirty-six went to formal adjudication.[38] As in Britain, complainants must first seek redress with appropriate officials at the paper involved before approaching the press council. The council will seek informally to settle most complaints it receives after this initial filtering, and thus only a relatively small number become the subject of adjudication proceedings. Again, as with the British model, the Ontario Press Council has no coercive authority. Its member newspapers agree only that they will publish the council's adjudication reports. Procedures are similar in the cases of the other press councils in English-speaking Canada.

Like the British Press Council, its Canadian counterparts have been criticized, primarily on these grounds: lacking the authority to impose fines or exercise some form of punitive power, the mere publication of adjudication reports can never be expected to work important improvements in the quality of the press; and for failing to establish a formal code of journalistic ethics. There also have been complaints that the Canadian councils have failed to seek out problems in the practice of journalism, treating them after the fact when the only possible action is one of reaction. Such criticisms are not entirely appropriate.

The Ontario and Quebec councils in recent years have conducted seminars for journalists on various issues of concern within the craft, and both have produced publications on specific themes. The OPC, for instance, has produced brief monographs under the following titles: *Trial by Media* in 1984 (a discussion of problems relating to pretrial publicity); *To Name or Not to Name* in 1974, revised in 1981 (on the vexing ethical question of when names should or should not be published); and *Press Ethics and Freebies* in 1978. The Quebec council has a similar list of publications to its credit. In addition, both councils publish detailed annual reports containing summary descriptions of the year's more consequential adjudication proceedings. Both have taken it upon themselves in recent years to submit briefs to various government commissions on matters relating to the media industries.

The British council and its various Canadian counterparts all have been reluctant to publish documents seeking to describe codes of ethics for journalism. As Stanley Cunningham has pointed out, reflecting historic philosophic uncertainties: "codes are rigid, restraining and antithetical to the spirit of consensus and free acceptance which characterize voluntary press councils."[39]

Finally, there is the question of whether or not press councils should have powers beyond those of moral suasion that they now possess. Apart from the notion that coercive powers would be "anti-thetical to the spirit of consensus and free acceptance," the criticism ignores a vital fact. The most important feature of these adjudications is that they represent the gradual accumulation of an already large storehouse of comment in the jurisprudential style on media ethics and performance. Given enough time and adjudications, the craft of journalism will soon possess a detailed, all–embracing statement of precedent—in effect, a professional code. Most importantly, this will be a statement both conventionally accepted, and created in an atmosphere of sustaining freedom.

There are two important remaining questions. The first of these is whether or not journalists themselves will give the press council movement the time it needs to mature according to principles of free association and non-coercion. The British experience at the moment is not promising. The departure of the National Union of Journalists was a serious blow to the organization. Also, too many editors continue to ignore the moral authority of the council, and "often react with indifference, hostility or contempt to adverse adjudications."[40] In Canada in recent years, editors generally have been polite about the council movement. But one cannot ignore that the great majority of Canada's dailies belong to press councils as death bed converts, seeking last-minute escape from the legislative measures proposed in 1982.

The second great question over the future of the press council movement is whether or not public critics of the press, and the governments who listen to them, will be prepared to wait out the long years that it may take for the movement to mature. Too few journalists and publishers seem to recognize (with reference to the British council, but applicable in the Canadian context as well) that it "functions as a device for condemning journalistic misbehaviour of a kind which, if left undeterred, would almost certainly be curbed by Act of Parliament."

NOTES

1. Jim Fleming, "Government Proposals on Freedom of the Press in Relation to the Canadian Daily Newspaper Industry," an address to the Graduate School of Journalism, the University of Western Ontario, London, Ontario, 25 May 1982.

2. Toronto Star Ltd., "Submission to Special Senate Committee on Mass Media," Ottawa, 30 January 1970.

3. John C. Merrill and Ralph L. Lowenstein, *Media, Messages and Men*, 2nd ed. (New York: Longman, 1979), 85.

4. Harold Herd, *The March of Journalism* (Westport, CT : Greenwood Press, 1973), 130.

5. Ibid., 223–4.

6. Michael Schudson, *Discovering the News: A Social History of American Newspapers* (New York: Basic Books, 1978), 18.

7. Boston Daily Times, 11 October 1837, as quoted in Schudson, *Discovering the News*, 19–20.

8. Herd, *The March of Journalism*, 223.

9. Schudson, *Discovering the News*, 61–2.

10. Bruce H. Westley, *News Editing*, 2nd ed. (Boston: Houghton Mifflin Company, 1972), 208.

11. Ibid., 227.

12. Randall P. Harrison, The Cartoon: Communication to the Quick (Beverly Hills: Sage Publications, 1981), 86.

13. Schudson, *Discovering the News*, 92, 111.

14. Schudson, *Discovering the News*, 110.

15. Herd, *The March of Journalism*, 248.

16. Paul Rutherford, *The Making of the Canadian Media* (Toronto: McGraw-Hill Ryerson, 1978), 2

17. Marshall McLuhan, "Canada: The Borderline Case" in *The Canadian Imagination*, ed. David Staines (Cambridge: Harvard University Press, 1977), 227.

18. C. Edward Wilson, *Teeming Invective: 300 Years of Vigorous Journalism* (London, Ontario: Western Journalism Library, 1976), 111.

19. Ibid., 93–7.

20. Mary Vipond, *The Mass Media in Canada* (Toronto: James Lorimer and Company, 1989), 11.

21. Mitchell V. Charnley and Blair Charnley, *Reporting*, 4th ed. (New York: Holt, Rinehart and Winston, 1979), 37.

22. Paul Rutherford, *A Victorian Authority* (Toronto: University of Toronto Press, 1982), 212–3.

23. Westley, *News Editing*, 137.

24. Theodore Peterson, "The Social Responsibility Theory of the Press" in *Four Theories of the Press*, ed. Fred S. Siebert et al. (Urbana: University of Illinois Press, 1956 and 1973), 88.

25. Fred W. Friendly, *Due to Circumstances Beyond Our Control....* (New York: Vintage Books, 1967 and 1968), 23–67.

26. Michael L. Johnson, *The New Journalism* (Wichita: University Press of Kansas, 1971), 48.

27. Merrill and Lowenstein, *Media, Messages and Men*, 223–4.

28. Ibid., 224.

29. Joseph Fletcher, *Situation Ethics: The New Morality* (Philadelphia: The Westminster Press, 1966), 27.

30. John C. Merrill, *Existential Journalism* (New York: Hastings House, 1977), 55.

31. Geoffrey Robertson, *People Against the Press* (London: Quartet Books, 1983), 1.

32. Ibid., 17.

33. The Press Council, *The Press and the People: 29th/30th Annual Report of the Press Council 1982/1983* (London: The Press Council, 1984), 12–5.

34. Canada, *Report*, The Special Senate Committee on the Mass Media, vol. 1, "The Uncertain Mirror" (Ottawa: Queen's Printer for Canada, 1970), 257.

35. Conseil de presse du Québec, "Rapport des activités du conseil de presse du Québec pour l'année 1980-1981," Québec, 1981.

36. Fleming, "Government Proposals on Freedom of the Press in Relation to the Canadian Daily Newspaper Industry."

37. Ontario Press Council, "13th Annual Report," Ottawa, 1985, 54–5.

38. Ibid., 4.

39. Stanley B. Cunningham, "Press Councils in Canada," a paper presented at the Annual Conference of the Canadian Communications Association in Montreal, May 1977 (unpublished).

40. Robertson, *People Against the Press*, 4.

The

Consuming

Symbiosis:

Journalists,

Politicians,

and others

T here is an illusion about news suggesting that it springs to life randomly in unexpected places; perhaps like mushrooms erupting overnight wherever the soil is rich enough, and the climate warm and damp enough to stimulate growth. This is far from the truth. Journalism is too structured a phenomenon to exist in anything but circumstances of ordered cultivation. Nowhere is this more evident than in the remarkable patterning that exists in its relationship to the sources of information upon which it feeds.

To have legitimacy, news must be seen as originating with, or at least being affirmed by an official source. Even spontaneous and eminently newsworthy events as, for instance, fires, volcanic eruptions or bank robberies, must be officially proclaimed before they can be said to have happened for broadcast or publication. The fire marshal must state how the conflagration started, measure its dead and injured, and estimate its dollar cost before it can be entered into the journalistic record. By the same token, no bank can be journalistically described as being truly robbed until an investigating police officer has told reporters officially when, where, who, and how much. Even such natural events as floods, hurricanes, and volcanoes first must have their estimators, seismologists, and other proclaimers of official reality before they can be admitted as news.

A Net for Large Fish

News is a remarkably ordered phenomenon in the manner in which it derives from its official sources. But it also is important to recognize that the journalists who gather and process the news co-exist in structured relationships with these official sources. In fact, these relationships are so close as to be symbiotic in nature. Gaye Tuchman observed some years ago that newsgathering is not a process of "blanketing" a community as is often metaphorically supposed. Newsgathering is more like spreading a net "intended for big fish," with spaces in the webbing large enough to allow easy escape for bits of information deemed unimportant or inconsequential. (Often this simply can mean information that is not formally and officially sourced.)

> today's news media place reporters at legitimated institutions. [T]hese locations include police headquarters, the federal courthouse, and City Hall, where reporters' daily reports bring them into contact with official meetings, press releases, and official documents....The gleanings of reporters stationed at these and similar locations are supplemented by monitoring the police

and fire department's radio dispatches, and by assigning other reporters, based in the main office, to follow activities of such legitimated organizations as the Board of Education, the welfare department and the metropolitan transit authority.[1]

It makes no fundamental difference that news may fall into such diverse areas as education, religion, the arts, the courts, or the prisons. It is only that individuals who are recognizably official in some way or other—superintendents of education, professors, art critics, judges—be available to mouth those all-important affirming words prior to broadcast or publication.

The official sources syndrome is ubiquitous, touching all places where journalists look for news. It is most powerfully evident and its effects most consequential in the broad area of government and politics. The scope and intensity of journalism's relationship with government's official sources may be drawn from the fact that no fewer than 234 reporters were accredited members of the Parliamentary Press Gallery in Ottawa when the Royal Commission on Newspapers counted their numbers in 1981. By 1990, membership had reached 347.[2]

In a study of Toronto's metropolitan daily newspapers, it was observed that 42.6 per cent of all news items carried in the *Toronto Star* in a seven-day sample in January and February of 1989, originated with formal government sources at all levels. The *Globe and Mail's* total during the same period reached 60.8 per cent.[3] In an earlier study in the late 1970s, 32.3 per cent of the domestic content of the national wire of the Canadian Press was shown to have originated with formal sources in the federal establishment at Ottawa.[4]

While these figures give the reader a clear sense of the important place politics has in journalism's schedule of priorities, it is important to realize that this is a two-way street. The relationship between journalism and politics is a symbiotic one. It has evolved in this century to a point where journalism is every bit as important to politicians and to the processes and rhythms of their working lives, as their activities and pronouncements are to the substance of journalism. The authors of the Kent report remind us of William Lyon Mackenzie King's famous description of the press gallery as "an adjunct of Parliament." They also usefully quote the 1969 report of the federal Task Force on Government Information in its assessment of the gallery as "the most important instrument of political communication in the country."[5]

Arthur Siegel has suggested that there are specific ways in which journalism influences the political process, thereby deriving significant elements of political power in its own right: "Mass media political power flows from five major sources: the media as providers of information, the political linkage role, the agenda-setting role, the editorial offerings, and the direct influence the media have on political actors."[6] Obviously, the mass media have become the greatest single source of political information to the voting public, and the media doubtless derive a certain power as custodians of the basic information "pipeline." In his reference to political linkage, Siegel observes that the media also have a basic power-bestowing role in providing citizens a sense of connectedness to the political system, and thereby are instrumental in defining that sense of connectedness. Agenda-setting, one of journalism's more potent sources of political power, refers to the media's responsibility for selecting, processing, and prioritizing news information, in effect establishing the public agenda. (The concept is more fully discussed in chapter 2.) Siegel also proposes that the media may influence public opinion to some extent through opinion offerings of various kinds. Finally, Siegel offers this caution: "Politics has a seductive influence on journalists, but the liaison must not become too close. Press and politics cannot live without each other but they must also keep their distance."[7]

Living by Disclosure

Thus, while the relationship is absolutely necessary to each party, it can harbour great dangers for each because journalists and politicians tend to view the purposes of the relationship very differently. The classic description of the relationship, especially of the tension that naturally lies at its heart, was provided by the *Times* of London in 1852. When the British foreign minister of the day, Lord Derby, found himself embarrassed by press disclosures relating to sensitive discussions with the government of France, he told Parliament: "The press should remember that they [sic] are not free from the responsibility of statesmen, and that it is incumbent upon them, as a sacred duty, to maintain that tone of moderation even in frankly expressing their opinions on foreign affairs, which would be required of every man who pretends to guide public opinion."

But the *Times* fired back with this editorial retort, and in the process provided the first and best description of the tension phenomenon: "The press lives by disclosures, whatever passes into its hands becomes part of the knowledge of our times, it is daily and forever appealing to the enlightened force of public opinion...the statesman's duty is precisely the reverse. He cautiously guards from the public eye the information by which his actions and opinions are regulated."[8]

The problem of discontent in the relationship between journalist and politician is no small matter. Until recent decades, there never was any doubt as to where the ultimate power resided. In the final analysis, it was clear that it lay with the governors. Any ancillary power journalists might possess could be seen only as deriving from vaguely expressed constitutional conventions such as those relating to freedom of expression. (This, and perhaps nothing more complex than those uncertain and informal, unwritten, and traditional public perceptions relating to the proper conduct of public business in a democracy—the way things *should be* done, because that's the way they *are* done.) As the American columnist, George Will has aptly explained, the exercise of formal power is the constitutional prerogative of the elected politicians of the day, while in the public eye the business of journalism has to do with "consequences."[9]

A great question for modern times asks whether or not new technological conditions, and expectations in reaction to evolving social circumstances may have increased the intensity of those journalistic consequences. Perhaps, in turn, this has generated a shift in recent decades of significant power across our symbiotic equation from the side of the governors to that of their attending journalists. The resulting consequences may have at last made the natural tension in the traditional symbiosis intolerable to those who traditionally and properly have held the greater part of power, namely the elected politicians of the day.

An Intolerable Tradition?

That such a circumstance may have come to exist in the modern equation first suggested itself to this writer in research conducted for the Canadian Radio-television and Telecommunication Commission's Committee of Inquiry into the National Broadcasting Service in 1977.[10] As a part of this research, several members of the House of Commons were interviewed. Most questions related to the members' perceptions of the effectiveness of the news media as political communicators. It also asked members to describe a proper role for news media in the political arena.

The MPs revealed a widely held belief that in applying traditional news values, journalists tended to skew meaning and thrust away from the original intent of the source (mentioned by eleven of the seventeen MPs in the sample). Complaints of "distortion" or "sensationalism" in reporting were frequent (nine mentions) and seven cited laziness, superficiality, or lack of initiative in Parliamentary reporting. Thirteen members complained that Parliamentary news relating to their own regions and ridings was inadequately reported, and fifteen felt news of their regions was inadequately chronicled in the national media. A view often expressed by the members in the study was that Parliamentary journalists tended to ignore information offered to them by MPs and that these journalists generally failed in their responsibility to serve as information conduits to the regions and ridings of the country.[11]

Historically, Canada's federal politicians enjoyed a number of effective alternatives for communication with their electors. First there was the direct process of one-on-one communication, the simple business of talking with people about the issues of the day. This was not difficult in an earlier time when Parliamentary sessions were shorter, and members typically spent a greater portion of their time at home in the riding. It also was easier to keep in touch, virtually on an individual basis, when ridings contained many fewer voters than the 80 000 or more that has become the modern norm.

At the turn of the century, politicians usually made their speeches before large, live, and often enthusiastically critical audiences. This is a far cry from today's more common circumstance involving the throwing of phrases containing only fragments of meaning toward the empty eye of a television camera, in the hope that they may find their distant mark. The traditional Parliamentary privilege of free use of the postal system obviously had far greater significance in an earlier age when the periodic partisan newsletter was an effective "mass medium" in its own right. No list of traditional alternative channels of communication once effectively used by elected politicians, would be complete without reference to the church. In days gone by, when almost everyone went to church and clergy were more inclined to speak their minds on matters temporal as well as spiritual, many a political message was effectively conveyed from the pulpit, especially if it was one with a moralistic flavour.

A century ago, the print media already constituted the democratic politician's primary channel to the community. Apart from newspapers and magazines being obliged to compete with other forms of communication, the consequences of journalism clearly must have been much more tolerable to politicians of the era. The reality is that until quite recent times, newspapers were not as independent of direct partisan influence as that brave *Times* editorial of 1852 suggested, or as much of the romantic mythology of twentieth century North American journalism would have us suppose. Newspapers were commonly subsidized in one way or another by partisan organizations until well into the present century, and as historian Paul Rutherford has said of Canada's nineteenth century press, "a pure, lasting independence was very, very rare."[12]

This is not to suggest that the tension between journalist and politician was of no real consequence in earlier times. Far from it. Even partisan newspapers could be disagreeable at times, as Canada's federal Liberal Party found, for instance, when the *Globe*, the *Toronto Star*, and the Manitoba *Free Press* broke ranks in 1917 over the wartime conscription issue.[13] And even the most partisan of individual reporters and editors always retained a contextual semblance of their assumed right and responsibility to select, process, and prioritize published information as they saw fit.

Most importantly, from the politician's point of view, the ephemeral nature of journalistic power based in the vagaries of public opinion, along with the historic partisan connection, served for many years to ease the worst effects of the tension. Journalism's power was thus not only tolerable but perhaps even acceptable. George Ferguson, the influential mid-century editor of the *Montreal Star*, once described the attitude toward the press of that era among those he called the country's politically-minded minority: "Like Hamlet, it would rather bear those ills it has than fly to others it knows not of."[14]

Conditions touching the relationship between journalist and politician nonetheless changed gradually and greatly during the course of the twentieth century. As early as 1900, developing technologies and expanding market conditions were transforming daily newspapers (individually, and already as links in chains in a few cases) into economic entities too large for direct control or manipulation through partisan coffers. The tradition of journalistic partisanship lingered in waning circumstances to mid-century, and even beyond. But this was more on a voluntary than an obligatory basis, as in the case of the *Toronto Star*'s consistent loyalty to Liberal Party causes, at least to the end of the Trudeau era in the mid-1980s. In fact, it has only been in these latter years of what has been called the era of the "multimedia,"[15] that indifference to partisan pressures and values has become the editorial norm.

Modern media organizations are economically strong corporate entities in their own right, and therefore are free from the temptations of more obvious forms of partisan influence. But media technologies have also been revolutionized, increasing the media system's capabilities. Indeed, the multimedia now so dominate the processes of public information dissemination that the politicians' traditional alternatives simply have ceased to be of much consequence. Modern politicians must rely on the mass media as never before, and in a very real sense these are media transformed, and not at all susceptible to traditional patterns of influence. Whatever evils the old ways and old technologies may have harboured, they provided a certain leavening quality that made the tension phenomenon tolerable, and even comfortable from the political perspective. Given more recent changes that seem effectively—and perhaps dangerously—to mean a considerable loss of control over their own information environment, modern politicians, like Hamlet, may have become less inclined to bear with known ills.

A Proper Pipeline

There are many factors contributing to the present intense state of affairs. Importantly, there are many remarkable differences in perspective and opinion held by politicians as opposed to journalists with regard to journalism's proper place and purpose in politics. As that early *Times* editorial (quoted in part above) suggests, much of the traditional tension between journalists and politicians derives from precisely this source. The problem was also recognized in the 1969 Task Force on Government Information. As the reader may recall from concepts offered in chapter 1, the members of the Task Force felt that a great amount of government information never reaches members of the public who might use it, at least not through the mass media. Expressing a widely held governmental point of view, their report suggests: "the reason it's failing to get there is not that someone is suppressing it, but simply that this information does not help in the peddling of papers."[16]

Another observer, Edwin Black stands in agreement arguing that politicians feel a strong sense of dissatisfaction with the system. "Instead of a direct 'hotline' to and from the citizen grassroots—which would make the work of governing both easier and pleasurable—all they have is a rival, business-oriented, institution which uses them, ignores their legitimate needs, and offers a heavily filtered communications channel only marginally better than nothing."[17] In other words, most politicians likely would prefer to live and work with a much tamer journalism than presently exists, a journalism serving as a sort of mindless pipeline connecting Parliament with the voters. In the politician's ideal world, news releases issued from members' offices would be conveyed verbatim, dutifully and routinely, through printed page and airwave. Information could be relayed via the national media, when the member felt moved to address a national issue, or through local media when the political skids at home in the riding needed a touch of the grease of publicity. News conferences and photo opportunities would be faithfully attended, and their messages as faithfully conveyed through the pipeline. Also important to this vision of a politically domesticated journalism, opinion pieces and backgrounders would be few, and accurate to the member's satisfaction. Editorials would be polite.

Such would be the conduit journalism of the pipeline. Of course, few journalists would agree with much, if any, of this. A cursory examination of the content of daily journalism demonstrates a remarkably different perception of democratic purpose among political journalists and their editors and news directors. But most members of the craft would regard anything akin to pipeline journalism as nothing less than a dereliction of duty. The pipeline circumstance that Black describes, and that our sample of Parliamentarians prefer, runs against the grain of journalism's traditional perception of purpose. Since the time of Milton, the idea of journalism standing as public watchdog at the bar of government precludes any such role, and makes it entirely unthinkable. The argument has been presented in these words: "The great battleground for public opinion is, of course, the mass media. The media carry messages from the government to the people. Their function, however, is not just to transmit the message, for then they would be little more than propaganda outlets for the authorities."[18] Moreover, most modern journalists tend to see their independent role as an expanding, and increasingly complex one. There is the inclination among them to make the unfounded assumption that the latter-day tenets of a "socially responsible" press[19] impose weighty obligations upon political journalism relating to agenda-setting, and to news interpretation and analysis.[20] A senior editor of the *New York Times* has thus expressed his understanding of journalism's modern interpretive role in public affairs reporting:

> News now means more than factual coverage of spot events; it includes the broader trends, the recording and appraisal of currents that run in the far-from-pacific ocean that is the world

today. The factual reports that sufficed in the time of simple journalism are no longer adequate to provide understanding; interpretation—that is BACKGROUND: survey of the past and analysis of the present; and FOREGROUND: illumination of the future—has become essential.[21]

Thus modern political journalists now feel encouraged and even morally bound by the capacities of their new technologies, their new economic independence from political thraldoms of various forms, and their sense of an expanded "social responsibility," to participate more actively in the arena of politics and government than journalism has ever done before.

Glibness and Superficiality

Paradoxically, it is precisely as journalists have identified an expanded role for themselves, and have moved enthusiastically toward it, that it has become evident to many observers that the mass media are ill-equipped to assume such untraditional and unfamiliar responsibilities. Their agendas and purposes move them far from anyone's reasonable sense of service to the public good. In this sense, and noting the irony of the paradox, while the media have become vastly more powerful as social communicators in recent decades, the political journalism they contain has become less efficient and more superficial.

One of Canada's most senior political journalists, Jeffrey Simpson, sees a growing cynicism and its associated evils as being used increasingly by journalists to mask to their own ineptness in the modern circumstance of growing media power. In his words: "it pains me to see the glibness and superficiality, the rushed judgements, and worst of all, this developing cynicism, which at heart is nothing more than a refusal to accept the admission of ignorance and the need to rectify it."[22]

A sort of protective shorthand is implied here. Without a depth of understanding or a capacity to reach it, modern journalists tend to hide behind a formula generating a political journalism that is confrontational in its style; judgemental and controversial in its content. Journalists have long recognized (usually not in a mean-spirited sense, or even consciously much of the time) that violent information scenarios generate the most obviously newsworthy items for publication or broadcast, and that they often do so with the least expenditure of talent, intellect, or energy. From this, journalists also have recognized that where the overt ingredients of violence are not present in a given news scenario, then those surrogates of violence, controversy and confrontation, can provide excellent substitutes.

Modern political journalism thus has become mainly a matter of presenting information in contexts of confrontation and controversy. The effect on public perceptions of reality is every bit as distorting as are the more widely recognized consequences of an undue emphasis on violence.

A Case Study: The Mohawk Crisis

The trends discussed above became evident in research conducted jointly by the writer and a colleague, Andrew MacFarlane, into press behaviour during 1990's summer of hostility and confrontation involving members of the Mohawk communities at the Kanesatake (Oka) and Kahnawake reserves south of Montreal.[23] Longstanding frustrations existed among the region's Mohawks over territorial claims, and other dealings with provincial and federal authorities. Emotions peaked when officials at the non-Native community at nearby Oka on the south shore of the Saint Lawrence River sought to enlarge a municipal golf course by using land claimed by the Mohawks. Tempers flared, and tragedy soon followed: a police officer died in an exchange of gunfire in mid-July, and the whole affair quickly escalated into a major confrontation. Members of the Sûreté du Québec (the provincial police force) and, later, units of the Canadian Armed Forces confronted militant Mohawks, members of the so-called Warrior faction. The stand-off lasted until the dying days of September when the army, which had effectively laid siege to the Mohawk communities, forced the Warriors to lay down their arms and surrender. While there was much posturing and brandishing of weapons during those hot and dramatic summer months, thankfully the only directly attributable death, was that of Sûreté Corporal Marcel LeMay who died in the initial golf course challenge.

Our work involved a quantitative content analysis of eleven daily newspapers, including five francophone papers from Montreal and Quebec City. All four Montreal dailies, *Journal de Montréal, La Presse, Le Devoir* and the *Gazette* were included; as were the three Toronto dailies, (the *Globe and Mail,* the *Toronto Star* and the *Toronto Sun*); the *Ottawa Citizen* and Quebec City's *Le Soleil.* More distantly, the *London Free Press* and the *Winnipeg Free Press* also were analyzed. All non-advertising material (news, features, editorials, letters, background articles) relating to the Mohawk crisis was subjected to analysis for eighteen sample days through the crisis period from 12 July until 29 September, 1990.

Each item was catalogued according to a set of eleven subject themes. The most important of these were:

> 1. Military, paramilitary, or police action: Physical confrontation or manoeuvring between the primary disputing parties.
>
> 2. Violence and/or criminal activity: Real, threatened, otherwise described, but not appropriately covered by (1) above.
>
> 3. Political activity of any type: Including negotiations involving any official body including native or mainstream political organizations, the military, police, or paramilitary organizations.
>
> 4. Community well-being: Any information not touched upon in (1) or (2) above, but involving social concerns; the physical, psychological well-being of members of the Native communities involved.
>
> 5. Native religious and/or cultural concerns: Any item not more appropriately categorized elsewhere and touching an issue of religion or culture, or both, including matters relating to the longhouse and native cultural tradition.

By far the largest number of individual items fell into one or another of these categories. This aspect of the research examined "hard" or current news items. We found that percentages among the six representative papers described in Table 1, for instance, ranged from a high of 60.1 per cent of all relevant hard news items in the case of Montreal's *Gazette*, to a low of 54.8 per cent in the case of *Le Devoir*. Typically, the largest number of these news items treated themes of violence or direct confrontation. The second area (numerically the first, in the case of *Le Soleil*, and marginally so in the case of the *Globe and Mail*) treated political matters, with all the potential this category holds for the development of themes of confrontation and controversy.

It is interesting that in the case of each newspaper, only a relatively small fraction of news items was devoted to the rich potential of non-violent, non-confrontational themes relating to Mohawk life, religion, and culture.

In another aspect of our analysis, we created profiles of the work of eight journalists (two from each of four major newspapers) who covered the crisis from its tragic beginning in mid-July until uneasy peace finally was restored at the end of September.

T
A
B
L
E

1

The Mohawk Crisis of 1990: News Themes Comparison

Total	Themes 1 and 2 Confrontation		Theme 3 Political		Themes 4 and 5 Cultural	
	Items	Column Inches	Items	Column Inches	Items	Column Inches
Gazette	91	2643.0	51	1290.0	25	647.5
N = 278 items N^1 = 6839.0 ci	32.7% of N	36.0% of N^1	18.3%	18.9%	9.0%	9.5%
Globe & Mail	22	776.0	23	659.5	11	244.5
N = 96 items N^1 = 2683.5 ci	23.0%	29.0%	24.0%	24.6%	11.5%	9.1%
Le Soleil	40	967.0	53	1152.5	11	237.0
N = 174 items N^1 = 3492.0 ci	23.0%	27.7%	30.5%	33.0%	6.3%	6.8%
Le Devoir	43	879.5	29	644.5	2	25.0
N = 135 items N^1 = 2526.5 ci	31.9%	34.8%	21.5%	25.5%	1.5%	1.0%
Journal de Montréal	82	2457.5	55	1210.0	12	213.0
N = 238 items N^1 = 6285.5 ci	34.5%	39.1%	23.1%	19.3%	5.0%	3.4%

Note: N in each case represents the total number of hard news items analyzed in the sample for this newspaper.
N^1 in each case represents the total number of column inches for hard news.

Almost without exception, these profiled journalists stressed violent/confrontational and political themes at the expense of a potentially wide range of cultural and other non-violent and non-confrontational thematic possibilities (table 2). Such cultural information would have provided the background media consumers needed to reach a deeper understanding of the social context of the Mohawk rage. Moreover, as table 2 also indicates, the overwhelming tendency among these journalists was to use the dramatic Warriors, and to a somewhat lesser extent, members of the Canadian military, as their

The Mohawk Crisis of 1990: Journalist Performance Profiles

	Gazette		Le Devoir		Journal de Montréal		Globe and Mail	
	1	2	1	2	1	2	1	2
	N = 17	N = 13	N = 17	N = 27	N = 27	N = 15	N = 21	N = 13
Themes								
Confrontation 1, 2	7	6	9	2	9	6	6	5
Political 3	7	2	7	5	6	3	8	3
Cultural 4, 5	2	2	0	0	0	0	3	2
Other	1	3	1	0	12	6	4	3
Background Articles	0	0	0	0	6	0	0	1
Primary Sources Used								
Warriors	6	3	0	0	2	4	6	7
Other crisis-area Mohawks	3	2	2	0	1	1	2	0
Other Native	1	0	1	1	1	1	1	1
Federal government	0	1	4	4	4	0	2	3
Quebec government	2	1	3	0	1	0	2	0
Army	2	1	4	2	9	2	2	2
Non-native community	0	2	0	0	6	4	0	0
Other	3	3	3	0	3	3	6	0

TABLE 2

Note: N represents the total of crisis-related articles appearing during the sample period under each selected journalist's byline.

primary news sources. In the meantime, references to non-militant natives, and to other important players not directly involved in violent or confrontational scenarios were significantly downplayed or even ignored. It is disappointing to note that only one of these involved journalists, perhaps surprisingly a writer for the sensationalized tabloid, *Journal de Montréal*, made any serious effort to reflect on the issues by providing readers with background articles.

Television's technological imperatives have moved all of journalism in these dangerous directions. Anyone who reflects upon events of the summer of 1990 will remember those television images of Canadian soldiers standing jowl to jowl and toe to toe with those mysterious woodland guerrillas, patriots but also with a touch of the gangster in each of them—the Mohawk Warriors. These were images of violence, confrontation, and drama. But at the same time they were shallow images that provided little real information, not just about what was happening but also about what it all meant. Television has thus terribly intensified journalism's tendency to deal with all news, but especially political news, in such a manner.

A Canadian soldier and a Mohawk Warrior stand face to face in the Kanesatake (Oka) stand off in the summer of 1990. Television may have emerged as the only "winner" in this confrontation over land use and other differences between Mohawk and non-Native interests in the Montreal and Cornwall regions. (Canapress Photo Service/Komulainen)

"Lied to rather a lot..."

It should be recognized that the conditions of political journalism in recent decades have done little to engender mutual trust or good will in the difficult relationship between journalist and politician.

George Will has noted that modern political journalism is characterized by circumstances in which editors expect comparatively small numbers of reporters to cover all aspects of government. The reporters find themselves "outgunned by a government of intimidating size, daunting complexity, and much energy when advocating its own version of the news."[24] Add to this the atmosphere of confrontation and painful mistrust that came to characterize political reporting during the 1970s rundown from Vietnam, and that was intensified through the Watergate experience. This atmosphere continues to persist with the entrenchment of a tradition in the manipulative partisan processes that have dominated every national election in the United States, Canada, and most of the Western world in modern decades. It is small wonder that political journalists have come to believe that, as George Will claims "they have been lied to rather a lot in recent years."

A majority of political journalists have become untrusting and defensive in their work, taking something of a foxhole approach to reporting. An important ingredient, mistrust on the part of journalists, is thus added to the circumstance that seems to have its major source in journalism's own ineptness to its task. The whole problem tends to be made more obscure by the overlying and romanticized Woodward and Bernstein mythology of "investigative journalism." As already noted, such smoke and mirrors tactics often amount to little more than a cloaking of ordinary things, often readily available information under distorting layers of controversy and confrontation.

At best, this cloaking process provides fundamentally little information, and hides the reality that much political news represents very little in the way of independent reportorial initiative and research. The hidden truth is that a great majority of political news items actually come into being easily derived and largely predigested from official sources—the brouhahah of the Parliamentary question period, the hand-delivered news release, the distributed text of a speech, the staged media event, the photo opportunity and all the rest. In the worst scenario, public perspective on politics, the received truth becomes skewed toward the impression that confrontation and controversy are both normal and necessary. Kindlier and more constructive processes of conciliation and compromise seem impossible.

As Simpson has suggested, journalists cover their sins by putting on that awful mask of cynicism. The end result is a "political agnosticism, if you will, or...a sustained surliness toward government."[25] It is a surliness that can, and does, infect the entire political process with its poison, touching every political decision—from those made by prime ministers, to those made by the humblest of voting citizens.

Carman Cumming, who teaches journalism at Carleton University, has described the overall process more gently but no less critically as a "judgemental style" of journalism. In his words:

> The salient feature of the age is a tendency to impose or accentuate win/lose patterns in political happenings, through emphasis on conflict, personalities and strong point-of-view reporting...it is no longer good enough to report the terms of government legislation; the journalist must show whether it is good or bad legislation. It is no longer enough to report what [the] prime minister did...the journalist must say whether it was a success or failure. The judgements are not always overt; sometimes they are done by fact selection. But the result is the same: A kind of sports page approach to public policy.[26]

The sports page allusion seems unfortunately apt. The escalating tension between journalists and politicians certainly has reached a point where something analogous to warfare exists. Rationales justifying defensive behaviour are present on both sides, and obvious stratagems have been put in place as advantages are sought.

The Infocan Experience

In 1970, in response to the recommendations of its 1969 Task Force on Government Information, an early priority of the first government of Pierre Trudeau was to establish Information Canada, a federal media and information management agency. Infocan's life was short, largely because it committed a cardinal sin among propagandists and public relations practitioners; it developed a highly visible public image. Thus, it stood as a lightning rod, drawing media scorn and public contempt, and quickly became dysfunctional and a political liability. It was disbanded under the pretext of a government economy drive in 1975, but clearly it was an interesting experiment in the search for avenues around the mass news media. As Joe Clark stated in a House of Commons debate in 1973: "It [Infocan] is, in short, an attempt to get around the normal filters of democracy; an attempt not to present information, but to manage it."[27]

Though Information Canada died an untimely death, the idea of news and information management in the era of the modern media has remained very much a perceived need among politicians and bureaucrats. Information Canada never really died; most of the services it provided to government were shifted to less visible places. Within a year of Infocan's demise, a low-profile Task Force on Service to the Public had been established within the federal Department of Supply and Services and was busily engaged in successfully providing a wide array of information services. The government had "gone into the marketing business; the product it is trying to sell is itself."[28]

The process continues. Political campaigns have become exercises in sophisticated partisan manipulation as, for instance, Clive Cocking demonstrated in his diary of Canada's 1979 federal election.[29] Occasionally, we have seen the manipulative purpose escalate to something different and considerably more dangerous, namely the attempt to control by legislation. This seems to have been one purpose among others contained in the recommendations of the report of the Royal Commission on Newspapers. It most certainly was a very clear purpose of the subsequent legislation, the draft Daily Newspapers Act that died on Order Paper some months after being introduced in the House of Commons in July, 1983.

A Moral Right of Media?

For their part, the media insist on a form of moral right justifying their actions. As discussed in chapter 3, many journalists have used the mid-century social responsibility theory to assume an enhanced role for themselves and their craft in society, especially in their relationship with government. Since the passing of the Charter of Rights and Freedoms in Canada in 1982, there have been a number of challenges from the media, seeking protected and privileged positions under the law. (These themes are discussed more fully in chapter 6.) Most of the challenges involved the circumstances under which journalists may or may not be required to reveal secret news sources in courts of law, or before the various boards and commissions with powers to subpoena.

While such efforts have not met with much success in the courts, the language of their arguments is instructive. Inevitably, in one form or another, the position seems to be that journalism morally and ethically serves to protect citizens from the state, and thus merits special safeguards before the law. By definition in such arguments, journalism tends to assume the moral high ground for itself while relegating formally constituted authorities to some lesser place.

Consider, by way of example, these words from a CBC public affairs producer's affidavit to a 1989 Ontario Supreme Court hearing on a question of privilege relating to sources. The distressing implication is that journalism may be the only secure place where an individual with dangerous information may turn in the modern democracy.

> Often...sources require protection because they would suffer serious repercussions with regard to their employment or

income or in rare, but significant instances, because disclosure would threaten their safety and security....In my opinion the public interest is served if the media are protected as a "secure system" by which people with important inside information... can communicate with others on matters of public concern.[30]

Finally, it is interesting to note that there is at least one other movement in Canada urging the release of journalism from restraining law. A moral crusade for the reform of libel law has developed in recent years within the journalistic community. The underlying notion is that libel (a concept more fully discussed in chapter 6) has been used frivolously by powerful organizations and individuals in recent years as a means of containing journalism. Journalists complain that libel laws inhibit free journalism and impose a "chill effect" on the work of journalists. Many have begun to actively participate in efforts to eliminate or reduce the restraint that libel law imposes on their craft. Here again, the argument is that the public interest can only be properly served by an unfettered journalism, and that somehow journalism is the only public institution with the moral strength to enjoy such freedom. It is an interesting argument, if somewhat dubious in its logic. This argument was very much at the core of things in November, 1990, when the Writers' Union of Canada organized a demonstration in Toronto protesting libel suits then before the courts. Actions were commenced against various journalists and their employers by groups and individuals such as the Reichmann family with its enormous real estate investments; financier-publisher Conrad Black; and by lawyer and public servant Allan Gotlieb.[31] The libel issue is particularly interesting in this context. It demonstrates that tension, with its capacity for distortion that lies between journalist and politician, also exists, to some extent, wherever journalists relate to the public.

Other Institutions

Society's organizations and guiding institutions: businesses, educational and charitable institutions, and religious organizations, all maintain public relations services. In some cases these responsibilities may be left to a single individual who may write a few press releases, and make a few media contacts in addition to other duties; sometimes costly and sophisticated agency services may be contracted in, or full-scale corporate departments of public and media relations specialists may be established.

Much of the dynamic behind this expensive activity has to do with the modern reality that many people have messages they urgently wish to lay before the public, and they are very much in competition with each other in the scramble for limited media space. It is also true, however, that these observations concerning the relationship between journalism and the political system (the agendas of the media; the search for newsworthy information, or for information that can be forced into those newsworthy molds of violence, controversy, or confrontation) applies to journalism's relationship with all other social institutions.

Like politics and politicians, other institutions and the people who work within them often feel uncomfortably defensive in their relationships with the mass news media. Where other institutions have a different set of public concerns as their major reasons for being, "the so-called Fourth Estate is more concerned about profit, entertainment, and audience-building."[32]

In at least one other institutional circumstance, that of organized religion, journalism's insistence upon making all information fit the molds of its own design has been especially destructive. As Northrop Frye once suggested, we exist in a modern world where those ideas and activities that have to do with the spirit, have been expunged from the range of things that the forms of modern language allow us to imagine. These are the *linguistic* forms of detachment, the popular modes of the emotionless, descriptive language of the science laboratory that during the twentieth century have escaped into the streets in the form of journalism's stripped formulas of objective and distanced expression. Frye described our modern linguistic circumstance as a third phase of language, a "demotic" phase, essentially following upon an originating era of metaphor at the dawn of Western civilization, and the rich historic middle epoch of allegory. He noted that "for the third [modern] phase of language, the word 'God' becomes linguistically unfunctional."[33] The substance of religion thus becomes something that the language of journalism cannot deal with or comprehend.

Expressing these concerns in simpler terms, the Canadian religion journalist Tom Harpur has written: "The coverage of religion, morals and spiritual values by media in North America is a journalistic wasteland." Most media people, he adds, seem "locked into an outdated and narrow view of what religion and spirituality are about." And later in the same piece, "because the religious and the spiritual may *seem*, to the lightweight journalistic imagination, to be irrelevant…shamefully few newspapers, TV or radio stations have journalists with professional training to do the job."[34]

In other words, whereas politics often seems to excite the journalistic imagination to a perilous excess, religion has had a different effect. The journalistic imagination simply has failed to allow religion a serious place in the modern information mix. The exception is when news about religious organizations has little to do with religion itself. For instance, such non-spiritual matters as sexual scandal in a Newfoundland orphanage, or fraud in an American television evangelism operation are bound to covered. Indeed, they should be. But they do not convey much about religion as a human experience.

Each circumstance says much in its own way about modern journalism's impact within the communication symbiosis it shares, not just with government and the political process, but with all of society's institutions. The situation has not always been so, of course. Tension has always existed, and there has been information distortion in the flow of meaning as long as there has been a reasonably free journalism struggling to make the world interesting for its readers. But as will be shown in the next sections, modern technology has taken the issue to new extremes.

Television's Impact

There are a number of ways in which television and related technology contribute to the new and dangerous departures in the media's relationship with institutions. One factor is the sheer speed of the modern process. "Sometimes, everybody, whether prime minister or fish-packer, learns of the crisis at the same time—through the mass media. What is more, normal journalistic activity generates demands for action NOW!"[35]

The following scenario should illustrate the point. A member of Parliament gives a brief speech in the House during the daily question period. He or she plays for a bit of media attention, and perhaps is successful on this hypothetical occasion. Minutes later, there is some elaboration of a point of view; responses to media-generated ancillary questions in one of those much-microphoned corridor "scrums" with cameras and pencils grinding furiously. An hour or so later, our MP flies or drives back home to his or her own riding.

By the time home base is achieved, news of that Parliamentary encounter likely will have been processed for broadcast—perhaps already have been on the air, or even in print. In all likelihood, the news will have beaten our MP home and public opinion will already have been established. Our member will have no recourse but to react

The classic *scrum.* Claude Ryan, the publisher and journalist who became leader of Quebec's Liberal Party in the early 1980s fends off journalists with "one-liners" that provide the brief clips so valued by the electronic media. Print journalists are always part of the scrum, but usually on its outer edges. (Canapress Photo Service/J. Boissinot)

to the media's collective analysis. The issue is out of the MP's hands, and will have assumed a life and dynamic of its own. If our member is invited to offer further comment, this necessarily will take the form of reaction to an already established public record.

In a word, the speed of the system is such that members lose control over the pace and rhythm of their own communications. When the electronic reality of modern politics is added to journalism's self-assumed right and responsibility to select, prioritize, and interpret the news, then one can see why many politicians (and others, in other institutions) feel that they have lost control over their own communication processes.

As McLuhan might have put it, journalism is now conducted at electric speeds. But this alone does not even begin to describe the full complexity of modern processes at work in the conduct of political communication, the result of the new technologies.

Consider, for a moment, Black's words about the impact of television (regarding politics in this case, but with clear application to most other public concerns): "Our politics is all about ideas, and often subtle and complicated ones. Where newspapers were virtually invented to serve the needs of those discussing public affairs, broadcasting was not. The discursiveness so characteristic of politics makes it poor fodder for television…its operational values are those of mass entertainment."[36]

Sacrificing traditional ways of doing things, the technological imperatives of television have imposed conditions that are in the process of profoundly changing our entire perception of the nature and purpose of discourse in the public forum.

A Rapid-Fire Flow

Television is the communication technology that requires dramatic information clips in rapid-fire succession, a continuous flow of up-tempo excitement. It is the technology that demands an endless and unbroken stream of graphic images to meet the demands of the screen's insatiable appetite. Technology, therefore, makes television overwhelmingly an entertainment medium, and journalism is very much a part of the the the entertainment provided.

Thus, the considered political statement (in the House, in a speech, or in the context of a journalistic interview) becomes transformed into television's arresting one-sentence comment or one-liner. Imperatively, that one-liner will be easily photographed because, as we have seen, television is nothing if not a visual medium. It is of little consequence to television if the politician's words disappear altogether in the process. The words can be substituted with his or her video image set against an interesting background, or engaged in some dramatic event. The politician becomes an actor, but with most crucial dialogue left to the anchor's smooth, professional voice-over, or authoritative head-and-shoulders pronouncement. These changes make for better television.

The anchor, guiding his or her team of familiar electronic journalists, takes over the whole information environment. These people are the stars—the authorities. It is they who have the advantage of the "re-ask"; whose makeup is impeccable; who control the rhythms, the script, and the questions to be asked. Often, the camera shoots up to them and down to the politicians they interview. Certainly, it is the television news team members who always have the last word.

The electronic journalist serves as referee in the modern arena of public affairs communication. The politician (or the activist or union leader, for that matter) is often reduced to the position of supplicant—an amateur pleading to make a point, or seeking permission to argue a case; but only at the discretion of the professional media authority figures. In the long-term, television audiences at the very least, must come to view many public figures, especially politicians, as persons of less consequence than the media people who cover their activities.

For precisely these reasons, Robert Fulford has described the television newscast as the most influential form of modern mass communication.[37] He reasons that television provides a technically seamless form with no facts or questions seemingly unattended. The world is thus presented in its entirety, in however many broadcast minutes allocated for the newscast. For many viewers, the viewing experience becomes so powerful and so complete that it conjures patterns of meaning in a chaotic world that once were provided by the structures of religious belief.

The on-air personalities who deliver these patterned packages derive a power from their participation in the process that no print journalist ever possessed. As Fulford has expressed it, when television news personalities address an audience,

> they maintain an even, cool tone and a direct, noncommittal gaze. They are affable but never effusive. Their intonation betrays neither delight nor anger. They are surprised by nothing. They apparently never get excited. Someone being interviewed may shout or burst into tears—that makes "good television"—but the reporter will remain calm. In general TV reporters take their subjects, particularly politicians, less seriously than the subjects take themselves. Often they speak of the people they cover with a certain easy disdain. Sometimes...this reflects the cynicism of long experience; sometimes it appears to be nothing more than a mannerism picked up from other reporters, an attitudinal twitch.[38]

And, all the individual news items in a given broadcast end "tidily—always in the same way. Covering a routine fire, or the most terrifying hostage-taking, the reporter never fails to conclude with the same earnest glance into the camera, the same dying fall ("Mike Duffy, CBC News, Ottawa"). The reporter is saying: no matter what happens, we are in control."

NOTES

1. Gaye Tuchman, *Making News: A Study in the Construction of Reality* (New York: The Free Press, 1978), 21.

2. *Matthews List*, April, 1990.

3. Andrew M. Osler, "Routine and Hidden Sources: A Content Analysis of the Globe and Mail and the Toronto Star." A report of commissioned research to the Attorney General for Ontario, 1989. Altogether, 383 news items—all the general news items printed in *Toronto Star* during the sample period—were analyzed; while 273 were analyzed from the *Globe and Mail*, which is physically somewhat smaller than the *Star*.

4. Andrew M. Osler, "An Analysis of Some Aspects of French and English Content in the Canadian Press Wire Service." A report of commissioned research to the Canadian Radio-television and Telecommunications Commission, Committee of Inquiry into the National Broadcasting Service, 1977.

5. Canada, *Report*, The Royal Commission on Newspapers (Ottawa: Supply and Services Canada, 1981), 141.

6. Arthur Siegel, *Politics and the Media in Canada* (Toronto: McGraw-Hill Ryerson Ltd., 1983), 14.

7. Ibid., 20.

8. Harold Herd, *The March of Journalism* (Westport, CT: The Greenwood Press, 1976), 142.

9. George F. Will, "The Problem Isn't Bias," *Nieman Reports*, Autumn, 1977.

10. Andrew Osler, "No One is Listening: Media Voices from the Regions of Canada." A report of commissioned research to the Committee of Inquiry into the National Broadcasting Service, Canadian Radio-television and Telecommunications Commission, 1977. The writer presented the data more fully in a later invited paper, "The Conflicting Purposes of Journalists and Elected Federal Politicians in Canada," at the Conference on Media and Foreign Policy, sponsored by the Canadian Institute for International Affairs and the Department of Political Science, University of Windsor, Windsor, Ontario in October, 1983.

11. The sample was selected in manner which made it representative of the political parties in the House of Commons at the time, and with regard to such matters as age and seniority of the members, geographical and cultural background.

12. Paul Rutherford, *The Making of the Canadian Media* (Toronto: McGraw-Hill Ryerson, 1978), 28.

13. Ibid., 69.

14. George V. Ferguson, "Freedom of the Press," in G.V. Ferguson and Frank Underhill, *Press and Party in Canada: Issues of Freedom. The Chancellor Dunning Trust Lectures, Queen's University, 1955* (Toronto: The Ryerson Press, 1955), 7.

15. Rutherford, *The Making of the Canadian Media*, 78.

16. Canada, *Report*, Task Force on Government Information, vol. 1, "To Know and Be Known" (Ottawa: The Queen's Printer, 1969), 10.

17. Edwin R. Black, *Politics and the News* (Toronto: Butterworths, 1982), 222.

18. Siegel, *Politics and Media in Canada*, 19.

19. Theodore Peterson, "The Social Responsibility Theory of the Press," in Fred S. Siebert, Theodore Peterson and Wilbur Schramm, *Four Theories of the Press* (Urbana: University of Illinois Press, 1956), 73–103. In this essay, Peterson provides

one of the better summaries of the work at Chicago of the mid-century Commission on the Freedom of the Press that generated the so-called "social responsibility theory of the press."

20. There has been a tendency on the part of journalists and media organizations over the years, to accept those aspects of the social responsibility theory that would seem to enhance journalism's importance and prestige in society, while rejecting those that might be seen as limiting press freedom. This is evident, for instance, in the *Toronto Star*'s brief to the 1970 Senate committee on the mass media in which an educational responsibility is enthusiastically accepted, but such possibilities as press laws or even press councils, stand rejected. The matter is discussed more fully in chapter 4. See Toronto Star Ltd., "Submission to Special Senate Committee on Mass Media," Ottawa, 30 January 1970.

21. Lester Markel, "Definition of News," *Nieman Reports*, Autumn, 1972.

22. Jeffrey Simpson, "Everybody wants to be a critic: Canadian journalism could do with a lot less cynicism," *Globe and Mail*, 2 May 1988.

23. Andrew Osler and Andrew MacFarlane, "How Eleven Newspapers reported Oka." An invited paper presented at the annual meeting of the Canadian Communication Association, Kingston, Ontario, 30 May 1991, and at *Journalists and the Mohawk Crisis—Summer 1990*, a colloquium at the Université du Québec a Montréal, 1 June 1991. The Osler-MacFarlane research (conducted under the auspices of the Centre for Mass Media Studies at the University of Western Ontario) was part of much larger project involving a television content analysis directed by Professor Ross Perigoe at Concordia University, Montreal; an in-depth interview project directed by Professor Armande St. Jean at Université du Québec à Montréal; and a study of radio hotline shows directed by Professor Florian Sauvageau at Université Laval, Québec.

24. Will, "The Problem Isn't Bias."

25. Simpson, "Everybody wants to be a critic."

26. Carman Cumming, "The Coming Battle Over Media Power," *Carleton Journalism Review*, Spring, 1977.

27. *Hansard*, July 23, 1973.

28. Robert J. Jackson, Doreen Jackson and Nicholas Baxter-Moore, *Politics in Canada Culture, Institutions Behaviour and Public Policy* (Scarborough, ON: Prentice-Hall Canada Inc., 1986), 169.

29. Clive Cocking, *Following the Leaders A Media Watcher's Diary of Campaign '79* (Toronto: Doubleday Canada Ltd., 1980).

30. Linden MacIntyre, *Affidavit*. Supreme Court of Ontario (Divisional Court) in the matter of the Public Inquiries ACT, R.S.O., c.411 and the Royal Commission of Inquiry into the Niagara Regional Police Force between Judge W.E.C. Colter, Commissioner and Gerald McAuliffe.

31. H.J. Kirchhoff, "Writers' union to demonstrate Members protesting against 'libel chill,'" *Globe and Mail*, 29 November 1990.

32. Black, *Politics and the News*, 6.

33. Northrop Frye, *The Great Code* (Toronto: Academic Press Canada, 1981), 15.

34. Tom Harpur, "Religion coverage lacks expertise," *Toronto Star*, 13 March 1988.

35. Black, *Politics and the News*, 11.
36. Black, *Politics and the News*, 139.
37. Robert Fulford, "NOTEBOOK: The Grand Illusion," *Saturday Night*, June 1984.
38. Ibid.

Social

Control:

A Basis

in Law

CHAPTER

6

As the law touching journalism has accumulated over the centuries, it has provided some of the most important benchmarks in identifying journalism's place in society—its purposes, the nature of its freedom, and its responsibilities. This chapter will look at the outcome in lawmaking of journalistic values, and traditions of freedom of expression that have evolved since the time of Milton.

In their summary of the law as it touches journalism in Canada, Robert Martin and Stuart Adam make an interesting distinction between the right to express opinions, on the one hand, and the right to know, or to acquire information on the other. These may be seen as twin principles fundamental to the whole idea and tradition of free communication, a combined concept "so fundamental to democratic societies that it can be limited only for clear and pressing reasons."[1] For the practical purposes of the journalist, the right to know probably is a clearer and more absolute concept in law than the right to publish information, or to express an opinion about it. Again, as Martin and Adam have stated: "The right to know—that is, the right to gather information—is one thing; the rights to pass it on and express opinions about it are another."[2] The Quebec "Padlock Law" is an example of the harsh laws of restraint on the dissemination of information and the expression of opinion found in Canadian legal history. This law made the publication of communist points of view illegal, from the time of its adoption in the late 1930s until the Supreme Court of Canada declared it unconstitutional in 1957. In Alberta, short-lived legislation enacted in the 1930s and soon disallowed, was intended to give the provincial government a measure of control over news published about itself.

Despite the inclination of the courts to strike down these dangerous legal peculiarities over the years, federal and provincial governments still possess certain powerful authoritarian legislative instruments that apparently are acceptable to the courts. These range from the Official Secrets Act of 1939 (and several earlier British and domestic versions dating to the 1880s), to the Emergencies Act passed in 1988 to replace the much-criticized War Measures Act. The War Measures Act was last applied amid great controversy, and with an effective suspension of civil liberties, during Quebec's FLQ terrorist crisis of 1970. The Official Secrets Act and the Emergencies Act are discussed more fully later in this chapter, as is the FLQ crisis and its implications for the practice of free journalism in Canada. For the moment it is sufficient to note that the Official Secrets Act and the Emergencies Act stand (apparently within acceptable Constitutional parameters) as the most severe measures available to Canada's federal government. Yet, they are not the only elements in the genre of potentially coercive legislation. The seemingly much more positive Access to Information Act of 1985, for instance, is designed to carefully control the outward flow of government information, as well as to provide orderly public access to it. The same may be said of the various provincial information access laws. Even the Charter of Rights and Freedoms in the Constitution Act of 1982, Section 2(b) describes "freedom of thought, belief, opinion and expression, including freedom of press and other media of communication" as one of four fundamental freedoms. But it also notes in Section 1 that these and other freedoms are guaranteed "subject only to such *reasonable limits prescribed by law* as can be demonstrably justified in a free and democratic society." The italics are added here to show that the Supreme Court will have an important responsibility in years and decades ahead in determining precisely what *reasonable limits* suitably frame a *fundamental* freedom.

Whatever limits may exist under statute, ultimately to be defined by the courts, these limits primarily deal with the public expression of ideas. No practical bounds can be placed on private thought. Even though no attempt is made in the Charter or elsewhere to describe newsgathering as a "right," to all intents and purposes, few limitations can be placed on the process. (This provided one goes about gathering news information in a civil manner; does not resort to theft, blackmail, or other forms of criminal behaviour proscribed by the Criminal Code; and does not violate statutory limitations, such as those contained in the Official Secrets Act—all being "reasonable limits," one presumes.)

Prior Restraint

This discussion of limitations indirectly points to a concept called *freedom from prior restraint.* A philosophic value more than a principle in law (at least in its rather vague Canadian application) this concept underlies almost everything else having to do with journalism, public communication, and the definition of freedom of communication in our laws. As Martin and Adam have explained: "In the twentieth century, we would say we ought to be free to speak and publish and broadcast without prior restraint, subject to the laws."[3] Thus, freedom has few limits concerning the individual going about the more or less private business of gathering information. We come even closer to this ideal of absolute freedom in our thoughts and private conversations. It is only when information and ideas are published or broadcast that the full range of restricting laws and legal limitations comes into effect.

First of all, freedom to communicate means freedom from prior restraint. Without this first principle, nothing else much matters. Laws governing what may happen to information and opinion after publication or broadcast, and by implication to its author, is another matter. But here, too, the tradition, at least until the present century, has been to generate as little law as necessary to maintain reasonable order in the democracy. The priority is to protect both individuals and institutions from the malicious or unintended damage that can arise, on occasion, from unrestrained public communications.

Contempt of Court

Largely formulated before the beginning of the present century, traditional law touching journalism has two important components—contempt and libel. The concept of contempt of court has roots in English common law dating to the twelfth century,[4] and it remains in the unique position of being the only criminal offence that is not specifically described in the Criminal Code.[5] Contempt as a concept in law exists to protect the courts and the people who appear before them from any force or behaviour that might threaten to disturb the fair and orderly operation of the judicial system, or interfere with the due process of law. It is for this reason that the determination of contempt, alone among criminal offences, has been left mainly to the discretion of judges.

Contempt is particularly interesting from the journalist's point of view because it creates one of the very few places in law where the right of free expression and press can stand in conflict with other basic rights. For the most part, Canadian courts have recognized the validity of both, and sought to protect them. An example was provided by a Vancouver judge who declined to cite contempt in a 1957 case in which two of the city's newspapers had used an accused person's name in their coverage of a violent crime scenario, thus possibly compromising the fundamental common law principle that the accused stands innocent until guilt is proven. Media treatment included such iridescent headlines as: "I'll Kill Anyone! Four Held Prisoner by Crazed Gunman."

It is interesting that the judge not only showed considerable restraint, but also provided an excellent look at the contempt concept and the philosophy of its application as these have evolved in Canada: "It is the business of newspapers to gather and publish information to their readers of matters of public importance and that right will not be interfered with unless the higher right of the courts to determine the guilt or innocence of an accused is thereby prejudiced or interfered with."[6] Contempt generally has been applied in Canadian courts with restraint, recognizing that its application usually arises in circumstances where fundamental rights are in conflict. From the journalistic point of view, it is important to realize that contempt is also a broad and sweeping concept. It can touch a potentially great amount of the journalist's work.

Contempt can be committed almost anywhere, inside the courtroom itself or outside in the form of a public statement, publication, or broadcast. In the latter case, which is much more likely to be a source of trouble for the working journalist, the offence is described as *constructive contempt*. It falls into three basic forms:

> 1. Publications tending to pervert the impartiality of the judicial process in criminal cases;
> 2. Publications scandalizing the court or members of the judiciary through undue criticism; and
> 3. Publications unnecessarily abusing parties involved in civil [non-criminal] causes before the courts so as to make them compromise or refrain from using the courts.[7]

The third of these forms has been applied rarely in Canada. In fact, there has been only one Canadian instance of the offence being committed, and that was in 1934.[8]

For many years, the second listed form of constructive contempt, scandalizing the court, was more troublesome to the working journalist in Canada. Until the passing of the Charter, any journalist who commented critically about courtroom routines, the behaviour of a particular judge, or about the conduct of a given case even after any possibility for appeal had passed, was taking a certain risk. The problem was that journalists who routinely criticized the workings of social institutions were much more circumspect when the object of criticism lay among the offices, persons, and institutions of the judicial system. It was not that judges routinely slapped down reporters who dared to criticize, so much as the possibility that they *might* do so. There were no clear rules or guarantees. Thus in these circumstances of very real uncertainty, a genuine "chill" psychology existed among working journalists. This despite the fact that as J. J.

Robinette, a noted Canadian criminal lawyer of the pre-Charter era has suggested, journalists had no real cause to feel under particular restraint, so long as their criticisms were temperate. "The courts have no right to be protected, they don't work in private. If they are going to perform public duties, they are entitled to be criticized honestly, temperately, severely, if you like; but they don't enjoy special protection."[9]

The problem remained until the contempt by scandalizing issue became one of the first of journalism's professional concerns before the law to receive clarification by judicial interpretation of the provisions of the 1982 Charter.

In 1987, a Toronto lawyer, Harry Kopyto, appealed a contempt conviction from the Ontario Supreme Court. He had made critical comments in the media relating to a civil small claims court case, which he had lost, suggesting among other things that the decision was a "mockery of justice. It stinks to high heaven...and I have lost faith in the judicial system to render justice." The Ontario Court of Appeal overturned Kopyto's contempt conviction, ruling that Section 2(b) of the Charter, pertaining to freedom of expression issues, extends constitutional protection to criticism of the courts.[10]

Though it constitutes an important step, the new protection is neither complete nor absolute. It has been noted, for instance, that protection is more certain in cases of criticism deriving from "political speech," meaning political and social discourse as opposed to less exalted forms of public communication. But despite these elements of relatively minor uncertainty, journalism's position with respect to contempt by scandalizing is clearer, and substantially less inhibited. As a result of *R. v. Kopyto*, journalists now feel more comfortable about being forthrightly critical. This is an important and necessary development.

> Unhampered criticism of the courts has always been important to Canadian society, even if its importance had not been fully judicially recognized before the Charter. It is increasingly essential during the Charter era. Since 1982, Canadian courts frequently deliberate upon critical and often controversial policy issues, such as abortion, minority language rights, and gender equality. Judicial decisions in these cases must be open to intense scrutiny and criticism, in light of their profound impact on Canadian Society.[11]

By far the more consequential form of constructive contempt from the point of view of the journalist and his or her daily routine is the first form listed above—"Publications tending to pervert the impartiality of the judicial process in criminal cases." As a general rule, journalists covering criminal proceedings are obliged to restrict their coverage, in the main, to the provision of fair, balanced, and accurate summaries of evidence given under oath. Precisely what constitutes a fair, balanced, and accurate summary may be a matter of opinion, on occasion. And the only opinion that matters in such situations is that of the presiding judge.

Moreover, journalists covering criminal proceedings must be careful to abide by a large number of special provisions and proscriptions. The primary concern from the judicial point of view is that the court, and in particular members of juries, not be prejudiced by anything that may be read, heard, or seen in the mass media. Among the general rules are these:

- A person accused of a crime cannot be directly associated with the crime, or otherwise presented as guilty, until guilt has been established in court. "Even after a criminal trial is over, [the media] are not completely free to comment on the facts or the decision or the sentence until the time for appeal has passed or until the appeal has been heard and judgement pronounced."[12]

- Media are allowed to cover proceedings at preliminary hearings, but must refrain from any mention of confessions presented in evidence. This also applies at coroner's inquests.[13]

- Media are prohibited from publishing or broadcasting any reference to an accused person's previous criminal record during the course of a trial or in any pretrial publicity.

- A judge may specifically forbid publication of evidence when such publicity might prejudice the outcome of a trial. Such a prohibition may occur at any time during a trial, but is most likely when the jury has been removed from the courtroom while the judge considers a point in law, for instance, or the admissibility of a piece of evidence, or when the judge deems it appropriate to protect a witness. Also, where he or she feels that an accused person's rights may be compromised, a judge may choose to hold all or part of a preliminary hearing *in camera*, in effect in private and without publicity.

- The media must be remarkably careful not only about formal courtroom proceedings, but also about initial reporting of events that might result in charges being laid, even though an actual trial might be months away.

It is in this last aspect of the news media's relationship with the judicial system that the inherent conflict between freedom of expression, and the "higher right" of the court to protect itself and individuals appearing before it becomes especially evident. The pro-social purposes of free expression (freedom of information in our present context) is to warn society about criminal danger in its midst, and at the same time to protect society from its own institutions—in this case, the courts and the police. When the names of persons charged with crimes, and details relating to criminal acts themselves, appear in the news media, it ensures that *habeas corpus* remains an effective principle in criminal justice. Unlikely as it might seem in modern Canada, the publicity process is the best guarantee that individuals charged with crimes do not disappear into the sort of bureaucratic nightmare conjured in the novels of Franz Kafka.

These conflicting rights occasionally can place the media in a most uncertain position with regard to potential constructive contempt charges. For instance, "newspapers will co-operate with the police in publishing a photograph of a wanted man. As commendable as this practice would appear to be, it would not exculpate a newspaper from a possible contempt charge should identification be a key issue in the trial."[14]

In summary, it should be noted that there are Criminal Code provisions that specifically preclude or limit certain types of publicity. For instance, the identities of individuals charged and tried as young offenders may not be published. Victims in sexual assault cases are similarly protected (though at the time of writing, there was developing uncertainty as to the precise nature of this protection),[15] and there are limitations relating to information that may be published in divorce and family law cases.

Libel and Defamation

As a concept in law, libel is central to historic efforts to impose social controls on journalism and on all other forms of mass communication. In the early years of journalism, a libel was deemed to exist whenever anyone of sufficient social importance said it did, and chose to bring the complaint to the attention of the courts. Many eighteenth-century journalists (and even an occasional nineteenth-century one) were jailed, or worse, in effect at the whim of a judge rubber-stamping a socially privileged person's outrage. To appreciate the psychology of this draconian practice, it is helpful to keep in mind that in those early days when democratic values were emerging from authoritarian antecedents, "the law was designed to protect the state from the individual instead of the other way about."[16]

As discussed in chapter 3, more humane and enlightened approaches appeared in Britain, first with Fox's Libel Law in 1792, and later with the Libel Act of 1843. With the first of these, determining whether a published statement was libelous became a matter for juries to decide. The Act of 1843 further refined the application of libel, and brought it closer to its modern form by making truth without malice and truth for the public benefit a sufficient defence. The best and simplest modern definition of libel may have been expressed in England by Mr. Justice Cave in 1882: "A libel is a false statement about a man to his discredit."[17] While such a general definition continues to apply throughout the modern English-speaking world, the concept is complicated by the fact that it has both civil and criminal applications. In Canada, its criminal aspect is described in the federal Criminal Code; its civil aspect is generally provided for in provincial statutes.

Civil Defamation

It is libel's civil aspect that is most likely to affect the modern journalist. This is the non-criminal circumstance that arises when an individual feels he or she has been damaged by published information or comment, and seeks relief from the courts. The word "publication" has a very broad meaning in this context, covering the print and broadcast media in all their forms; films and videotapes, photographs, cartoons—virtually any imaginable method of mass communication.

Libel is described in the various provincial statutes under the general rubric of civil defamation, and it actually covers two related concepts, libel and slander. Libel is the term traditionally applied when an offending passage is rendered in a published form, including defamatory statements in the content of radio or television. Slander, which is not often an issue in journalism, primarily occurs when an alleged abuse is verbal, but not mass mediated. The difference has been explained in these words: "Libel involves publication of defamatory matter in permanent form; slander involves publication of defamatory matter in transitory form. Thus, although spoken defamation, uttered over the back fence, constitutes slander, broad-cast defamation constitutes libel."[18]

The various provincial statutes covering defamation vary in detail, but are more or less consistent in principal elements. Thus, while there may be slight variations in other jurisdictions, the procedures described in the Ontario Libel and Slander Act relating to initiating an action are similar to those in most other provinces. In this regard, the Ontario statute states "limitation periods requiring a person allegedly libeled in a newspaper or broadcast to give the defendant written notice of a libel action within six weeks of its coming to his knowledge, and requiring that any action be commenced within three months."[19]

In all jurisdictions, a journalist who has been hailed into court as defendant in a libel action has three basic courses of defence.

The truth

Such a defence seems simple enough, but "the burden of proof rests upon the defendant."[20] In other words, it is up to the allegedly offending journalist to prove the truth of his or her words; not to the plaintiff to prove their falsehood. Proving truth is not always an easy thing to do. It is far more difficult than merely proving the existence of a reasonable doubt, which is the law's more usual requirement.

Fair comment

The courts have long recognized that freedom of expression, if it is to have any useful purpose in a democracy, must often involve comment on the work and behaviour of other people. Newspapers engage in "fair comment" on a daily basis in their editorial pages and letters-to-the-editor columns. Background and feature articles, and radio and television documentaries regularly contain this sort of material. And, of course, reviews of theatrical performances, concerts, works of art, and literature, all fall within the genre.

The problem is determining precisely what is "fair." Generally, this means that the item in question must be written without malice, and that it must be based in fact. But the limits remain uncertain.

Germane to the legal realities of modern Canada, Atkey tells us: "Statements of opinion made upon matters of public interest fall under the protection of this defence [fair comment] if they are made in good faith and without malice."[22] He also suggests that one of the best definitions of fair comment that likely will influence future decisions in Canadian courts, comes from Lord Denning's 1968 decision in a libel action brought against the *Daily Telegraph* and a writer of letters-to-the-editor published in that English newspaper. In part Lord Denning wrote of the *Telegraph's* correspondent: "If he was an honest man expressing his genuine opinion on a subject of public interest, then no matter that his words conveyed derogatory imputations; no matter that his opinion was wrong or exaggerated or prejudiced; and no matter that it was badly expressed so that other people read all sorts of innuendo into it; nevertheless, he has a good defence of fair comment. His honesty is the cardinal test."[22]

Absolute and qualified privilege

There are some specific situations in which journalists enjoy the indirect benefit of complete protection, *absolute privilege*, regardless of the fundamentally libelous nature of words reported. There are other situations where journalists may benefit from a similar, but more limited protection, usually described in the law as *qualified privilege*. The essential difference between the two, is that absolute privilege pertains even when words are uttered with malice. In the case of qualified privilege, the protection disappears when malice can be shown.

It has been suggested that there are two places where absolute privilege touches the work of journalists. First, the classical examples of absolute privilege are statements made in the House of Commons by a Member of Parliament, or in the Senate by a Senator, or in any of the Legislative Assemblies of the provinces. The second area involves proceedings in court. Anything that a judge, a witness, or a lawyer says in court, is absolutely privileged.[23]

Absolute privilege pertains in these situations for the reason that free expression is vital to the important work being done, and because "bringing out of truth is more important than a possible injury to a person's reputation." Journalists are cautioned, however, that absolute privilege pertains to the participants in these situations, and not to the observing journalist who is covering them. While journalists who quote such material are generally safe, they must bear in mind that reports may be protected, but not in the same unqualified way.

For the most part, it is the concept of qualified privilege that applies to journalism. The Ontario Libel and Slander Act, for instance, enumerates a wide range of circumstances where qualified privilege applies to the journalistic product where reports are fair and accurate, and are published without malice. The list of such privileged sources includes proceedings of any legislature or any part or committee thereof; proceedings of the administrative bodies of public authorities, such as a provincial municipal board or securities commission; proceedings of commissions of inquiry; and proceedings of crown corporations. Qualified privilege may even apply to the decisions of governing bodies of social institutions, such as educational, sporting, scientific, and religious organizations.[24]

Libel as a Crime

The crime of *defamatory libel* is most simply explained as the equivalent in criminal law to the concept of civil defamation. It is described in part in the Criminal Code as publication of material "without lawful justification or excuse, that is likely to injure the reputation of any person by exposing him to hatred, contempt or ridicule."[25]

As with the civil equivalent, defamatory libel is not restricted to print, but applies to virtually any means of mass communication, "in words legibly marked upon any substance, or...by any objects...other than by words."[26] By the same token, defences against a criminal charge are entirely similar to those that might be used in a civil action: proof of truth, fair comment, and statements made in a circumstance where absolute or a qualified privilege apply. Kesterton makes the interesting observation that in the case of the first of these, truth alone is not always an adequate defence in the criminal context, but that "public benefit" should be shown as well in justifying the publication.

Finally, it is important to note that the criminal charge of defamatory libel is very rare in Canada. Most such questions are treated as civil matters, and the state only becomes involved with the laying of criminal charges when the matter is very serious. There would have to be a question of breach of the peace, or the possibility of violence being incited against an allegedly libeled individual, before a criminal charge would be considered.

Robinette has described defamatory libel as being "virtually dead" in Canadian practice. Before such a charge is laid, "it is necessary to do something more than merely do injury to an individual's reputation. It has to be considered as so outrageous as to offend the state's concept of what is right and proper. In other words, there has to be criminal intent to it."[27]

An example is a case in the 1960s in which the *Georgia Straight*, an iconoclastic underground Vancouver newspaper, was convicted of criminal libel. Robinette explained the situation in understated terms: "the newspaper disagreed with a magistrate's finding and compared him to Pontius Pilate, publishing a number of remarks that the court found to be in very bad taste." The *Georgia Straight* case is one of very few instances in modern Canada in which a charge of defamatory libel has been laid and successfully prosecuted.

There are other elements in law that fall close to the general rubric of libel though they have been applied even less in modern usage than defamatory libel. *Blasphemy,* or *blasphemous libel* is a good case in point. To blaspheme is in effect to libel God, and as Kesterton has pointed out, this is a law that has "slept in obscurity" in a Canada that has found its identity in an age of increasing secularism. There are only two or three judicial references to blasphemy throughout our entire colonial and mature history.[28]

Blasphemy remains an offence described in the Criminal Code, however, and Kesterton quotes William Wickwar as noting that as early as the 1820s, "the essence of blasphemous libel came to consist in its offence against 'the peace of our Lord the king, his crown and dignity'—[in other words, the state, and the fabric of social values]— more than its being 'to the high displeasure of Almighty God.'"[29] This interpretation may be worth noting in the light of furious public reaction in the United States to a Supreme Court ruling that burning the American flag was an act of free expression, and therefore not illegal. As one observer put it: "The idea that abusing it [the flag] is included in the principle of free speech struck most Americans as preposterous, verging on blasphemous."[30] It is unlikely that laws relating to blasphemy as they presently stand in Canada, the United States and elsewhere, are about to be reactivated. However, the U.S. flag affair and other comparable issues suggest that the idea of blasphemy still exists, especially in the sense of offending revered institutions and cultural icons.

Related to the idea of blasphemy is the concept of *sedition*. Here the idea of libel implies libeling the state and its institutions. According to the Criminal Code, sedition exists when anyone "publishes or circulates any writing that advocates the use, without the authority of law, of force as a means of accomplishing governmental change within Canada." In other words, while criticism of Parliament or its members is always legitimate, it is that fateful step of advocating the unconstitutional overthrow of sovereign institutions that becomes sedition.

Except in time of war or other national crises (and its application has been rare even in such dire circumstances as these) the law pertaining to sedition has been infrequently applied in Canada. Canadian law is equipped with other devices (the Official Secrets Act and the Emergencies Act most prominent among them) for dealing with those who would use pen, microphone, or camera to threaten the state and its perception of our national well-being.

Obscenity and the Media

Canadian law on the subject of obscenity was dramatically clarified by the Supreme Court in February, 1992. In the wake of the court's ruling in *R. v. Butler*, it seems likely, moreover, that the law has not only been clarified, but it has also been made more enforceable. (David Butler, a Winnipeg video shop owner, had been charged five years earlier with 173 counts of selling obscene tapes or possessing them for the purpose of distribution. He was convicted by a lower court on eight counts, and his appeal eventually reached the Supreme Court.)[31]

Section 163 of the Criminal Code stated that "any publication a dominant characteristic of which is the undue exploitation of sex, or of sex and any one or more of the following subjects, namely crime, horror, cruelty and violence, shall be deemed to be obscene." Criticisms have included the observation that sex is the operative factor in this definition; that crime, horror, violence, and so forth technically are not obscene in their own right. This concern does not appear to have been answered by the 1992 ruling, and it could become the subject of further high court review at a later time.

In 1984, the federal government seriously considered a rewording that would have eliminated the pivotal position of sex in the definition, and at the same time would have made it entirely clear that an obscenity can be committed in any medium (any "matter or thing") and not just in publications. The wording of the 1984 proposal, which was never adopted, would have made "any matter or thing" obscene where "a dominant characteristic…is the undue exploitation of any one or more of the following subjects, namely sex, violence, crime, horror or cruelty, through degrading representations of a male or female person or in any other manner."[32]

Apart from the definition, there is the problem of determining when a given printed passage, film, broadcast, or other medium has crossed the theoretical line separating that which is obscene from that which is not. Various legal tests have emerged over the years, none of them entirely satisfactory.

The so-called Hicklin Test, provided by England's Chief Justice

Cockburn in 1868 (*R. v. Hicklin*) suggests that obscenity exists where "the tendency…is to deprave and corrupt those whose minds are open to such immoral influences and into whose hands a publication of this sort may fall." The main problem with the Hicklin test is that it must use the weakest members of society as a standard for all. "Thus, because adolescent or emotionally unstable persons may get hold of the material…[it] is denied to more mature, stable and discriminating people."[33] The Hicklin Test also leaves unanswered the question of whether or not an entire book or film, regardless of overall merit, should be condemned as obscene for a single passage it may contain.

The "dominant characteristic" limitation in Canadian law removed this concern, and in effect, it is unlikely that any single passage or clip taken out of context could have become the entire basis for an obscenity conviction, at least not in recent decades. But this still did not resolve the primary concern about sacrificing the interests (the freedom of choice, in effect) of the mature and stable for the sake of the immature and unstable. Attempts to expand and complete the Hicklin concept in modern times by applying a "community standards" test had not helped much prior to the 1992 ruling. This approach had obliged judges to measure alleged obscenities against vaguely defined community standards. In effect, they were required to draw a line between that which is obscene and that which is not, depending upon the individual judge's perception of society's relative degree of moral conservatism or permissiveness. Such a test had been used by Canadian courts, but the judges usually opted for broadly based interpretations. Judges had been placed in the lonely and inappropriate position of being obliged to determine the meaning of obscenity, more confused than guided by the the law as it governs the concept.[34]

The unanimous ruling of the Supreme Court in February, 1992, should change all of this. Written by Mr. Justice John Sopinka, it first rejects the argument that the obscenity provisions in the Criminal Code constitute a violation of the guarantee of freedom of expression as outlined in Section 2(b) of the Charter of Rights. In the language of the ruling: "the harm associated with the dissemination of pornography in this case is sufficiently pressing to warrant some restriction on full exercise of the right of freedom of expression." The court built its decision around the concept of a much-clarified community standards test. Lower court judges are to be guided by the application of a community standard of tolerance test, "concerned not with what Canadians would not tolerate being exposed to themselves, but what they would not tolerate other Canadians being exposed to."[35]

The ruling also provides several more specific tests for application in the lower courts. Generally, any material will be considered obscene, and therefore illegal, if it contains: sex coupled with violence; exploitive sex that degrades or dehumanizes any person, female or male; or explicitly sexual material that employs children in its production.

Fortunately, there have been very few cases, if any, involving obscenity in daily journalism in Canada. Modern practice seems to suggest, in fact, that no subject matter, regardless of its inherent prurient qualities, will place a daily newspaper at risk provided the connection to news is legitimate. Many of the larger newspapers in Ontario established this ground clearly in 1978 when they applied unprecedented frankness in publishing testimony in graphic anatomical detail from the trial of three Toronto men charged in the sex-linked murder in 1977 of a Toronto shoe shine boy, Emanuel Jaques.[36] While a qualified privilege applied indirectly to the journalism of this situation, the interesting fact remains that this did set a precedent. Nothing this frank and graphic had been published previously in Canada's mainstream daily press. And there was no legal challenge.

Newspapers are thus reasonably free from concerns relating to obscenity, at least within the confines of news presentation and comment, but the environment remains somewhat more restricted in the case of broadcast journalism. For one thing, there is a qualitative difference, a matter of societal expectations, between vulgarities obscurely nestled in a sea of type on the printed page, and the same words blandly mouthed by the well-groomed voice of a radio or television announcer. Apart from conventions of good taste that would make such a presentation unlikely, the regulations of Canadian Radio-television and Telecommunications Commission specifically exclude "any obscene, indecent or profane language." The same regulations also frown on broadcast discussions of matters such as birth control and venereal disease, unless the programming "is presented in a manner appropriate to the medium of broadcasting."[37] What this may mean, is anyone's guess in an age of endemic AIDS and urgent mass media condom advertising.

Questions of Hate

Another difficult corner of the law has to do with efforts to prevent the use of the media for the spread of hatred, particularly hatred directed toward religious and ethnic minorities. As with obscenity, the law relating to hatred and hate literature does not often touch the mainstream print and broadcast media. Not because the law does not apply, but for the simple reason that these media tend to go to extremes in their good intentions to avoid prejudice. However, the law does touch the subject in several places in the Criminal Code.

In essence, to advocate the genocide of "an identifiable group" constitutes an offence, so does the "communicating of statements in any public place" that might incite "hatred against any identifiable group where such incitement is likely to lead to a breach of the peace." The word "communicating" is defined in the governing sections of the Code as including not just printed material, but "words spoken or written or recorded electronically or electromagnetically or otherwise, and gestures, signs and other visible representations."[38]

Originally passed into law in 1970 in the wake of incidents in Toronto several years earlier involving the activities of a neo-Nazi group, these "Hate Literature" provisions were applied most recently in the case of James Keegstra, an Alberta high school teacher. Keegstra ultimately was convicted on charges stemming from activities that included instructing his pupils that the Holocaust of World War II may not have taken place.

Another section of the Criminal Code makes it an offence to publish "a statement, tale or news" that the publisher "knows is false and that causes or is likely to cause injury or mischief to a public interest."[39] It was under this "False News" provision of the Code that charges were laid in the much publicized Ernst Zundel case of the mid-1980s. Zundel's 1985 conviction (under appeal at the time of writing) relates to pamphlets that he produced and distributed, and in which he is alleged to have falsely represented the historic evidence of the Holocaust.

As with obscenity concerns, it is difficult to imagine a circumstance in which any reputable daily newspaper, magazine, radio or television station might face charges under either the hate literature or the false news provisions of the Code. Moreover, the language of the Code goes to some lengths to protect legitimate discussion of issues that, in another context, might be questionable. In the case of the hate literature provisions, for instance, truth is a stated defence as is an attempt in good faith to argue an opinion on a religious subject. Comment, including quotation from objectionable material, also is allowed provided this is done in good faith and with public benefit as the intent.[40]

Emergencies and Official Secrets

Democracy is about the values collectively held by the ordinary members of a society, more than the high-flown words officially mustered in constitutions and other documents of state. It is important that this be the case because in order to ensure the continuance of democratic order in extraordinary circumstances, even the most democratic of states requires the availability of legal devices that are fundamentally undemocratic in nature. Canada has its share of these. Fortunately they rarely touch journalism (which is a telling sign of the fundamentally healthy state of democracy over time in this country), but they do exist in the statute books. The two most consequential items in the genre, both federal statutes, are the Official Secrets Act, and the Emergencies Act.

The former is a device that deals with espionage, but it is also the legislative mechanism governments use to legitimize their conduct of many elements of public business in cloaked circumstances of the strictest security and privacy. Often there are good reasons for this. Much information relating to defence planning logically falls into the category; as do many matters concerning international treaty negotiations or internal police investigations. By the same token, one can imagine the chaos that might result if governments were obliged to do all their budget construction and financial planning in public.

Few journalists and civil libertarians are wholly comfortable with the existence of such a statute, but most understand the need for it, and fortunately journalists rarely run afoul of its provisions. Until 1981, there had been just twenty-one prosecutions under its provisions. No fewer than seventeen of these had derived from the Igor Gouzenko defection and extensive related Soviet espionage revelations of the late 1940s. Of the remaining four, only one directly involved the mass media.[41]

This isolated case dates to 1978 when the *Toronto Sun* and two of its employees were charged in connection with their possession of a classified RCMP document relating to Soviet intelligence activities in Canada, and subsequent publication of its contents. At a preliminary hearing, the defence showed that much of the "secret" information involved had been previously aired in a television broadcast, discussed in the House of Commons, and reported in Hansard. No fewer than sixty-seven copies of the document in question had been distributed to various government offices. The court thus discharged the *Sun* and its two employees on the grounds that the document, stamped "Top

Secret," in fact was not secret at all within the meaning of the act.[42] The case points to an important practical reality about journalism and secret government information; simply that journalism deals primarily in public information. Secrets rarely come to it, unless they are purposefully "leaked" as was the case with the Sun and that RCMP document in 1978.

The only recent case connecting journalism and the Official Secrets Act was a 1989 episode involving Global Television political reporter, Doug Small. Small acquired a copy of a federal budget document on 26 April 1989, a day before the Finance Minister, Michael Wilson, had intended to read it in the House of Commons. No investigative or deeply researched journalism took place here; the document was leaked to Small by one or more civil servants who sought him out. In any event, having literally stumbled into the situation, Small broadcast the information and subsequently was charged with possession of stolen goods. The trial, more than a year later, was halted in its early stages by Ontario Provincial Court Judge James Fontana. He described the charges as constituting an "abuse of process," and was critical of what he described as the aggressive behaviour of investigating RCMP officers and Crown attorneys involved in the prosecution.[43] Small's experience clearly indicates the reluctance of the courts to prosecute reporters who may stumble over secrets dropped in their way, and

Global TV reporter Doug Small was charged with possession of stolen goods when a federal budget document was leaked to him a day before Finance Minister Michael Wilson was to present the April 1989 budget in the House of Commons. Though Small used the information on air, the charges against him were eventually dismissed. (Canapress Photo Service/Chartrand)

who make journalistic use of them in circumstances of technically dubious legality. The Small case had nothing to do with the Official Secrets Act, but all the principles concerning journalism practised in the shadow of such legislation were apparent.

More troubling to the interests of free journalism than the Official Secrets Act, has been our national experience with emergencies legislation. Since 1988, the Emergencies Act has been the legal instrument available to the federal government to deal with perceived national emergencies of various kinds. The provisions of the act are wide-ranging, and describe the basic forms of national emergency.

> There are four levels of emergency distinguished in the new act: a Public Welfare Emergency caused by natural disaster, disease, industrial accident or pollution; a Public Order Emergency caused by a "serious" threat to the security of Canada; an International Emergency caused by acts in which Canada is entangled "of intimidation or coercion or the real or imminent use of serious force of violence," and a War Emergency which means "war or other armed conflict, real or imminent, involving Canada or any of its allies that is so serious as to be a national emergency."[44]

The act had not been tested in any important way to date, thus its potential impact on basic liberties, including freedom of expression, remains conjecture. The provisions of the act require that it be activated for specific and appropriate purposes by the Governor General in Council, in effect, the federal cabinet. Once in place, however, it would appear that in circumstances of a declared public order emergency, or of a war emergency, the cabinet would have very far-reaching powers, including the power to limit or suspend civil liberties.

The new Emergencies Act replaces the War Measures Act that dates back through various British and domestic antecedents to the 1880s. Created early in World War I, the recently superseded War Measures Act gave the federal government powers to impose extraordinary security measures, including the suspension of basic civil rights, in times of extreme national emergency. Ordinarily, it lies dormant in the statute books, and can be activated only by Order-in-Council when a national emergency is declared by the government. During its lifetime, the War Measures Act was invoked on three occasions: for the duration of the two world wars; and in 1970 when Prime Minister Pierre Trudeau and his cabinet described a state of "apprehended insurrection" relating to separatist activities in Quebec.

The consequences of having such a piece of legislation in the statute books are significant. By 27 March 1941, about eighteen months after the invocation of the act for the duration of World War II, no fewer than 325 periodicals had been suppressed or banned.[45]

The 1970 October Crisis application, however, is the only one of real interest here, and there can be no question that the circumstances leading to its promulgation were extraordinary. The British Trade Commissioner, James Cross, had been kidnapped on 7 October 1970 by an organization describing itself as a cell of the Front de Libération du Québec. On 10 October, a second FLQ cell kidnapped the Quebec Labour Minister, Pierre Laporte. After days of increasingly dramatic activity, the government imposed the War Measures Act, effectively suspending civil liberties on 16 October.

The terrible drama continued with the immediate murder of Mr. Laporte that proved to be the climax of the historic sequence of events. The location of the FLQ cell holding James Cross was discovered on 3 December, and intense negotiations resulted in his release, and safe passage for his kidnappers to an exile in Cuba. Finally, three FLQ members allegedly involved in the Laporte murder were arrested on 28 December at a farm near Montreal.[46]

The media were inexorably drawn into the affair, and in retrospect there seems to be little doubt that government officials overreacted. There were a number of instances of direct media censorship; many journalists experienced interventions in the routine course of their lives ranging from midnight searches of homes, to actual arrests. There were reports of beatings by police, and some of those arrested appear to have been held without being charged for a number of days.[47]

Freedom of expression applies routinely in ordinary times, but in times of crisis, its application becomes more difficult. The media have become such a consequential influence in our society that they cannot stand entirely apart from situations they cover. This becomes dangerously evident when the situation at hand is on the scale of consequence of the October Crisis. Noting that certain radio stations broadcast FLQ "communiqués" without first consulting authorities, for instance, and observing that the journalistic news purpose in such situations does not always coincide with official purposes, LaTouche makes this observation: "media can be said to do more than reflect the outer reality: they are intervening, becoming actors in social systems, rather than merely reporting events."[48]

None of this eases the uncomfortable realization that events such as those surrounding the October Crisis could occur in modern Canada, sequence of the October Crisis. Noting that certain radio stations broadcast FLQ "communiqués" without first consulting authorities, for instance, and observing that the journalistic news purpose in such situations does not always coincide with official purposes, LaTouche makes this observation: "media can be said to do more than reflect the outer reality: they are intervening, becoming actors in social systems, rather than merely reporting events."[48]

None of this eases the uncomfortable realization that events such as those surrounding the October Crisis could occur in modern Canada, but it helps to explain the situation a bit. Possibly the most disconcerting issue is research evidence suggesting that the media, specifically newspapers in this case, were not unduly disturbed about the effective suspension of their liberties during the time of the crisis. One analysis of comment in eighteen English-language daily newspapers across Canada during the the two weeks immediately following the imposition of the War Measures Act in 1970 produced just sixty-one keyword assertions suggesting that the government should explain

Soldiers guarding public figures; detainment and questioning of journalists; and even press censorship—Canadians experienced all of these when the War Measures Act was invoked in October 1970 to deal with the perceived threat posed by FLQ terrorists in Quebec. (Canapress Photo Service)

The Constitution

Much of the content discussed in this chapter stands subject to change or influence in the light of the provisions of the Charter of Rights and Freedoms. The 1982 Constitution Act, of which the Charter is a part, significantly alters Canada's approach to constitutional matters of all sorts. The Act "substantially expands the scope of judicial review in Canada," moving us considerably closer to an American model in such matters. Fundamentally, this means that our founding presumption of Parliamentary supremacy diminishes under the new constitution, giving the courts markedly increased powers in the area of law review.

Possibly the most important element in this remarkable philosophic change has to do with the great significance of the Charter itself: "judicial review now embraces the whole field of fundamental freedoms, civil liberties and human rights."[50]

Section 2 of the Charter describes the fundamental freedoms of Canadians, with Section 2(b) providing specifically for "freedom of thought, belief, opinion and expression, including freedom of the press and other media of communication." Like the other three fundamental freedoms (touching conscience and religion, peaceful assembly, and association) Section 2(b) is limited only by the wording of the general guarantee in Section 1, where it is noted that our fundamental freedoms are "subject only to such reasonable limits prescribed by law as can be demonstrably justified in a free and democratic society." Some journalistic cynics have dubbed this latter provision the "weasel clause," noting that being free is absolute; either one is, or one is not.

There is no question that the workload of the courts, especially that of the Supreme Court of Canada, has increased enormously since the arrival of the Charter, with many interests seeking judicial interpretations of their rights in specific situations under the general provisions of Sections 1 and 2. The media industries have been among these active interests, and it is not yet clear how varied and numerous the challenges may be and how many judicial rulings will be required, before the media find themselves in a settled position under the provisions of the Charter, especially with regard to their relationships with government and agencies of government.

The media have benefited more or less as bystanders in a number of instances before the law, the contempt by scandalizing clarification resulting from *R. v. Kopyto*, for instance. To date most challenges directly touching the news process have emerged in one important area. This has to do with circumstances under which journalists might be required to reveal veiled news sources in courts of law or before various boards and commissions empowered to subpoena witnesses. A number of Canada's more influential journalists have argued, at least cautiously, in support of a form of privilege not shared by other citizens. Murray Goldblatt, a Carleton University journalism professor, has argued that society requires a free investigative journalism more or less uninhibited by a judicial practice that can require journalists to reveal sources or to submit notebooks and other forms of retained work product information. In Goldblatt's words: "It is counterproductive for journalists to be terrorized by the fear of easy exposure of their work product. Journalists ought to be accountable, but not defensive. The editorial process and journalist's work product ought to be available to the justice system only as a last resort."[51]

For the moment, the consensus seems to be against having any form of special status or privilege under law. In 1987, a reporter for the *Edmonton Journal* lost an appeal to the Alberta Supreme Court that she not be required to reveal her sources in stories relating to a labour dispute she had been covering. She had been ordered to do so by the province's Labour Relations Board. In its decision, the court suggested that the reporter was inappropriately seeking an "exclusionary enclave" that the Charter could not be interpreted as providing. In the words of the court: "there is here no common law privilege, qualified or absolute, marking the relationship of journalist and source which would excuse the appellant from providing relevant evidence and which might involve source disclosure."[52]

The Supreme Court of Canada declined an appeal from the Alberta ruling in June, 1989, and this seemed to settle the issue. But a greater question remains unanswered, namely: in a broad sense, is there any way that the journalist should enjoy a special status before the law, different from that of other citizens? The issue was considered at the international level in the late 1970s by the UNESCO International Commission for the Study of Communication Problems. Its chair, Sean McBride of Ireland, was one among a substantial minority of the commissioners who clearly saw a need for legislated protective status. He argued that the role of the working journalist in the global scheme, and the dangers the journalist regularly faces all point to "the need to afford journalists and media agents a special status and protection."[53] In its final report, however, the commission noted that however desirable special protection might be, it necessarily would mean defining the role of the working journalist. This, the report argued, could have the consequence of inhibiting rather than enabling free expression; "it is frequently contended that any hard and fast definition of the journalist may be dangerous for freedom of information…In this connection it is maintained that the adoption of any definition whatever generally leads to official licensing of journalists."[54]

Special status for the journalist does not seem a likely prospect in Canada at the moment, even though it remains an important issue without clear resolution. An answer will emerge only as more challenges under the Charter reach the courts, and indications are that there may be many of these in the years ahead.

NOTES

1. Robert Martin and Stuart Adam, *A Sourcebook of Canadian Media Law* (Ottawa: Carleton University Press, 1991), 25.

2. Ibid., 26.

3. Martin and Adam, *A Sourcebook of Canadian Media Law*, 26.

4. Wilfred Kesterton, *Law and the Press in Canada* (Toronto: McClelland and Stewart, 1976), 8.

5. Ronald G. Atkey, "The Law of the Press in Canada," *Journalism, Communication and the Law*, ed. G. S. Adam (Toronto: Prentice-Hall, 1976), 125.

6. Ibid., 126–7. Atkey here cites the decision in *Fortin v. Moscarella* (1957) 23 W.W.R. 91, 94.

7. Ibid., 125–6.

8. Ibid., 126.

9. J. J. Robinette, as quoted in *Libel, Defamation, Contempt of Court and the Right of the People to be Informed*, a Legal Seminar of Thomson Newspapers Ltd, Toronto, March, 1962, rev. ed. (Toronto: Thomson Newspapers Ltd., 1979), 42.

10. *R. v. Kopyto* (1987), 24 O.A.C. 81 (Ont. C.A.).

11. David Lepofsky, "Open Justice 1990: The Constitutional Right to Attend and Report on Court Proceedings in Canada," *Freedom of Expression and the Charter*, ed. David Schneiderman (Toronto: Carswell, 1991), 33.

12. Atkey, "The Law of the Press in Canada," 129.

13. Ibid., 131.

14. Ibid., 129.

15. By ethical convention supported in law, the names of victims of sexual assault are not ordinarily published or broadcast in Canadian media. Protection that once extended into the courts by making a sexual assault victim's previous sexual history inadmissible as evidence, was considerably weakened in August, 1991, when the Supreme Court struck down the so-called rape-shield provision, Section 276 of the Criminal Code, ruling that it could deny an accused person a fair trial, as guaranteed by the Charter of Rights. See David Shoalts, "Supreme Court quashes 'rape-shield' provision," *Globe and Mail*, 23 August 1991.

16. Kesterton, *Law and the Press in Canada*, 3.

17. Atkey, "The Law of the Press in Canada," 134. Atkey here quotes *Scott v. Sampson* (1882) 8 Q.B.D. 503.

18. Kesterton, *Law and the Press in Canada*, 42.

19. Atkey, "The Law of the Press in Canada," 136.

20. Ibid.,136.

21. Atkey, "The Law of the Press in Canada," 137.

22. Ibid., 138. Atkey here cites the decision in *Slim v. Daily Telegraph Ltd.* (1968) 1 E.R. 497, at 503.

23. Robinette, *Libel, Defamation, Contempt of Court*, 12–3.

24. Ibid., 15–8.

25. Criminal Code, R.S.C. 1970, c. C34, s. 262(1).

26. Kesterton, *Law and the Press in Canada*, 66. Kesterton is here quoting, in part, the Criminal Code, R.S.C. 1970, c. C34, s. 262(2).

27. Robinette, *Libel, Defamation, Contempt of Court*, 112.

28. Kesterton, *Law and the Press in Canada*, 73.

29. Ibid., 73.

30. Joseph Sobran, "An Unsound Constitution," *The Spectator*, 15 July 1989.

31. Jeff Sallot, "Ruling paves way for child-pornography bill," *Globe and Mail*, 28 February 1992.

32. Michael G. Crawford, *The Journalist's Legal Guide* (Toronto: Carswell, 1986), 197.

33. Kesterton, *Law and the Press in Canada*, 81.

34. Jeff Sallot, "Text/pornography: Community standard is test of tolerance," *Globe and Mail*, 28 February 1992.

35. "Community standard is test of tolerance," Globe and Mail, 28 February 1992. (Excerpts from a Supreme Court of Canada ruling written by Mr. Justice John Sopinka, upholding the constitutionality of federal obscenity law.)

36. "One acquitted, two convicted in murder of shoe shine boy," *London Free Press*, 11 March 1978.

37. Crawford, *The Journalist's Legal Guide*, 196.

38. Criminal Code, ss. 318, 319.

39. Criminal Code, s. 181.

40. Crawford, *The Journalist's Legal Guide*, 199–200.

41. Walter Tarnapolsky, "Freedom of the Press" in *Newspapers and the Law* (Ottawa: Ministry of Supply and Services Canada, 1981), 137–9.

42. Crawford, *The Journalist's Legal Guide*, 184–5.

43. "Judge halts budget leak case, calls charges 'abuse of process.'" *Globe and Mail*, 17 July 1990.

44. Martin and Adam, *A Sourcebook of Canadian Media Law*, 122–3.

45. Martin and Adam, *A Sourcebook of Canadian Media Law*, 130.

46. Daniel LaTouche, "Mass Media and Communication in a Canadian Political Crisis," *Communications in Canadian Society,* 3rd ed., ed. Benjamin D. Singer (Toronto: Addison-Wesley Publishers, 1983), 197–9.

47. No one would appear to have produced an entirely reliable inventory of actions taken against journalists and others during this time of suspended civil liberties. One of the better summary accounts was prepared shortly after the events by the Fédération professionnelle des journalistes du Québec. This has been published in English as "File: Dossier Z," *The Media Game,* ed. Dick Macdonald (Montreal: Content Publishing Limited, 1972), 85–103.

48. LaTouche, "Mass Media and Communication in a Canadian Political Crisis," 197.

49. Patrick J. Waters, "A Critical Analysis of Canadian Daily Newspaper Editorials in Reaction to the War Measures Act Published Between October 16, 1970 and October 31, 1970." Master's thesis in Wayne State University, Detroit, Michigan, 1975. 61–99.

50. Martin and Adam, *A Sourcebook of Canadian Media Law,* 73.

51. Murray Goldblatt, *Affidavit.* Supreme Court of Ontario, (Divisional Court), 1989. In the matter of the Public Inquiries Act, R.S.O. 1980, c.411, and in matter of the Royal Commission of Inquiry into the Niagara Regional Police Force.

52. *Moysa v. Labour Relations Board and Attorney-General for Alberta* (1987), 52 Alta. L.R. (2nd) 193., (Alta. C.A.).

53. UNESCO, *Many Voices, One World.* Report of the International Commission for the Study of Communication Problems (London: UNESCO and Kogan Page Ltd., 1980), 236n.

54. Ibid., 237.

Regulation:

The

Canadian

Way

C

H

A

P

T

E

R

7

anadians have a long history of looking to government for solutions to seemingly insoluble problems, especially those relating to
the struggle to maintain Canada's economic and cultural integrity on
a continent shared by accident of geography with the United States of
America. By their nature, Canada's media industries are among the
most vulnerable of the country's economic and cultural endeavours to
the shifting patterns and forces of American influence. At the same
time, it has long been recognized that in the interests of national survival the media must remain fundamentally Canadian in character.

For these reasons, Canadians have learned to accept an element of
compromise between their historic inclination to maintain a democratic environment of free expression, and a perceived need for a
strong and protective government hand intervening in the affairs of
the mass media. It is a compromise that contains inherent dangers for
free expression, especially when government assumes a monitoring
role with regard to quality, and therefore (however lightly and tangentially) with regard to subject matter.

Whether it stands in the final analysis as a good or detrimental element, the Canadian compromise exists as a fact of national life.
Broadcasting, of course, but magazine and book publishing as well
have been favoured with various forms of government intervention
over the years. In broadcasting these range from licensing and extensive formatting regulations under provisions of the Broadcasting Act,
to outright government ownership in the case of the Canadian
Broadcasting Corporation and the various provincial educational television authorities. Among the devices touching other media, there are
Income Tax Act provisions relating to advertising that serve powerfully to protect Canadian magazines from offshore competition in
their own domestic market. There also are grant programs in aid of
some aspects of book publishing and various foreign ownership
restrictions in the book industry.

It is one of the historic oddities in the evolution of Canadian media
law and regulation, however, that only our daily newspapers have so
far been left generally untouched by the mixed blessings of government involvement in their affairs. When intervention of one sort or
another has been proposed as, for instance, when the Royal
Commission on Newspapers recommended a federal grants scheme
to strengthen the Canadian Press wire service and other agencies of
news exchange among newspapers[1], publishers have always declined,
arguing that if government were allowed to pay the piper, then there
would be a real danger that it might end up calling the tune as well.

Public opinion, and opinion among most journalists, has tended to support such reasoning. This despite a lack of any evident logic in maintaining such a sensitivity in the case of daily newspapers, while government interventions of one form or another have become more or less routine in the cases of the other media. Historically, of course, the daily press has been most closely associated by venerable tradition with those powerful *laisser faire* political values that found early expression in John Milton's *Areopagitica* of 1644, for instance, or in John Locke's eighteenth-century concepts relating to the social contract. That daily newspapers should be more closely associated with such traditional values in our political imagination, and other media less so, thus becomes understandable, if not entirely logical. Be that as it may, there has also long been a certain unwritten public assumption that regulating entertainment media somehow is less problematic than regulating news media. Over the years, the electronic media, and perhaps magazines as well, have been more closely associated in our political imagination with entertainment values. On the other hand, newspapers have been linked much more directly with news and public affairs. The obvious reality that newspapers entertain as well as inform, and that radio and television, periodicals, and even books, obviously do as much to inform and educate as they as do to entertain, does not seem to enter the popular equation. Somehow it remains appropriate in our political imagination to regulate "entertainment" media, and intervene in their affairs in the public good; but not acceptable to intervene in the affairs of "news" media.

Despite the illogic, there nonetheless has been a certain wisdom in leaving newspapers more or less untouched. Simply put, a daily press standing beyond the reach of regulation can act as an uninhibited critic, should government intervention in the affairs of the other media be seen at any point as overstepping reasonable democratic bounds. As already noted in chapter 5, however, and to be discussed again later in this chapter, it is becoming less and less certain that Canada's daily press will continue for very many more years to enjoy its traditional status.

Periodicals

Long before Confederation, there was evidence of public concern about the chronically anaemic state of periodical publishing in the British North American colonies. W. H. Kesterton has described the precarious magazine business of the era, overwhelmed by British and

American competition, as generating publications that "did not contribute vigorously to the life of the colonies; much of their content was made up of borrowings from British and American writers, while colonial writing was usually imitative, derivative, and of inferior literary merit."[2] Even after Confederation, magazine publishing in the late nineteenth century and early twentieth continued to be financially risky, with few domestic periodicals surviving more than a year or two and many disappearing with their second or third numbers.

By the 1920s, public debate on the state of Canadian periodical publishing and the competition it faced from primarily American sources had become both vigorous and articulate. Arguments that will be entirely familiar to modern Canadians of the satellite television era were being made in Parliament, pulpit, and press urging the introduction of measures both to protect the domestic periodicals industry economically, and to preserve Canadian lifestyle and cultural values in the process. Several arguments were presented.

First, on a moral plane it was commonly and unfairly argued that the bulk of American magazines flooding the Canadian market in the 1920s consisted of salacious material that dissipated the morals of Canadian youth. Some of the depth of feeling is conveyed in an editorial comment from the Vancouver *Morning Star*. "[the] mentality and morale of impressionable young Canadians, which should be kept clean and apart to their own land, is being merged in the reeking gas cloud of the lower Americanism…Something should be done…to dam this trash which is flowing over the border."[3]

Second, it was contended that the content of American publications tended to lure young Canadians away from Canada to the glittering lights and perceived economic opportunities of the great republic to the south. Thus we have one of the earliest expressions of Canadian concern for a media-precipitated "brain drain."

Third, it was argued that all Canadians, not just Canadian youth, were being denied an opportunity to discover, experience and discuss their own culture. Even then, American voices were seen as drowning out domestic ones, to the presumed long-term cultural peril of the nation.

Fourth, on the economic side, there was the purely protectionist argument that homegrown publications could not hope to compete with foreign imports, especially given the economies of scale enjoyed by publications produced for the huge American market. Canadian publishers also argued that advertising revenues from Canadian sources were being drained away to New York and Chicago. Ironically in view of this concern, Canadian manufacturers felt that the presence of so many American magazines filled with alluring advertisements for American products was robbing them of their own domestic market.[4]

The cumulative effect of public debate around these themes was to generate the first significant government venture into the realm of protective policy making related to the mass media. In 1931, a duty scaled to volume of advertising was imposed upon imported publications. The scale ranged from no duty at all for magazines with less than 20 per cent of their content devoted to advertising, to five cents per copy where advertising exceeded 30 per cent. Periodicals devoted to religious, educational, scientific, and certain other specific subject areas, were admitted duty-free.[5]

While the 1931 duty may have generated modest revenues for the federal coffers, it proved to be an ineffective cultural device for controlling the northward flow of foreign periodicals and the allurements and attractions they might contain. Their importation continued apace. But concern for such matters was swept away for a time as Canadians found themselves caught up with the rest of the world in the more urgent demands of the Great Depression, and later of World War II. In fact, Canadians would not turn significant policy-making attention specifically toward the periodicals publishing industry again until the appointment of the Royal Commission on Publications, which reported in 1961. Chaired by Grattan O'Leary, this commission proposed changes to the federal Income Tax Act designed to make it impossible for Canadian advertisers to "write off" for income tax purposes, the cost of advertising in periodicals published in Canada but not owned by Canadians.[6]

The O'Leary commission established the political principle of the federal government's right and obligation to become involved for the good of the country in regulating aspects of the financial environment of the periodicals industry. Important encouragement was also given to the principle of government involvement in questions of journalistic quality and cultural influence. In the language of the report: "there must be few left to deny the right—indeed the duty— of government to act…if faced with demonstrable community necessity."[7] The recommendations of the O'Leary commission received a mixed but generally favourable reaction at home in Canada, but were roundly condemned in official Washington and by the powerful publishers of such American magazines as *Time* and *Reader's Digest.* Both these magazines at the time produced branch-plant Canadian editions with large circulations. The main Canadian complaint was that these and other American periodicals occupied such a huge share of the Canadian magazine market that homegrown periodicals had little chance to emerge or thrive against such competition.

Parliament eventually passed legislation in 1964 reflecting the O'Leary recommendations, but it was legislation with little substance. Effectively capitulating to American publishing interests, the Canadian government specifically exempted some forty U.S. publications operating in Canada, *Time* and *Reader's Digest* among them, from the effects of the new tax law requirements. A so-called "grandfather clause" in the legislation left these magazines untouched in their Canadian operations. Eventually the measures were given more solid effect when further legislation in 1976 eliminated the privileged list of foreign publications. Cries of outrage from south of the border went unheeded this time, and among other consequences, *Time* suspended publication of its Canadian edition.[8] This, in turn, made it possible for Maclean Hunter Ltd. to take advantage of the newly protected domestic magazine market, and to convert its venerable monthly, *Maclean's Magazine,* to today's familiar weekly news magazine format.

In addition to the arrival of the revamped *Maclean's* on Canadian newsstands, there was other immediate evidence of a new vitality in the Canadian magazine publishing industry. Among other useful changes some U.S.-based periodicals, *Reader's Digest* most significant among them, found it possible to alter both their corporate structure and their editorial policies sufficiently to meet the new tax law requirements of Canadian corporate citizenship in the magazine publishing industry. To all intents and purposes, *Reader's Digest* thus began to present itself to its Canadian readers as a Canadian publication. A variety of new Canadian periodicals also began to emerge.

Unfortunately, and despite the obvious benefits, the provisions of 1964 and 1976 were not without their price. As has already been suggested, the provision by law (in this case tax law) of a secure and protected base for any Canadian media sector necessarily means at least a theoretical compromising of the values of free and uninhibited expression in the marketplace of ideas. The so-called Cullen Rule of 1976 (Bill C-58 named for then Revenue Minister Bud Cullen) which at last gave solid effect to the intent of the O'Leary Report, required that to be eligible for advertiser tax write-off benefits, a periodical must be published in Canada, and must be at least seventy-five per cent owned by Canadians. This has been no real problem so far, but the rule also contains the provision that in order to be considered Canadian, and thus eligible for tax benefits, a periodical's content must be eighty per cent different from content published in foreign periodicals. Technically, this means that Canadian magazines must live with a form of self-imposed quota on foreign content.

As Geoffrey Stevens observed in his *Globe and Mail* column at the time Bill C-58 was being debated in the House of Commons: "If *Maclean's* decided to broaden its horizons with, say, 15 per cent of its contents purchased from *Newsweek* [published in the U.S.] and 15 per cent from *The Economist*, [published in Britain] that would total 30 per cent and *Maclean's* would cease to be regarded as Canadian."[9]

Taming the Airwaves

At about the time that Canada's federal government was taking early steps toward intervention in the magazine publishing industry, it also was moving toward ultimately far more extensive involvement in the broadcasting industry. In addition to those distinctions in the public mind already discussed between the daily press and other media, there was another reason why Canadians found it relatively easy to accept extensive government regulation of broadcasting. In its earliest days, broadcasting was popularly seen as having a magic, or even a spiritual quality. To ordinary people still acclimatizing to a world newly lit by electricity, the idea of pulling voice and song out of thin air was awe-inspiring. It seemed entirely logical to most that the airwaves should be revered as common property and safeguarded by a benign government for the common good. Conservative prime minister of the era, R.B. Bennett, expressed the general sentiment in 1932 when Canada's first major piece of broadcast legislation was before Parliament: "The use of the air...that lies over the soil or land of Canada is a natural resource...I cannot think that any government would be warranted in leaving the air to private exploitation and not reserving it for development for the use of the people."[10]

Popular acceptance of the principle of the airwaves as a natural resource lying necessarily and forever in the public domain led easily and quickly to several forms of government involvement in broadcasting. In fact, government in Canada already had been minimally involved for many years by the time Bennett made his 1932 statement of principle. The Wireless Telegraph Act of 1905, and its successor, the Radiotelegraph Act of 1913, imposed frequency control over the early use of radio, then envisaged as a device primarily to be used for the "wireless" transmission of private messages. By the 1920s, the act of 1913 was also being used to allocate frequencies to pioneer broadcasters, in effect to license them.[11] Canada's first radio station, XWA in Montreal, broadcast its first experimental program on 20 May 1920. By 1926, a total of ninety-one broadcast licences had been issued across the country, with forty stations actually on the air. In the United States, by way of comparison, 530 stations were operating by the middle of the decade.[12]

It was these American stations (their numbers mushrooming to more than 1 000 by the late 1920s) that caused the Canadian government to move in 1928 to establish the first Royal Commission on Broadcasting chaired by Toronto banker, Sir John Aird. Not only was the virtually unregulated American broadcasting industry pouring its signals into Canadian airspace, often drowning out domestic voices in the process, but those old fears of American media influence threatening the Canadian way of life took on a whole new urgency. Thus, when the Aird Commission reported in 1929 its recommendations went far beyond merely affirming the government's right and obligation to regulate the airwaves as a natural resource.

This commission proposed nothing less than the development of radio under government auspices as a national cultural resource; as a device both to encourage Canadian cultural development, and to foster national unity and identity. Among its other recommendations, the Aird Commission proposed the creation of a national broadcasting company with responsibility both to regulate all broadcasting in the country, and to establish a state broadcasting service. The commission recommended that the national service be equipped initially with seven powerful fifty kW transmission centres across the country, and that it be encouraged to develop an ambitious range of programming, including news and public affairs programming. The gradual elimination by expropriation of privately-owned commercial broadcasting stations was also envisaged, and the royal commission proposed that this new venture in state ownership should largely be financed through tax dollars and receiver set licence fees. Advertising was to be allowed in the Aird scheme, but only as indirect advertising (corporate identification announcements) and rather little of that.[13]

In a Quebec challenge to federal authority in the area of broadcasting, the Supreme Court of Canada ruled in June, 1931, that control of the airwaves was, in fact, a federal responsibility. The decision was later upheld in London by the Judicial Committee of the Privy Council, which still was at the time, Canada's final judicial arbiter in constitutional matters. In the process, broadcasting's importance to national well-being was thus powerfully affirmed, along with an equally powerful affirmation of the federal government's right to deep involvement in regulation of the new mass medium.[14] Lobbying by various groups, notably by the Canadian Radio League,[15] which was the inspiration of such visionaries as Graham Spry, Alan Plaunt, and Brooke Claxton, kept the Aird recommendations alive, despite the deepening crisis of the Depression. A reduced version of the Aird Commission's vision was finally passed into law in the form of the Canadian Radio Broadcasting Act of 1932.

In essence, this legislation provided for the creation of the Canadian Radio Broadcasting Commission (CRBC) as an intended national authority in radio, but with responsibilities beyond the modest appropriations it was to receive from Parliament. In the fiscal year 1932-33, for instance, it received just $400 000 and a rather begrudged $1 000 000 a year later. It has been suggested that this latter appropriation may have been considerably less than the total actually received by the government in payment of receiver set licence fees.[16]

The CRBC was never able to establish itself as the powerful regulatory authority envisaged by the Aird commission, and its efforts to create a national broadcasting service were less than successful. Nonetheless, the commission was more remarkable for its accomplishments than for its failures. For the sum of just $50 000, it acquired the radio facilities and more importantly, perhaps, the expert personnel who went with them that had been operated primarily in the Maritime provinces by the financially troubled Canadian National Railways. The commission also established affiliate arrangements by which a number of privately owned stations carried commission programming, and thus in a remarkably innovative if somewhat jury-rigged fashion, the national broadcasting service was born.

Actual broadcasting operations were launched with just two hours of programming per week early in 1933, but this had expanded to 48 scheduled weekly hours by the end of the first year.[17] Albert Shea has pointed out that by 1936 national service programming was reaching about fifty per cent of Canada's population. By that year, the system consisted of seven publicly owned stations feeding the programming of the national service through an extended network of forty-seven affiliated private radio stations.

Most importantly, the twin principles of a powerful state-owned radio system and a permanent federal regulatory hand, were established during the short life of the CRBC. These principles were greatly strengthened by the Broadcasting Act of 1936 that truly laid the foundations of Canada's modern broadcasting system.

The CRTC and on to the 1990s

Under the provisions of the 1936 Broadcasting Act, the CRBC was reorganized as a Crown corporation, the modern Canadian Broadcasting Corporation (the CBC) with considerably strengthened authority. The CBC was confirmed by the new legislation both as the national broadcast regulatory agency, and as the provider of the dominating national service. The structure established in 1936 remained essentially unchanged until 1958 when a new Broadcasting Act, reflecting the private sector-oriented values of the Conservative government, removed the CBC's regulatory authority, and provided for the establishment of a Board of Broadcast Governors (BBG) with direct regulatory supervision over both public and private broadcasting operations. The CBC was now obliged, like all its private sector competitors and affiliates, to submit to the regulatory overview of an independent agency of government, the BBG. Among other requirements, the CBC had to stand in line with private sector broadcasters and apply periodically for licence renewals.

Though much of the CBC's monolithic pre-eminence disappeared with the loss of its regulatory powers in 1958, its physical growth continued. It entered the modern era as by far and away the nation's major broadcaster, and one of the largest such operations anywhere in the world. By the early 1960s, the CBC was broadcasting in both AM and FM radio across the country, and had a mature television network in place. Altogether in 1962, the corporation owned and operated twenty-eight AM radio stations, four broadcasting in the French language. It also had affiliation arrangements with eighty privately owned AM stations, twenty-six of these broadcasting in French. On the television side, the corporation operated fourteen stations of its own (four in French) and had affiliation arrangements with forty-seven private operators, nine of these broadcasting in the French language.[18]

The general situation, including the separation of broadcasting and regulatory responsibilities, was reaffirmed by the passing of the Broadcasting Act in 1968. Under the provisions of this act (as amended a number of times in the subsequent years) the CBC continued to function as a Crown corporation and matured as the country's paramount broadcaster. It had no association with the regulatory function carried out by a new agency replacing the Board of Broadcast Governors, initially named the Canadian Radio-Television Commission (CRTC). Amending legislation having effect on 1 April 1976 added regulatory responsibility over a range of telecommunications activities to the CRTC's initial mandate. Its title was changed to the modern form, the Canadian Radio-television and Telecommunications Commission. A new Broadcasting Act, given royal assent on 1 February 1991, has served to consolidate the 1968 act and its various amendments. While it provides some changes in the wording describing broadcasting's cultural "mandate," the new act does not appear to have moved Canadian broadcasting policy in significant directions. The CRTC continues to function much as it has done since responsibility for telecommunications was added in the mid-1970s.

The primary difference between the BBG of 1958 and the CRTC as it has evolved from the initiating legislation of 1968 to the new Broadcasting Act of 1991, is that the CRTC was perceived by the 1960s Liberal government that created it as being a much stronger regulatory authority. In many ways, the BBG often appeared to be little more than a referee, keeping peace among the various public and private broadcast interests, and usually favouring the private sector. The CRTC clearly addresses broadcasting and telecommunications issues with greater authority, and has tended to reassert public sector pre-eminence in broadcasting.

The presence of a powerful government hand in broadcasting, both as regulator and as the country's paramount broadcaster, has meant a number of things for radio and television journalism that together, over the years, have created more confined perceptions of freedom of expression than is the traditional case with the print media. Unlike print journalism, the news and public affairs content of broadcasting is subject to a degree of official overview and assessment. Station owners in the private sector, and public sector managers at the CBC and at the various provincial educational television authorities that have emerged in more recent decades, are equally aware that the performance of their operations in news and public affairs will be as much subject to official quality assessment as any other aspect of programming during the processes of periodic licence renewal.

To what extent such concerns filter down to the working journalistic level is not clear. All journalists, print and electronic alike, are aware of such longstanding restraints in their work environment as the legal provisions pertaining to contempt of court, libel, obscenity, and so forth discussed in the previous chapter. For the most part, these provisions have worked well to encourage civility within the craft. But as we have also seen, many journalists will point out that the anticipation of potential legal problems occasionally discourages a journalist (or more likely, her or his editor) from including seemingly risky elements of information in the final published version of a given story. Some stories may never see the light of print or broadcast at all for such reasons, and thus a psychological "chill effect" may be generated, and a form of self-imposed prior restraint may come to exist. The presence of a regulatory authority, no matter how distant it may seem to be psychologically from newsroom concerns, unquestionably adds a further cautionary restraint to the work environment.

An "Air of Death"

One of the CRTC's first major acts after its creation, in fact, was to mount an inquiry in 1969 into allegations of biased journalism in a CBC public affairs documentary, "Air of Death," broadcast in November 1967. The program dealt with an air pollution problem in Ontario's Niagara Peninsula, and generated much-publicized allegations of journalistic bias from owners of a fertilizer plant said to be the source of the problem. In their report, published in 1970, the commissioners did not directly censure the CBC, or the producers of the program in question, but sought instead to establish general fairness guidelines for the production of such documentaries. The commissioners recognized that electronic journalists working with controversial material will find it difficult to avoid an "honest bias", but argued that such sentiment must not become "malicious, distorting, or taken to the point of propaganda." The closest the committee allowed itself to come to outright censure was in the somewhat obscure observation on the final page of its report: "…the credibility of broadcasters cannot be maintained if exaggeration is accepted as a legitimate technique."[19] This can only be interpreted as being an indirect censuring by the government regulatory body, if not of the documentary's content, then most certainly of the quality and style of the journalism involved.

In 1977, the CRTC again investigated allegations of journalistic bias at the CBC, this time touching the corporation's francophone arm, Radio-Canada, and at the direct request of the prime minister of the day, Pierre Trudeau. On this occasion, the CRTC established a committee of inquiry to investigate Parliamentary allegations of pro-separatist bias perceived to be infecting much of Radio-Canada's news and public affairs programming. The committee found no evidence of such bias, and generally reserved its criticisms of the corporation to such organizational matters as noting a regrettable lack of communication between the CBC's French and English operations. It is worth

noting that the members of the committee of inquiry chose to interpret their mandate quite broadly, however, and effectively commented in general terms upon the performance of the entire national
news media system, including private as well as public broadcasting,
and on the Canadian Press wire service among other components of
the printed media.[20] Among other things, the committee suggested
that news from the regions of Canada tends to be neglected in all the
media, while journalistic energies focus on events within the so-called
"golden triangle," roughly contained within imaginary lines drawn
between the cities of Toronto, Montreal, and Ottawa.

Perhaps more significant than the various public inquiries into
broadcast content, is the fact that all broadcasting, especially in the
public sector, has been frequently subjected to political criticism of
one form or another. As we have seen, the 1977 CRTC inquiry was a
response to Parliamentary criticism, and as late as 1980 (to cite just one
example) various members of the House of Commons including André
Ouellet, then Minister of Consumer and Corporate Affairs, were still
gnawing at the bone of alleged separatist bias in Radio-Canada's news
and public affairs content. The effect of this ongoing criticism from
the political masters was obvious to Geoffrey Stevens, then the senior
political columnist for the *Globe and Mail.* He said of Mr. Ouellet's
public comments on the subject: "He has so cowed the management
of the CBC that in several telephone calls yesterday to the offices of
Al Johnson, President of the CBC, in Ottawa, I couldn't find anyone
who was prepared to defend the integrity of CBC journalists."[21]

Political interference is thus a concern that must be taken into
account when government intervention is proposed as a means of
curing the perceived ills or limitations of the journalistic process.
Another is the natural inclination of government to use regulated
media as agents for the promotion of public policy. The potential
becomes evident when one notes that the Broadcasting Act contains a
general "mandate" requiring that all broadcasting outlets be effectively owned and controlled by Canadians, and that the broadcasting
system should "serve to safeguard, enrich and strengthen the cultural,
political, social and economic fabric of Canada." Broadcasters are also
required to use Canadian talent and resources wherever possible in
their programming. In addition to these general provisos, the CBC
(described in the Act as the national public broadcaster) has further
mandate obligations to provide all Canadians with a wide range of
programming that informs, enlightens, and entertains, and to do so
in both official languages.

Most importantly, the CBC must also "contribute to shared national consciousness and an identity," and reflect the "multiracial and multicultural nature of Canada."[22] Such considerations may seem entirely benign, and supportive of a conventional understanding of federal Canada and its purposes and objectives. But questions remain as to how such bromides will be interpreted in news and public affairs programming, and who shall do the interpreting as they are put into day-to-day practice as elements of public policy.

Regulation and the Daily Press

Canadians have not only allowed, but generally encouraged extensive government involvement in the regulation of broadcasting and done so with equanimity. The main reason for this has had to do with the comforting background perception that should the hand of government ever become too heavy in the regulation of broadcasting, the unregulated and uninhibited voices of the daily press soon would set matters to rights. There is a certain truth to this perception, but in 1982 it came very close to losing whatever validity it might have had when draft press legislation was tabled in the House of Commons.

Though never passed into law, it is interesting to note that had this legislation been passed, Canada would have been unique among the established Western democracies in the possession of such a statutory instrument. Directly inspired by the recommendations of the Report of the Royal Commission on Newspapers tabled in August, 1981,[23] Canada's press legislation was announced by the then Minister of State Jim Fleming in May, 1982.[24] The legislative measures were not strong ones in themselves, and likely would have had little immediate impact on the conduct of the nation's press. But they were remarkable, nonetheless, because they would have brought into being at least the framework of a general press law in Canadian democracy where no such law existed before. In fact, even in failure, they may have spaded the political ground, establishing a possible precedent for future action just as the recommendations of the 1961 Royal Commission on Publications put in place a principle that formed the basis of legislation years later.

The roots of the extraordinary Canadian position are complex but readily traced. As we have seen, federal interest in the print media as potential objects of policy concern, especially as the journalism of these media relates to questions of national unity and national cultural development, dates back to the early years of this century. It is a record that can be traced primarily through the reports of a remark-able number of royal commissions and other government inquiries that have treated media themes over the years; sometimes as their pri-mary focus, on other occasions tangentially. It is important to keep in mind that royal commissions and other temporary investigatory bod-ies have played an extremely important role in the long-term formula-tion of Canadian social policy in any number of areas, not just those relating to media concerns. As J.E. Hodgetts has written: "royal com-missions appear to remain the chief source of 'outside' inspiration for longer term programme development...they become temporary research institutes, assembling the best available outside [non-govern-mental] talent to carry on sophisticated analyses of complex social and economic problems."[25]

The beginnings of a clear pattern leading to the Kent report and to the subsequent draft legislation are evident at least as early as 1951 with the publication that year of the Report of the Royal Commis-sion on National Development in the Arts, Letters and Sciences in Canada. This commission, chaired by Vincent Massey, actually made only passing reference to the print media as a "chief source of knowl-edge to Canadians of their country,"[26] noting in a context of general concern about the media that "a vast and disproportionate amount of material coming from a single alien [American] source may stifle rather than stimulate our own creative effort."[27]

A statement of the obvious, perhaps. But the immense prestige and influence of this commission were enough to lend important cre-dence to later public arguments in support of the principle of a gov-ernment obligation to concern itself with the quality and social pur-poses of newspapers and magazines. A number of royal commissions, task forces, and other public inquiries have followed, and each has added its brushstrokes to the canvas put in place by Vincent Massey. As we shall discuss shortly, with the publication of the Kent report in 1981, and subsequent presentation of draft legislation, the portrait may now be nearing completion.

The 1961 Royal Commission on Publications was responsible for the first significant post-Massey developments in print media policy evolution. Its tax law provisions, eventually given full force in amend-ments to the Income Tax Act in 1976, were concerned with maga-zines, but as Geoffrey Stevens has noted, only arbitrary distinctions separate magazines from newspapers.[28] One cannot imagine that Commission Chair, Grattan O'Leary, himself a newspaper editor, had only magazines in mind when he wrote these words in his report:

"Only a truly Canadian printing press, one with the 'feel' of Canada and directly responsible to Canada, can give us the critical analysis, the informed discourse and dialogue which are indispensable in a sovereign society."[29]

Of the many commission and task force reports touching press-related media themes that dot the political landscape between Vincent Massey and Thomas Kent, one stands above the others as a special landmark. This is the exhaustive Senate examination of the mass media chaired by Senator Keith Davey, which reported in 1970. The Davey study not only provided Canada's first detailed and all-embracing public examination of media economics and ownership patterns, but it deeply explored such hitherto untrodden territory (at least in terms of government-sponsored research in Canada) as the values and traditions of journalism, newsflow and news definition patterns, journalism education and standards of professionalism, and working conditions in the industry. Public attitudes toward newspapers were explored, as were the dynamics of inter-media relationships, and a number of questions pertaining to the cultural impact of the mass press.

While the actual recommendations of the Senate committee were mild and often generalized, proposals were made for the establishment of a federal Press Ownership Review Board and a federal Publications Development Loan Fund. The committee also urged the industry itself to establish a voluntary national press council.[30] None of these suggestions was ever adopted in the legislative sense, but voluntary press councils were established not long after the publication of the Davey Report in the provinces of Alberta, Ontario, and Quebec, and, at the municipal level, in the City of Windsor, Ontario. Eventually the movement spread across the country, and by the 1990s, most of the nation's daily newspapers had become involved.

Most of the issues raised by the Davey committee were revived by the 1980 Royal Commission on Newspapers, and subsequently had their influence in the shaping of the draft press legislation. In identifying evolving patterns, it is interesting to note that except in certain limited financial areas, the authors of the great earlier studies— Massey, O'Leary and Davey—all refrained from proposing coercive legislative measures as cures for the perceived ills of the press. Massey and O'Leary both emphasized journalism's importance to national well-being, and O'Leary sought to protect it obliquely through the Income Tax Act. Davey proposed his ownership review board and loan fund as a devices to limit press ownership concentration, but his other recommendations were proposals urging voluntary action. In his proposal for a national press council, for instance, he urged the media themselves "to get together and set up a Press Council. You do have something besides profits to protect."[31] A decade later Thomas Kent was recommending something far different, a press law that would have provided for the establishment of a mandatory form of press council, a "Press Rights Panel," with authority not only to police ownership patterns and other economic circumstances within the newspaper industry, but to monitor the quality of journalism as well.

LaMarsh, Infocan, and others

While the several royal commissions from Massey to Kent, along with the Senate study of 1970, provide the most important landmarks in the evolution of Canada's federal press policy, a number of other task forces and inquiries have made their contributions. The broad interpretation of its mandate by the 1977 CRTC Committee of Inquiry into the National Broadcasting Service to include print media considerations has been noted, for instance.

Reference also should be made to the report in 1977 of the Ontario Royal Commission on Violence in the Communications Industry. This massive provincially sponsored study (which cannot be seen as having direct relationship to the various federal studies primarily

Judy LaMarsh was Secretary of State in the 1960s and a major architect of Canada's mature broadcasting policy. She went on to chair the Ontario Royal Commission on Violence in the Communications Industry. She is shown here with fellow commissioners, newspaper columnist Scott Young and Family Court Judge Lucien Beaulieu. (The Toronto Star)

under examination here) is interesting in the present context primarily because it was chaired by Judy LaMarsh. She served as Secretary of
State in the federal Liberal government of Lester Pearson during the
1960s, and was the principal author of the 1968 Broadcasting Act
that was developed under her ministry. It would not be inappropriate
to speculate that the powerful press legislation proposed by LaMarsh
in her 1977 Ontario report, complete with an elaborate press council
structure and various other devices for the regulation of print journalism and the improvement of its quality, may have had their beginnings in her earlier experiences as a federal minister. Be that as it may,
the draconian LaMarsh proposals certainly are not far removed from
those put by the Kent commissioners just a few years later.[32]

Of more immediate interest in the present discussion is the Task
Force on Government information which was created by Order-in-
Council to examine conditions in the federal government's various
public information and public relations services. Reporting in 1969,
the major recommendation of the Task Force was that a federal information agency be established; the cabinet acted almost immediately
with the creation in 1970 of Information Canada. Its life was short.
Information Canada was dismantled in 1975 as part of a government
austerity drive that year, and in terms of its contributions to an evolving national press policy, it might best be regarded as having been an
interesting experiment. It was, in effect, an attempt to find avenues to
circumvent the news media, rather than to seek to co-opt them more
directly to national policy purposes. As we have seen, Joe Clark criticized Information Canada in House of Commons debate as an
attempt to "get around the normal filters of democracy."[33]

Black Wednesday

The creation in 1980 of the Royal Commission on Newspapers was
an entirely logical political development given the nature of the
processes that had been unfolding in Canada since the Massey
Commission reported in 1951. This Royal Commission was chaired
by Thomas Kent, a long-time *éminence grise* of the federal Liberal
Party and professor of management studies at Dalhousie University in
Halifax. The commission's recommendations, and the general sense
of public urgency that surrounded its year-long processes of research
and public hearings, provided the catalyst that brought the long-
developing federal policy interest in the nation's press to new maturity
in the form of a draft press law.

The immediate government concern in 1980 was with economic patterns in the press industries, especially those that have led in recent decades to a most extraordinary concentration of Canadian newspaper ownership in very few hands. But for the longer run, the fact that the federal government came very close to producing a national press act in 1982, and apparently found the move to be much more unpopular with publishers than with the voting public, may have far greater implications. The historic trend is clearly toward a press law, and the abortive 1982 experience may well prove to have been something of a legislative breakthrough.

But to begin with the immediate economic issues, the processes of ownership concentration had accelerated dramatically during the 1970s, a fact which prompted the Kent royal commissioners to open their report with the words: "This commission was born out of shock and trauma."[34] Indeed it was. Two major dailies, the Ottawa *Journal* and the Winnipeg *Tribune*, had been permanently closed by their respective owners, Thomson Newspapers and Southam Inc., within hours of each other on 27 August 1980. On the same day, Thomson sold its fifty per cent interest in Pacific Press Ltd., which publishes Vancouver's two dailies, the *Sun* and the *Province*, to the firm's only other investor, Southam Inc. Meanwhile, in Montreal, Thomson sold to Southam its one-third minority interest in the Montreal *Gazette*.

Southam thus was left as the sole owner of the only English-language daily newspaper in each of Montreal and Ottawa, and the two dailies in Vancouver. The Thomson interests, with their *Free Press*, became the only daily newspaper in the lucrative Winnipeg advertising market. These arrangements subsequently were investigated by the federal Department of Corporate and Consumer Affairs. Seven charges were laid against the Southam and Thomson interests on questions involving the merger, conspiracy, and monopoly provisions of the federal Combines Investigation Act.[35] Though no convictions ultimately were obtained, the fact that such charges were laid in the first place demonstrates the importance that the government attached to the whole affair.

In addition to the dramatic events of 27 August 1980 (since dubbed "Black Wednesday" in Canadian journalistic circles) a number of other dailies either disappeared altogether, or were reduced in status during the 1970s. The Toronto *Telegram*, the Montreal *Star*, *Montréal-Matin*, and *l'Action* of Quebec City all ceased publication. The Calgary *Albertan* also folded, but was resurrected by the Toronto Sun Group, which bought it from Thomson Newspapers and reestablished it as the Calgary *Sun*. In Quebec City, the venerable English-language *Chronicle-Telegraph* ceased daily publication and became a weekly when it was sold by the Thomson chain into independent hands. And on the west coast, the *Times* and the *Colonist*, published in Victoria, were merged to form the single Thomson-owned *Times-Colonist*.[36]

By far the most significant development of the decade, however, was the purchase by Thomson in January 1980 of what was then English Canada's third, and perhaps most important newspaper chain, FP Publications. In this single move, the Thomson group acquired eight of Canada's finest daily newspapers, among them the Toronto *Globe and Mail*, the Winnipeg *Free Press*, and the *Times* and *Colonist* in Victoria. The corporate rationalizations that followed in the wake of this Thomson takeover produced the already-noted merger in Victoria, the closure of the Ottawa *Journal*, the sale of the Calgary *Albertan*, and the sale to Southam of Pacific Press and *Gazette* interests in Vancouver and Montreal respectively.

The takeover left the Thomson organization with forty of Canada's 117 newspaper "titles."[37] Southam Inc., on the other hand, with just fourteen titles, emerged from the activities of 1980 with the largest newspaper group in terms of circulation statistics. With some notable exceptions, such as the *Globe and Mail* and the Winnipeg *Free Press*, Thomson papers tend to be small, while Southam Inc. contains many of the country's largest under its corporate umbrella, including such properties as the two Vancouver papers, the *Windsor Star*, the *Calgary Herald*, the *Edmonton Journal*, and the Ottawa *Citizen*. In 1980, Southam Inc. controlled 32.8 per cent of English-language Canadian daily newspaper circulation, while the Thomson organization controlled 25.9 per cent.

New newspapers also emerged during the 1970s, but the more significant of these in terms of circulation figures were all in the format of morning tabloids. Their presence on the publishing scene clearly is a mixed blessing from the point of view of anyone concerned about the quality of daily journalism and the richness of the public forum. Pierre Péladeau's *Journal de Montréal* and *Journal de Québec* began publication early in the decade, as did the Toronto *Sun*, spiritual successor to the defunct *Telegram*. The *Sun* subsequently expanded to mini-chain status with its purchase and transformation of the old Calgary *Albertan*, and its earlier launching of a new tabloid in Edmonton, predictably christened the *Edmonton Sun*. The Sun group, launched on a relative financial shoestring when the *Telegram* died, was always a risky financial venture when one considers its Toronto competition, the mighty Torstar Corporation and the Thomson-owned *Globe and Mail.* It achieved financial security in February 1982, however, when Maclean Hunter Ltd., the large Toronto-based magazine publisher with extensive television, radio, and nationwide cable television interests, became the Sun group's major shareholder.

These sorts of events are not unique to the newspaper industry. Indeed, they are descriptive of a generalized private sector trend in the last few decades, accelerating in very recent years towards the acquisition of smaller firms, whatever their service or product of manufacture, by a relatively small number of very large conglomerates. Nowhere have the negative effects of industrial concentration been so singled out as objects for both public and political concern as in the newspaper business.

These issues became clearly focused as problematic in the minds of citizens and politicians with the publication of the 1970 report of the Davey Committee. In the language of this report:

> What matters is the fact that control of the media is passing into fewer and fewer hands, and that the experts agree that this trend is likely to continue and perhaps accelerate. The logical ...outcome of the process is that one man or corporation could own every media outlet in the country except the CBC. The committee believes that at some point before this hypothetical extreme is reached, a line must be drawn.[38]

By 1981 when the recommendations of the Kent report were being publicly debated, Senator Davey, who chaired the 1970 study, was using much more urgent language:

> The situation that confronted the Kent Commission was alarmingly simple. Press concentration in Canada has become almost total. Fewer and fewer voices are speaking to more and more Canadians. Ten years ago the Senate committee reported that 77 per cent of Canadian daily newspaper circulation was involved in some form of common ownership. Three big chains controlled 44.7 per cent of readership. Comparable figures today are 88 per cent with just two big chains controlling 47.2 per cent of all English-language readers. And one of these chains, Thomson, dominates the Canadian department store business and has enormous holdings in travel and resources.[39]

The Draft Legislation

Further concentration would have been prevented by the proposed legislation of 1982, the long-term objective being to limit newspaper holdings of any single owner or ownership group to twenty per cent of the country's total average daily newspaper circulation.[40] In his policy announcement of May 1982, Minister of State Jim Fleming also spoke of a need to encourage the Canadian Radio-television and Telecommunications Commission to use its regulatory powers under the Broadcasting Act to break up local mixed-media monopolies and near monopolies.[41]

The fact that the federal government of the day found it both desirable and politically feasible to bring such draconian economic measures relating to the daily newspress to the floor of the House of Commons was in itself a profoundly important development in the evolution of government involvement in the nation's media system.

Of far greater importance, however, was the clear intention evident in both the 1980 Kent Royal Commission Report, and in the subsequent draft legislation, that there should be federal regulatory involvement in matters related to the quality and social purposes of journalism. Consideration of these substantive concerns was often masked in the agendas of public discussion at the time by a much greater focus on those dramatic economic issues. The government of the day was at least as interested in matters of quality and content, as is evident in the draft legislation's provision for a Canadian Advisory Council on Newspapers. It was intended that this agency should "have the objectives of receiving complaints about press reporting in daily newspapers that are not members of effective press councils, promoting public debate, complementing the press councils and ombudsmen that already exist locally, and reporting biennially [to Parliament] on the state of the industry on the basis of its own research and analysis."[42]

The council was never established, but even as a short-lived legislative concept it had its influence. The remarkable growth of the press council movement in Canada during the early 1980s was directly attributable to publishers anticipating passage of the legislation, and rushing to take advantage of its important "loophole" provision that would have allowed mandatory membership in the proposed federal Advisory Council on Newspapers to be waived in most instances for those newspapers already belonging to established voluntary councils. In a further statement in January 1983, Minister of State Fleming said that the national council concept would be reviewed if momentum was maintained in the growth and development of the voluntary press council movement.[43]

It is useful to observe for the record that the recommendations of the royal commission were significantly different from the legislative proposals only in their greater severity. There was little difference in principle. Instead of the twenty per cent ownership limitation contained in the legislation, for instance, Professor Kent and his colleagues of the royal commission (retired Toronto Star ombudsman Borden Spears, and Laurent Picard, a former president of the CBC) sought to place the general ownership limitation at five per cent of total national daily circulation.[44] "Grandfather" loopholes were to have been granted to the large existing chains, but none of these would have been left entirely untouched. The Thomson organization, for instance, would have been required to divest itself either of the *Globe and Mail,* or of all the other newspapers in its possession. The rationale behind this proposal was that the *Globe,* which prints simultaneously via satellite transmission in five Canadian cities, and has significant same-day circulation in most major population centres in the country, would be in a form of regional or local competition with many other Thomson newspapers.[45]

The Royal Commission also recommended establishment under federal statute of a so-called Press Rights Panel. This proposed body (much more powerful in concept that the Advisory Council on newspapers described in the legislation) was envisaged as having authority to review all proposals for newspaper ownership changes, including proposals for newspaper closures, and generally to monitor journalistic performance. Working through a network of local councils, it was also intended that the panel would monitor legislatively established contracts between publishers and their senior editors.

In the final analysis, the question of power and its applications may be the most important reason behind the move toward press legislation early in the 1980s. In the language of the Royal Commission: "Too much power is put in too few hands; and it is power without accountability. Whether the power is in practice well used or ill used or not used at all is beside the point. The point is that how it is used is subject to the indifference or to the whim of a few individuals."[46]

The royal commission clearly had in mind concerns relating to the unbridled use of private power, in this case the vast potential power associated with the ever-increasing concentration of newspaper circulation in fewer and fewer hands. When asked for his opinion on these matters, Lord McGregor of Durris who was chair of Britain's Royal

Commission on the Press between 1974 and 1977, saw equal if not greater danger existing when too much power over the press falls into government hands. Asked to comment on proposals for a press regulatory board (the "Press Rights Panel") contained in the 1981 Report of Canada's Royal Commission on Newspapers, he made this observation:

> It is here that we meet the fundamental difference between the Canadian and the British reports. The British commission was urged by several groups to recommend the creation, by or through government intervention, of new agencies to control the press. It rejected all such proposals on the ground that government intervention would undermine the independence of the press and soon involve persons who owed their position to government acting in practice as censors.[47]

The Royal Commission on Newspapers commissioned a number of cartoons for inclusion in its 1981 report. This one, by Anthony Delatri of Louiseville, Quebec, says all that needs be said about the evolving impact of television on daily newspapers. (Reproduced with the permission of the Minister of Supply and Services Canada, 1992)

A History of Concern

It is possible to make arguments supporting special legislation to regulate most industries based on social concerns. But the journalists of the newspaper industry, and the already well-regulated broadcast industry, are closer to politicians and bureaucrats, touch their lives more directly, than workers in any other field of endeavour, with the possible exception of the civil service itself, thus making legislation a difficult issue.

The tradition of federal concern with the daily newspress and its potential regulation is long and complex. However, it is important to emphasize one particular point that has been made several times in this chapter: the press legislation of the early 1980s must be regarded as the most dramatic and most assertive expression, for the moment, of an ongoing process begun much earlier in Canada's national development. The shape of policy emerged only gradually, eventually arriving some thirty years after the Massey commission at the detailed analysis and recommendations of the Kent report. The process not only created draft legislation; it also produced the political climate necessary for public acceptance of extensive federal policy involvement in the affairs of the print media.

The measures given such serious consideration early in the 1980s would have been politically unthinkable at the time of the Massey commission. The question remains as to whether they are any more appropriate in modern Canada than they would have been at mid-century. The fundamental argument in both the royal commission report, and in the resultant draft legislation, was that economic trends in the newspaper industry have created a threat to press freedom (and by implication, to national development) at least as great as any potential threat from an overweening government.

The point is well taken. But it does not consider the inextricably related point on the other side of the coin, that an invitation to government to rectify these presumed economic ills is also an invitation to government to concern itself with the quality and social purposes of journalism. That government has quite willingly accepted this second "invitation" has been amply demonstrated in modern Canadian experience. The influences of a revolutionary technology (if one is to consider the thesis of Harold Innis) and certainly those influences generated by the continuing struggle for cultural survival on the American margin may be seen to be at work here. This is, perhaps, to the good of the long-term national survival agenda as perceived by federal policy makers, but not necessarily to the spontaneous flow of news and public information.

NOTES

1. Canada. *Report.* The Royal Commission on Newspapers (Ottawa: Supply and Services Canada, 1981), 254–5.

2. W. H. Kesterton, *A History of Journalism in Canada* (Toronto: McClelland and Stewart, 1967), 25.

3. Isaiah Litvak and Christopher Maule, *Cultural Sovereignty: The Time and Reader's Digest Case in Canada* (New York: Praeger Publishers, 1974), 19.

4. Ibid., 19–21.

5. Ibid., 23–4.

6. Canada. *Report,* Royal Commission on Publications (Ottawa: Queen's Printer, 1961).

7. Ibid., 2.

8. Printed in the United States, *Time*'s Canadian edition usually boasted a cover that reflected a Canadian theme. A cluster of half a dozen inside pages, produced by a small editorial establishment that *Time* maintained in Toronto, contained Canadian information. Except that the Canadian edition was rich in Canadian advertising content, it was otherwise indistinguishable from its American cousin. Since 1976, Canadian subscribers have received the basic American version of *Time.* A liberal sprinkling of Canadian advertising still finds its way into the magazine, despite unfavourable income tax provisions.

9. Geoffrey Stevens, "The Cullen Rule," *Globe and Mail,* 28 October 1975.

10. As quoted in Frank W. Peers, *The Politics of Canadian Broadcasting 1920-1951* (Toronto: University of Toronto Press, 1969), 102.

11. Ibid., 15–6.

12. E. Austin Weir, *The Struggle for National Broadcasting In Canada* (Toronto: McClelland and Stewart, 1965), 1–2.

13. Ibid.,107–9.

14. Marc Raboy, *Missed Opportunities The Story of Canada's Broadcasting Policy* (Montreal and Kingston: McGill-Queen's University Press, 1990), 34–5.

15. Ibid., 117–23.

16. Peers, *The Politics of Canadian Broadcasting 1920-1951,* 107–30.

17. Albert A. Shea, *Broadcasting: The Canadian Way* (Montreal: Harvest House, 1963), 105.

18. Ibid., 31.

19. Canadian Radio-Television Commission, Public Announcement, 9 July 1970.

20. Canadian Radio-television and Telecommunications Commission, Committee of Inquiry into the National Broadcasting Service, *Report* (Ottawa: CRTC, 1977).

21. Geoffrey Stevens, "Disgusting," *The Globe and Mail,* 17 April 1980.

22. These mandate provisions are described in the Broadcasting Act, 1991, Section 3. The place of the legislated mandate is described in an internal CBC policy document, *Journalistic Policy* (Ottawa: Canadian Broadcasting Corporation, 1988). This document on journalism recognizes the mandate provisions as the "legislated objectives by which the corporation is governed."

23. Canada, *Report.* The Royal Commission on Newspapers (Ottawa: Supply and Services Canada, 1981).

24. Honourable Jim Fleming, "Government Proposals on Freedom of the Press in Relation to the Canadian Daily Newspaper Industry," an address to the Graduate School of Journalism, the University of Western Ontario, London, Canada, 25 May 1982.

25. J. E. Hodgetts, *The Canadian Public Service: A Physiology of Government* (Toronto: The University of Toronto Press, 1976), 217.

26. Canada, *Report,* The Royal Commission on National Development in the Arts, Letters and Sciences in Canada (Ottawa: The King's Printer, 1951), 61.

27. Ibid., 18.

28. Geoffrey Stevens, "The Cullen Rule," *Globe and Mail,* 28 October 1975.

29. Canada, *Report,* Royal Commission on Publications (Ottawa: Queen's Printer, 1961), 2.

30. Canada, *Report,* The Special Senate Committee on the Mass Media, v. 1, "The Uncertain Mirror," 255–60.

31. Ibid., 257.

32. Ontario, *Report,* The Royal Commission on Violence in the Communications Industry, v. 1 (Toronto: The Queen's Printer for Ontario, 1977).

33. Hansard, 23 July 1973.

34. Canada, *Report,* Royal Commission on Newspapers, 1981, xi.

35. *London Free Press,* 6 May 1982.

36. The Royal Commission on Newspapers, *Report,* 4–9.

37. Ibid., 90. The royal commissioners noted a number of local situations in Canada where two seemingly separate newspapers were published under common ownership, printed on the same presses, and even produced by common news, advertising and business staffs. Examples include the *Times* and the *Transcript* in Moncton, and the *Chronicle-Herald* and *Mail-Star* in Halifax. In order to produce realistic statistics, the Royal Commission selected the word "title" to describe each newspaper production situation. Thus the Ottawa *Citizen* is designated a single "title", but so are each of the fictionally multiplied newspaper clusters in Moncton, Halifax, and elsewhere.

38. Canada, The Special Senate Committee on the Mass Media, *Report,* v. 1, "The Uncertain Mirror" (Ottawa: The Queen's Printer, 1970), 6.

39. D. Keith Davey, "Newspapers jolted into hysteria," *The Globe and Mail,* 16 September 1981. In his reference to department store and resources holdings, Senator Davey is here noting the fact that Thomson controls, among its other assets, the Hudson's Bay Company, and is a major investor in Britain's North Sea oil properties. The Thomson organization, of course, has extensive newspaper and other media holdings in the United States, Britain, and overseas.

40. The two largest chains, Thomson and Southam, already exceeded the proposed twenty per cent limitation. A "grandfather" clause in the draft legislation would have left these chains in tact for the foreseeable future, but unable either to acquire new newspaper properties, or to sell existing holdings to other large chain organizations.

41. The Blackburn Group in London, Ontario, owner of that city's daily newspaper and a number of electronic outlets, was mentioned at the time as a possible candidate for enforced divestiture. In fact, the CRTC did subsequently consider the London, Ontario, situation in 1986, but took no action.

42. Honourable Jim Fleming, "Government Proposals on Freedom of the Press in Relation to the Canadian Daily Newspaper Industry," 15.

43. From an interview with the Honourable Jim Fleming on "The Nation's Business," CBC Television, 16 January 1983.

44. Royal Commission on Newspapers, *Report*, 239.

45. Ibid., 243.

46. Royal Commission on Newspapers, *Report*, 220.

47. Lord McGregor of Durris, "Commissions differ on state of newspaper industry," *London Free Press*, 23 October 1981.

Toward
Tomorrow:
Changing
Patterns

In the world of journalism, tomorrow dawned for Canadians on 6 September 1952. That was the day the Canadian Broadcasting Corporation's English language channel in Montreal, CBFT, began the first scheduled television programming in Canada. CBLT went on air two days later in Toronto, and journalism was never to be the same again.

As a new technology, with new capacities and certain limitations, television forced the restructuring of journalism in a number of ways. The consequences of the new medium's arrival were not immediately obvious in those early days, but journalists quickly realized that when the traditional characteristics of news and newsworthiness were transplanted to the television environment, they tended to assume an unprecedented intensity and urgency.

Print journalism's traditional preference for graphic qualities in news became markedly more intense. Newspaper journalists who made the pioneering transition into the new medium nearly half a century ago found themselves painfully and very suddenly conscious of the little screen's insatiable appetite for the visual and the visceral.

From the outset, television instilled in journalism a whole new sense of temporal urgency. In its time, radio had forced print journalism to treat deadlines with a more competitive sense of time and timeliness. But radio never was able to replace the daily newspress as society's gatekeeper medium; thus its influence on the ways of the printing press was limited. Television's influence has been much more powerful, and among other things, it has forced the entire news gathering and news disseminating process into more demanding time frames. In the older print-ordered environment, news remained fresh for at least twenty-four hours; often longer if the information was coming from abroad. Television, however, has forced a twelve-hour lag on all journalism. After these short hours, all news becomes stale, regardless of its consequence in any absolute sense. It must be updated with fresh ingredients or it must be abandoned.

Immediacy in the sense of real or physical closeness also has taken on a whole new meaning in the modern era of an ascendant television journalism. In earlier times when print was predominant, datelines labeling news from far places tended to enhance the reader's romantic feeling of distance and of separation from fascinating far-away events. But television has reversed this, opening windows of urgent proximity on news wherever in the world it occurs. It is the journalism of television that gives significant meaning to Marshall McLuhan's notion of all humanity dwelling in a village of global proportions. This is a village in which powerful events, wherever they may occur, are far too close to viewers to retain much romance.

But of all the traditionally understood characteristics of news, it is the imperative to entertain that has been most powerfully enhanced in journalism's transition to television. To a much greater degree than the print media, television is popularly understood to be a medium of entertainment. Those who plan and create its content firmly believe that if television is to attract and hold audiences, all its programming must be designed primarily to entertain. The news of the day must contribute as fully to this overarching imperative as any sitcom, drama, or sporting event. It is especially with this emphasis on entertainment values that television has changed all of journalism.

A Subtle List

The list of television's effects on journalism is long. Many of its entries are subtle, and it would not be unfair to say that many, if not most have negative consequences for the health and richness of the democratic forum. Television simply provides vastly less information than can be provided in a typical daily newspaper. This is true even after the average of at least sixty per cent advertising content has been removed from the reading,[1] along with advice, bridge and health columns, and all the other non-news components of a typical modern daily. The point will become clear to any news consumer who tries this simple experiment: begin at the top left corner of any daily's front page, and carefully read what is there for a timed twenty or twenty-five minutes, the typical duration (stripped of ads and promotional segments) of a half-hour television newscast. Where numbers of words alone are the measure, a television newscast will be found to provide not much more than the equivalent of a column and a half of print, or about a quarter of all the content on a typical printed news page. (Obviously an experimenter would cover more ground in twenty to twenty-five minutes in one of the photo-heavy tabloids. Even so, it would be impossible to reach beyond the second or third of the *Toronto Sun*'s eighty or so pages, for example, in the time available.)

Television compensates by abbreviating the information it provides, and by taking great care to select words that will be immediately understood by all audience members, both in their definition and in their context. Further cues are provided through powerful visual components. Where it is all done well, the result gives the impression of a remarkably tidy, thorough, and authoritative news package.

It is a package that evidently is seen by a majority of the modern news-consuming public as being neater, more complete, and more comprehensive than its printed equivalent. Various recent opinion polls have clearly shown that television news is influential, despite the relatively meagre amount of information it offers. An Environics Research Group poll in 1988, for instance, produced statistics based on a question asking sample members to indicate the main medium through which they keep up with the news. The results suggested that forty-seven percent of Canadians use television for the purpose, while newspapers are the choice of thirty-one per cent and radio of just fifteen per cent.

In the same survey (based on a national sample of 2013 home interviews) a more telling question was asked: which medium is "most likely to give in-depth analysis of the [news] situation?" In this context, thirty-five per cent named television, while magazines were selected by twenty-seven per cent, newspapers by twenty-three per cent, and radio by just six per cent.[2] More recently in a poll commissioned by the Canadian Daily Newspaper Publishers Association in 1991, Environics identified a decline in the number of Canadians "who believe the newspaper is important" from forty-five per cent in 1986 to just thirty-seven per cent in 1991.[3]

Robert Fulford, the well-known Canadian essayist and editor, is correct in describing television news as a "grand illusion," a powerful and influential phenomenon that has reduced news to a level where it has become more a matter of form than of substance. "What counts is the form, because the form will determine how we see the world." Fulford then continues:

> The result [the television news package] is a structured and carefully crafted little drama, without unexplained facts or unanswered questions. Television news stories are much more persuasive than their newspaper equivalents because they appear to make good sense and the reporters appear to be in complete control of their material. The style of TV reporting makes us believe that the whole story has been told, whereas the style of newspaper reporting—with its loose ends and incomplete thoughts—makes us believe we are receiving only a partial account....What TV people have in place of knowledge or wisdom is technique and an unerring sense of ritual. They can fit the world together, make sense of it, in a way that other journalists cannot....They never bore us with the more cumbersome details of reality or the awkward corners of events.[4]

Much of television thus can be seen as having replaced substance with form providing a sort of junk-food journalism, appealing but low in informative value. Nonetheless, the fast food diet that it provides has become remarkably attractive to a great many people, if statistics such as those cited above are accurate. In the process, television also has created news announcers and commentators who have become personalities of greater presumed importance, presumed stability, and presumed trustworthiness in the minds of viewers than the actual newsmakers whose faces and words flash in brief clips throughout a typical newscast.

Journalism of the Stars

Clive Cocking provided the flavour of all of this in his description of a 1979 election campaign visit by then Conservative leader Joe Clark to the town of Tillsonburg in southwestern Ontario. The media retinue that follows political leaders on such occasions included the CBC's Peter Mansbridge, and Peter Desbarats, then a news personality at Global TV. "Joe is being upstaged, heads turn when a voice says, 'there's Peter Mansbridge.' Other members of the audience keep coming over and shaking Peter Desbarats' hand. One lady has him pose for a snapshot, and then can't remember his name....Outside, while waiting for the bus, some youthful voices are heard in the milling throng saying, 'I've never seen so many movie stars.'"[5]

These voices were not far off the mark; in fact the phenomenon has been appropriately described as the "star syndrome." It occurs when television journalists, especially those who serve as highly visible anchor persons, become public celebrities. It is an inevitable aspect of television's entertainment imperative and once it occurs it becomes an entirely moot point as to who is more important, more respected, and above all more powerful, in the ordering of public business: is it Barbara Frum, for instance, who presided so prominently over the CBC's "The Journal" until her tragic early death in 1992, or is it the national political leader she and her producer had selected on a given evening to interview?

In his study of American TV news and its personalities, Ron Powers joins other observers in suggesting that during the late 1960s Walter Cronkite may have influenced President Lyndon Johnson in shifting from a policy of force to one of negotiation in the Vietnam struggle. After a 1968 visit to the war zone, Cronkite returned in a troubled mood to his CBS anchor desk, and expressed a newly

Peter Mansbridge, anchor of CBC's "The National" and "Sunday Report" is one of several high-profile television journalists to have reached celebrity status. (Courtesy CBC)

acquired opposition to the war at the conclusion of several broadcasts. The effect, as Powers has put it, was this: "[President] Johnson saw and raged—but he knew a straw in the wind when it blew in his face. If the bearded, unkempt kids in the streets preached against the war, that was piecemeal agitation—containable. When Walter Cronkite said the same thing, in different language, it was as if the soul of America had opened up."[6]

Since the Cronkite era, the commercial networks in the United States have come to regard their senior journalists as personalities, celebrities to be valued primarily for their ability to attract and hold large audiences. As expressed in a 1989 *Time* cover article on these themes: "Although most [TV news celebrities] are competent reporters, they have reached their positions largely because of qualities that have little to do with journalism; the way they look, the tone of their voices, their on-camera charm." The danger is simply that "as stars become more and more important in the high-stakes world of TV journalism, they are overwhelming the news they purport to report." The same article notes that in the late 1980s there were at least a dozen of these American network news stars drawing salaries well in excess of $1 000 000 annually.[7] Many others had salaries approaching that figure.

The star syndrome is an integral part of television's imperative to entertain. But it is also a form of static in the medium, a noise that often hinders viewers' comprehension of the meaning of mass-mediated messages as intended by the originating sources. It is ironic, given this intervening noisiness of the modern mass media that the proper meaning of the word suggests something very different.

The Oxford dictionary defines "medium" as the "middle quality or degree; intervening substance through which impressions are conveyed to senses." In other words, and in the way that an artist might understand the concept, the ideal medium is something that will retreat; it will not be easily visible, in and of itself, to a person viewing a great work of art. The actual paint and canvas of Van Gogh's "Cornfield with Crows," for instance, are rendered effectively invisible to any attuned viewer. The viewer feels only for that moment the light, the madness, and the agony in the artist's soul. The medium has merely and silently transmitted all of this.

Mass media, especially television, are very different. Unlike Van Gogh's transcending paint and canvas, mass media vigorously announce themselves, and often stand more as barriers to communication than enablers of it. Even the vocabulary of the news craft, words such as "newsworthy" or "gatekeeper;" "editor" or "news director," suggest that the active sorting and shaping of news is more important to these media than the useful business of conveyance.

The newspress always has been "noisy," of course, filled with its own agendas and capacities to skew and distort the information it conveys. And in part it must risk these things. There isn't enough room to publish all the information in the world that is potentially newsworthy on a given day. Thus, selections must be made and there is useful purpose in sorting news items according to an experienced editor's sense of priorities. Ideas often need interpretation if they are to be understood by all readers, and often, it can be appropriate to seek to contain the more blatant expressions of self-interest that skilled public relations professionals may insinuate into the news of the day. Despite their obvious imperfections as media, newspapers traditionally have regarded the conveyance of information to readers as their prime purpose.

Television has proved not to be so inclined. This becomes apparent when one looks at the career paths of journalists who, decades ago, left print and moved into the new electronic environment. When television first arrived on the cultural scene, it drew most of its journalists from the world of print. Walter Cronkite who read the nightly news on the American CBS network for nearly twenty years until his retirement in 1981, remains one of the better-known of these transplants.

His road to television included wire service work as a war correspondent during the 1940s, and later for the old United Press in Joseph Stalin's postwar Moscow. Cronkite never felt entirely comfortable in the television environment. *Time* described him at his retirement as a man who "persists in the mannerisms and discipline of the older medium as if this guarantees his integrity—and the integrity of the news—in television's less pure environment of hucksters, big money and pizzazz." Cronkite reviewed and gave final edit to everything he read on air, and insisted on such unusual vanities as refusing to wear contact lenses for the sake of the camera and insisting on reading the evening news from behind a battered desk rather than a modern news set. In his own words: "I don't want to be a personality, a presenter, a show-biz thing."[8] Despite his protests Cronkite became all of these during his years as the leading American news anchor. In effect, he became a "star."

Various writers and observers have pointed out that in the years since Cronkite's arrival in television, the medium has increasingly produced more of its own news people, and has learned to rely less on recruits from print newsrooms. Many of today's television journalists have had little or no experience in print, with the result that there are few TV news personalities today who make an effort to resist the "stardom," or the power granted to them through constant public exposure in this newer medium. Most gladly accept these personally gratifying new dimensions, and are entirely undisturbed by them.

In 1989, Diane Sawyer, a one-time press aide in Richard Nixon's White House, was earning $1 600 000 as a rising news star at ABC. Her Hollywood-style view of news and its purposes was this: "I love the breathtaking way we walk into people's lives and ask them anything we want and then leave. For a moment you have available to you the whole universe of a person's life—the pain and the suffering and the joy and the struggle. You can learn from it and take it with you, and then come back the next day with somebody else. That's what I like to do."[9]

The Imperative to Entertain

The star syndrome is not only part of television's entertainment imperative, but its contribution is critically important to what Peter Trueman has called "the awful power of the tube."[10] Trueman has described the television journalist's problem with the fuller scope of the entertainment imperative in these words: "To hang onto an audience, to hold the ratings, the producer of a half-hour [news] program must somehow entice an audience which the producer of the previous half hour assembled or held onto for another purpose. To do that, the emphasis must be on entertainment rather than information."[11] This means that the entertainment characteristics of the rest of television find their way all too readily into the value system of the television newsroom. The edges between journalism and fiction can become entirely blurred. This happened when Connie Chung of CBS, one of those influential $1 000 000 plus news stars, crossed an invisible barrier into the world of TV fiction to play herself in a 1989 episode of "Murphy Brown," the popular sitcom about television journalism. This is not an isolated instance; U.S. news personalities appear routinely on talk shows and variety shows of all kinds. Then there are the syndicated American trash-journalism programs such as those featuring Geraldo Rivera or Oprah Winfrey. Their shows exist because of their ability to provide sensationalized entertainment in the guise of serious journalism. In the process, they provide "an extreme example of a trend some TV critics say has begun to infiltrate the legitimate news and public affairs programming."[12]

Far more disconcerting is the modern trend to news dramatization in which actors and stage props are used to provide fictional replications of news scenarios. The phenomenon is simple, brief, and seemingly innocuous. Fox Broadcasting's documentary program, "A Current Affair" artificially illustrated a tragic bridge collapse that claimed thirty-three lives during the 1989 San Francisco earthquake. The producers at "A Current Affair" showed a pair of hands gripping a steering wheel, and a dashboard clock reading 5:04 P.M., the precise moment on 17 October 1989 when the earthquake struck.[13] This footage was staged after the fact. It wasn't real, and if news is to be news, then surely it must be about things that are real. Otherwise, it isn't news, and it isn't journalism, either.

More significantly, the same practice was employed on a much larger scale in a Canadian incident in October 1989. On this occasion, the CBC's "The Journal" used actors to dramatize purported closed-door discussions among Commonwealth leaders in London in 1986 relating to the sensitive issue of South African trade sanctions. At the time Mark Starowicz, executive producer at the "The Journal" justified the news dramatization on the grounds that it was "based on transcripts supported by eyewitnesses."[14] In his view, this was enough to justify airing the material on the country's leading news analysis program. The problem Starowicz failed to recognize is that no group of actors could possibly replicate the complexities and nuances of such a news situation. These dramatizations are bound to contain unintended misrepresentations, and they also present disturbingly rich opportunities for the purposeful placing of skewed interpretations on actual events. In other words, they present opportunities to generate powerful propaganda.

It would be inaccurate to leave the impression that television is the only medium that has been tempted to convert news and public affairs information into the substance of entertainment. The very definition of news, established in its modern form by daily print journalism many years before the arrival of television, recognizes the need to entertain readers. Print journalism acknowledges that the newspaper reader is a sort of volunteer who is under no obligation to read, and who may abandon the exercise when other more interesting stimuli command attention. By much the same token, and long before television arrived on the scene, most newspaper reporters were well aware that they possessed a modicum of power to influence events. All print reporters for instance, are aware that their arrival at a public meeting will immediately alter the psychology of the event. The platform speaker's words may be changed as they are uttered, and edited-on-the-go for the broader audience beyond the reporter's notebook. Members of the immediate audience, even when they number in the thousands, are somehow able to sense the presence of a single print reporter in the room. Print journalism has never been without its stars and well-developed egos, either. Pierre Berton and Gordon Sinclair, for instance, both products of the *Toronto Star*, were print-generated celebrities, long before television was invented in Sinclair's case, and long before it had achieved its present dominant position in Berton's situation.

What television has done is to intensify all news values to a point where an entirely new dynamic is created. Television continues in these last years of the century to work as a force for change, and to expand its influence in quantum fashion. Paradoxically, this is happening as the great commercial networks in the United States and in Canada, confronted with audience-fracturing competition from specialized cable channels, are at last showing signs of aging. As one observer has suggested, the old networks may be in decline and our viewing patterns may change dramatically as CNN, the Sports Network, and all the other cable channels carve out their own shares of the traditional audience. Yet, as an institution, television's hold on the public imagination continues to grow, "seeping into the courtroom and the diplomatic pouch and the military lair. Indeed even democracy itself seems to be emphasizing principles taken from mass pop culture, with pollsters to supply the ratings, with referendums and plebiscites and populist rhetoric. It's as if the tube is losing its grip on our minds but tightening its hold on our souls."[15]

A Struggle for Survival

For its part, the daily press of the late twentieth century has found itself involved in an unprecedented struggle for survival in an age dominated by television. The general mood in recent years is found in an observation in 1991 by Phil McLeod, editor-in-chief of the *London Free Press*: "our business has perhaps twenty years left unless we make some fundamental changes." These changes have to include a new definition of what is news.[16]

There is a sense of urgency shared by many print journalists and print newsroom managers. Some aspects of the situation are not new; print journalism has always existed in an intensely close relationship with advertising, and with a respectful awareness of the economic imperatives of the marketplace. Newspapers are businesses, where making a profit is the ultimate purpose. Senator Keith Davey once made the point in these effective, if somewhat jaundiced words:

> It seems harsh, but it happens to be utterly accurate, that editorial and programming content in the media serve the same economic function as the hootchy-kootch girl at a medicine show—she pulls in the rubes so that the pitchman will have somebody to flog his snake oil to. This notion may collide with the piety which most media owners view their social responsibilities, but the more you think about the analogy the apter it seems.[17]

The analogy is apt indeed. Despite their seemingly conflicting purposes, journalism and the advertising that largely supports it have lived together comfortably for many years within the nation's newspapers. Of course, there always have been instances of stories being altered or even suppressed because a major advertiser might be embarrassed by the content. But such instances are not common, and they are virtually unheard of in the largest news media. Organizations such as the *Toronto Star*, Southam Inc., or any of the major television networks, are simply too big and too powerful as business organizations in their own right to be so easily bought off. And for most of this century, few publishers have been effectively able to bring advertiser influence to bear when it conflicted with perceptions of things from the vantage point of the newsroom. A circumstance used to exist in which the interests of the newsroom and those of the advertising department ran on parallel and complementary courses. There was a balance in this, with each of the newspaper's purposes depending upon the other for survival.

It worked like this: the mentality of the advertising department (which in most cases approximated that of the business-oriented publisher) tended to view the newspaper as a package designed to carry and attractively display advertising. The more readers, and the more exposure for advertising the package contained, the more successful the newspaper would be as a business. Newspaper publishers and advertising executives recognized, however, that it was precisely the non-advertising content, the journalism that made the package attractive to readers. Thus the newsroom tended to be left alone, disturbed only when circulation figures and advertising revenues went into periods of sustained decline. As long as the bottom line of the balance sheet was satisfactory and as long as the newsroom was reasonably cautious about the money it spent, journalists were allowed to shape the package as they saw fit. Thus, the commercial and the social interests were mutually supportive.

In this situation, most publishers had the wisdom and inclination to leave journalism to the journalists. More precisely, the editorial side of the operation typically was entrusted to the care of a very senior journalist, an editor-in-chief. Though rarely wealthy in their own right, such individuals tended to be the equals of their publishers in terms of community regard, and often too, in the effective social power they wielded. The relationship between the publishers and senior editors was one of trust and respect, and usually it reflected the balanced symbiosis between journalistic and economic interests that characterized the typical newspaper. An example is the remarkable relationship between Grattan O'Leary (editor of the *Ottawa Citizen*) and the Southam family who owned the paper. The longstanding relationship between Richard Doyle and one-time publisher Howard Webster at the *Globe and Mail* was also remarkable. Arthur Ford, and later William Heine, successive editors of the *London Free Press*, and the Blackburn family, provide yet another good example.

One of the best expressions of this relationship comes from one who actually lived within such a symbiosis, Robert P. Clark, former executive editor of the respected *Courier-Journal* and the *Times* of Louisville, Kentucky. Here he describes the ownership philosophy that prevailed when the papers were independently owned by the Bingham family during his tenure in the 1970s and before the Gannett chain acquired the papers during the 1980s: "Over a span of three generations, the Louisville newspapers established a tradition of serving the public welfare. And the motive was not primarily money, but public service. With public service came money, which is one of my premises...that quality journalism leads to financial success. Too many newspaper owners, I fear, believe that shorting the readers on quality is the road to a nice bottom line."[18]

Whether or not Clark's assessment of the modern era is entirely correct may remain to be seen, but in recent years, largely in response to television's intense competitive pressure, newspaper publishers have chosen to distrust the provisions of the old unwritten contract of the symbiosis. Instead, they have introduced new forms of expertise into their newsrooms, severely limiting journalism's traditional discretion.

Journalism and the Marketeers

Few cities have room in the marketplace for more than one daily, and though such surviving papers generally remain profitable, circulation figures rarely keep abreast of population growth. In many instances they tend to show long-term gradual declines. Where new newspapers have been established in recent years, almost all have been in the tabloid format of the Toronto Sun group, and of Pierre Péladeau's *Journal de Québec* and *Journal de Montréal*. The reader may recall Péladeau's telling words to the effect that publishers tend to forget that television is the most important medium.[19] Such newcomers to print journalism tend to be entirely devoted to serving a television-attuned audience. Photos and other graphics dominate in busy design frameworks and even the many photos are often printed with rounded corners, possibly simulating frozen TV moments.

While established dailies have not moved toward blatantly TV-imitating formats, their publishers certainly have done much (often at terrible cost to traditional journalistic values) to move them in directions designed to reach a TV-oriented modern generation. The great example, one of the few modern full-sized papers new to the North American market in recent years, is the Gannett chain's *USA Today*. Distributed nationally in the United States, and with strong penetration into many urban Canadian markets as well, *USA Today* has been described as "the quintessential corporately planned and packaged, market-driven paper. Reporters' copy is simply grist for editors, who hack it and reshape it into the brief, graphically oriented copy that gives the paper its television feel."[20]

In effect, what has happened at *USA Today*, at the Canadian tabloids, and at many of the important traditional dailies in Canada and the United States, is that publishers no longer trust the journalistic instincts and traditions of the newsroom. The great editors, once entrusted to produce those acceptable commercial packages by producing acceptable journalism, have been replaced by managers more knowledgeable in the ways of business than in the traditions of journalism. These individuals rely more heavily on reader surveys and market analyses than they do on basic journalistic wisdom. Newsrooms are being increasingly managed and rationalized, structured as any other work unit in any other business, to maximize efficiency and minimize costs. The marketability of the product is what counts most.

One American newspaper marketing theorist, Philip Meyer of the Knight-Ridder chain, has suggested that there are three basic approaches to the marketing of modern daily newspapers.[21] First, there is the *referendum model*, or gallup editing, as described by some critics. This simple model involves polling readers, finding out the most popular information ingredients and emphasizing these accordingly in published content. The second or *target group model*, involves research to determine the basic demographic patterns in the community that the newspaper in question serves. This model presumes that one or more potential target groups may be identified that are not being served efficiently by the paper. Content in the paper is then enriched to accommodate the identified target group or groups, and presumably circulation will increase accordingly.

Finally, there is what Meyer calls the *Knight-Ridder model* that involves elements taken from both the referendum and target group

USA Today has been called "the quintessential corporately planned and packaged, market-driven paper." Distributed nationally across the United States, and with penetration into many urban centres in Canada, *USA Today's* busy, graphic treatment is designed for competition in the age of television. (Copyright 1992, USA TODAY. Reprinted with permission)

models. This third model adds the sophisticated demographic wrinkle of correlating subject matter with readership. Studies have determined that some forms of information (traditional hard news, for instance) have high reader interest, and high readership correlation. Other forms of information, such as consumer advice, child-rearing or budget-stretching service features, enjoy high referendum ratings, but are not strongly linked to actual readership patterns. These are seen as growth opportunity areas, as are those occasional areas where, the referendum factor is not strong but there is promising correlation with actual readership patterns. Finally, there is information that fails to score well in either of the referendum or correlation approaches, and these can be given "low priority."

The world of market survey journalism has become increasingly sophisticated since Meyer provided this description, but the basic elements of the approach remain as he described them. For journalism, the art of editing and the mystique of the newsroom have been largely superseded by modern business management methods. The greatest loss is the very marked disappearance from daily journalism of the balance that used to exist between business imperatives on the one hand, and the non-commercial social concerns of the traditional newsroom on the other. For better or worse, daily print journalism is now largely in the hands of the business people.

In summary, what is happening is a reduction in the traditional organizational importance of the journalist. In many newspapers this also can mean a substantial reduction in the actual number of journalists employed by the paper, along with a concomitant reduction in the variety and scope of journalistic specialization. In other words, it means newspapers, designed to complement the journalism of television, and to imitate the style of television, can thereby share in the perceived success of television.

Softer and Narrower News

In 1983, the author was commissioned by Canada's federal Ministry of Justice to undertake research into changes in the content of a major Canadian daily newspaper, the Montreal *Gazette,* in circumstances of management changes and economic pressures under discussion here.[22] This content analysis was in connection with the ministry's prosecution that year under the federal Combines Investigations Act of Thomson Newspapers, Southam Inc., and others, in the wake of the same-day closings on 17 August 1980, of the *Ottawa Journal* and the *Winnipeg Tribune,* and other industry rationalizations. This was the sequence of events that provided incentive for the creation of the 1980 Royal Commission on Newspapers.[23]

The object of the 1983 research was to observe changes in the content of the *Gazette* over a four-year period, changes that presumably related to shifting circumstances in the paper's overall competitive environment. For the purpose, a three-week sample drawn from August, September, and October, 1977, was compared with an identical sample drawn from the same three months in 1981. The results of the comparison were revealing.

The *Gazette* expanded enormously, almost doubling in size from a total of 125 252 column inches published in the 1977 sample to 240 786 column inches in 1981. This did not mean that readers enjoyed a doubling of their reading value. While there was an increase from about 42 000 column inches of news and other forms of non-advertising material to about 65 500 column inches, there was also a much larger expansion of advertising material from about 69 000 column inches to just over 155 000 column inches.

Thus, as a percentage of overall available space, the news and other non-advertising content of the *Gazette* dropped from 33.1 per cent to 26.8 per cent. With the death of the *Montreal Star* in 1979, an event that was a precursor to the later and more dramatic rationalizations in the industry, Southam's *Gazette* became the only English-language daily in Montreal. Its advertising volume increased considerably.

The data also revealed that the Gazette of 1981 gave the impression of being a much "softer" newspaper than it was in 1977. In order to comparatively measure aspects of content of the *Gazette* in the two sample periods, non-advertising content was separated into five categories according to journalistic style.

> 1.   Hard News: objective accounts of current events in standard, expository journalistic writing style.
>
> 2.   Soft News: feature-style reports of less consequential current events, typically with human interest as the primary news value.
>
> 3.   News Features: serious "backgrounder" articles providing interpretation and analysis of the news.
>
> 4.   Soft Features: longer articles, usually with little connection to current events. They are light and frequently subjective in writing style. Typically, they involve entertaining "lifestyle" pieces with heavily developed human interest qualities.

5. Columns: regularly appearing by-lined opinion columns.

With regard to hard information, (categories one and three—hard news and background and analysis material combined), there was a slight actual increase in allocated space from 24 500 column inches in 1977, to 28 000 in 1981. But as a percentage of available space, these numbers represented a considerable decline from 19.4 per cent to just 11.7 per cent.

More interesting was the fact that in the third category taken by itself (hard background and analysis material), there was a percentage decline in content from nearly eleven per cent available space to just over six per cent and also a decline in actual column inches from about 4500 column inches to just under 4000. This despite the fact that the 1981 *Gazette* was physically twice as big as the 1977 *Gazette*.

Journalism style was not the only measure taken in this research. In addition, there were also sixteen subject matter divisions. Among these were five categories of government information: Canadian federal, Quebec provincial, Montreal, other provincial, and foreign. Significant percentage declines were evident in all five of these categories, with absolute declines in numbers of allocated column inches of hard information in two, namely Quebec provincial and other provincial. Particularly dramatic was a decline in hard Quebec government news and news analysis from about 2300 column inches to just 1500. Absolute declines in hard information types in such important categories as business news, educational news, medical news, and religion also were noted.

On the other hand, when figures for soft journalism types were examined in the various subject categories, there were increases—sometimes very dramatic ones, almost everywhere. One information category, public well-being, (a category containing a range of social and community service information, self-improvement and lifestyle material) increased nearly threefold from 2400 column inches in the 1977 sample to more than 6400 in 1981. Nearly all of the increase was in the soft style of journalism, entertaining possibly, but less informative and typically treating rather inconsequential subject matter.

There was a similar evolution in sports information, entertainment information, and in the business information category. The latter increased from about 7000 column inches to just over 11 000, and almost all the increase here was predictably in soft categories mostly devoted to consumer information. As a matter of fact, business information in the hard categories actually declined dramatically from 5400 column inches to 4400.

Thus, we found the *Gazette* evolving into a softer, and arguably, a less informative newspaper. It might also be described as being narrower in the sense that it seemed less eclectic in its range of interests. Three information categories, provincial government information, religion, and educational information, showed actual declines in total column inches devoted to them despite the near doubling of the overall size of the paper. When one looks only at the hard journalism categories, there were total column-inch declines in no fewer than six categories; the three just mentioned, along with provincial government information from other parts of Canada, business information, and medical information.

The *Gazette* had reduced its presentation of non-governmental information from the province of Quebec outside the Montreal circulation area from 5.1 per cent of available news space in 1977 to just 3 per cent in 1981, representing a decline in actual column inch totals from about 2100 to 1900. Thus in an absence of newspaper competition, but in the presence of developing television competition, English-speaking Montrealers in 1981 were served by a *Gazette* that was twice the physical size of the *Gazette* of 1977. The later paper was also one in which hard journalism values had been scaled back in a number of important ways; the range of subject matter had been narrowed; and the bulk of new, non-advertising space had been devoted to largely entertaining material in soft and comparatively inconsequential subject areas.

At the Bottom Line

The developments examined above are also happening at many other Canadian dailies. They are a part of new business practices now prevalent in the industry, and intended to make print more competitive with television. The cumulative effect is one of considerable consequence. As one observer has put it: "One typical feature of bottom-line journalism is to react to the shift in expectations of readers suckled on television news. That means shorter news stories with less background, less overall space devoted to hard news, and more to features and specialty subjects."[24]

One result is the softer and narrower journalism of papers such as the *Montreal Gazette*. Don Gibb, who resigned as city editor of the *London Free Press* in 1988 when that paper introduced the new newsroom management approaches, has offered this summary observation of his experiences: "The reality for me is that the drive to make a fatter profit and the commitment of hard-hitting, credible, responsible journalism pull in different directions. Market surveys, as the Kent commission pointed out, search for readers' psyches, not for news. Tomorrow's *Free Press* will be the product the corporate managers think readers want."[25]

Ultimately, one supposes newspaper readers will be the final arbiters of whether or not they like these new products designed according to management perceptions of a measured public taste. In the meantime, there is always television.

Notes

1. Canada, *Report,* The Royal Commission on Newspaper, (Ottawa: Ministry of Supply and Services, 1981), 69. The commissioners reported that in 1980, editorial pages as a percentage of total published pages in aggregate weekly circulation ranged from 49 per cent in small circulation dailies under 250 000 average weekly circulation, to a low of 39 per cent in larger dailies with circulation in the range of 500 000 to 1 000 000 average weekly circulation.

2. Duncan McMonagle, "TV favored as source of news, survey finds," *Globe and Mail,* 27 January 1988.

3. These disturbing figures are cited by Phil McLeod, editor-in-chief of the *London Free Press* in a brief paper, "Needed: A New Definition of News," circulated to members of his newspaper's journalistic staff on 3 October 1991.

4. Robert Fulford, "The Grand Illusion—Television news suggests there's nothing in the world that can't be made comprehensible in twenty seconds," *Saturday Night,* June, 1984.

5. Clive Cocking, *Following the Leaders* (Toronto: Doubleday Canada Limited, 1980), 90.

6. Ron Powers, *The Newscasters* (New York: Saint Martin's Press, 1977), 195.

7. Richard Zoglin, "Star Power," *Time,* 7 August 1989.

8. Thomas Griffith, "The Age of Cronkite Passes," *Time,* 9 March 1981.

9. Zoglin, "Star Power."

10. Peter Trueman, *Smoke and Mirrors: The Inside Story of Television News in Canada* (Toronto: McClelland and Stewart, 1980), 94.

11. Ibid., 163.

12. Rae Corelli and William Lowther, "Packaging the News," *Maclean's,* 30 October 1989.

13. Corelli, Lowther, "Packaging the News."

14. Corelli, Lowther, "Packaging the News."

15. Rick Groen, "The Fragmented Viewer," *Globe and Mail,* 14 December 1991.

16. McLeod, "Needed: A Definition of News."

17. Canada, *Report*, The Special Senate Committee on Mass Media, vol. 1, "The Uncertain Mirror," (Ottawa: Queen's Printer, 1970), 39–40. This remarkably influential committee was chaired by Senator Davey, and the quotation is therefore attributed to him in the text.

18. Robert P. Clark, "A Threat in the '90s: Bottom-Line Journalism," *Nieman Reports*, Autumn, 1990.

19. Peter Brimelow, "A Sensational Canadian Export," *Financial Post*, 18 March 1978.

20. Doug Underwood, "When MBAs rule the newsroom," *Columbia Journalism Review*, March/April, 1988.

21. Philip Meyer, "In defence of the marketing approach," *Columbia Journalism Review*, January/February, 1978.

22. Andrew M. Osler, "A Content Analysis of the Montreal Gazette, 1977 and 1981." A report of commissioned research to the Ministry of Justice for Canada, 1983.

23. The events surrounding "Black Wednesday," (27 August 1980), that led to the creation of the Royal Commission on Newspapers of that year are described in some detail in this volume, Chapter VI, 178–81.

24. Jim Etherington, "Paper Cuts. There's a new threat to journalistic ethics: it's called the bottom line," *London Magazine*, October, 1988.

25. Don Gibb, "Profit motive driving paper into journalistic bankruptcy," *Content*, November/December, 1988.

The

Documents

of

Journalism

A P P E N D I X

The story of democratic journalism can almost be told through the pages of a handful of influential documents. This being so, it seems appropriate to bring this volume to its conclusion by providing the reader with a selection of these documents.

Areopagitica   *John Milton originally wrote his great essay on freedom of expression as a speech that he delivered from his place in Parliament in 1644. It was Milton's courageous purpose to protect writing and writers from state controls through licensing legislation that the Puritan-controlled Parliament was preparing to impose. Milton failed in his effort to drive back the legislation; licensing was introduced, and remained in place in Britain until it was allowed to lapse in the 1690s at the dawning of the Age of the Enlightenment. Despite failure in his immediate purpose for it, Milton's* Areopagitica *stands as the first great modern argument for freedom of expression published in the English-speaking world. Named for the Areopagus, the Athenian court where the rights of the citizen had their ultimate place of defence,* Areopagitica *is an imperfect document, rife with the religious prejudices of the era, for instance. But its basic principals form the foundation of modern concepts of freedom. What follows is not the complete essay, but excerpts that will provide a source of insightful comment for most modern readers.*

...This is not the liberty which we can hope, that no grievance ever should arise in the Commonwealth—that let no man in this world expect; but when complaints are freely heard, deeply considered, and speedily reformed, then is the utmost bound of civil liberty attained that wise men look for....

If ye be thus resolved, as it were injury to think ye were not, I know not what should withhold me from presenting ye with a fit instance wherein to show both that love of truth which ye eminently profess, and that uprightness of your judgment which is not wont to be partial to yourselves; by judging over again that Order which ye have ordained *to regulate Printing: that no book, pamphlet, or paper shall be henceforth printed, unless the same be first approved and licensed by such,* or at least one of such as shall be thereto appointed. For that part which preserves justly every man's copy to himself, or provides for the poor, I touch not, only wish they be not made pretences to abuse and persecute honest and painful men, who offend not in either of these particulars. But that other clause of licensing books, which we thought had died...when the prelates expired, I shall now attend with such a homily as shall lay before ye, first, the inventors of it to be those whom ye will be loath to own; next, what is to be thought in general of reading, whatever sort the books be; and that this Order avails nothing to the suppressing of scandalous, seditious, and libellous books, which were mainly intended to be suppressed. Last, that it will be primely to the discouragement of all learning, and the stop of truth, not only by disexercising and blunting our abilities in what we know already, but by hindering and cropping the discovery that might be yet further made both in religious and civil wisdom.

I deny not but that it is of greatest concernment in the Church and Commonwealth to have a vigilant eye how books demean themselves as well as men; and thereafter to confine, imprison, and do sharpest justice on them as malefactors. For books are not absolutely dead things, but do contain a potency of life in them to be as active as that soul was whose progeny they are; nay, they do preserve as in a vial the purest efficacy and extraction of that living intellect that bred them. I know they are as lively, and as vigorously productive, as those fabulous dragon's teeth; and being sown up and down, may chance to spring up armed men. And yet, on the other hand, unless wariness be used, as good almost kill a man as kill a good book: who kills a man kills a reasonable creature, God's image; but he who destroys a good book, kills reason itself, kills the image of God, as it were, in the eye. Many a man lives a burden to the earth; but a good book is the precious life-blood of a master spirit, embalmed and treasured up on purpose to a life beyond life. 'Tis true, no age can restore a life, whereof perhaps there is no great loss; and revolutions of ages do not oft recover the loss of a rejected truth, for the want of which whole nations fare the worse. We should be wary, therefore, what persecution we raise against the living labors of public men, how we spill that seasoned life of man, preserved and stored up in books; since we see a kind of homicide may be thus committed, sometimes a martyrdom; and if it extend to the whole impression, a kind of massacre, whereof the execution ends not in the slaying of an elemental life, but strikes at that ethereal and fifth essence, the breath of reason itself, slays an immortality rather than a life. But lest I should be condemned of introducing licence, while I oppose licensing, I refuse not the pains to be so much historical as will serve to show what hath been done by ancient and famous commonwealths against this disorder, till the very time that this project of licensing crept out of the Inquisition...

And that the primitive councils and bishops were wont only to declare what books were not commendable, passing no further, but leaving it to each one's conscience to read or to lay by, till after the year 800, is observed already by Padre Paolo, the great unmasker of the Trentine Council. After which time the Popes of Rome, engrossing what they pleased of political rule into their own hands, extended their dominion over men's eyes, as they had before over their judgments, burning and prohibiting to be read what they fancied not; yet sparing in their censures, the books not many which they so dealt with....Which course Leo X and his successors followed, until the Council of Trent and the Spanish Inquisition, engendering together, brought forth, or perfected those catalogues, and expurging indexes, that rake through the entrails of many an old good author, with a violation worse than any could be offered to his tomb.

Nor did they stay in matters heretical, but any subject that was not to their palate, they either condemned in a prohibition, or had it straight into the new purgatory of an Index. To fill up the measure of encroachment, their last invention was to ordain that no book, pamphlet, or paper should be printed (as if St.Peter had bequeathed them the keys of the press also out of Paradise) unless it were approved and licensed under the hands of two or three glutton friars....

And thus ye have the inventors and the original of book-licensing ripped up and drawn as lineally as any pedigree. We have it not, that can be heard of, from any ancient state, or polity, or church, nor by any statute left us by our ancestors elder or later; nor from the modern custom of any reformed city or church abroad; but from the most antichristian council and the most tyrannous inquisition that ever inquired.

Till then books were ever as freely admitted into the world as any other birth; the issue of the brain was no more stifled than the issue of the womb; no envious Juno sat cross-legged over the nativity of any man's intellectual offspring; but if it proved a monster, who denies but that it was justly burnt, or sunk into the sea. But that a book, in worse condition than a peccant soul, should be to stand before a jury ere it be born to the world, and undergo yet in darkness the judgment of Radamanth and his colleagues, ere it can pass the ferry backward into light, was never heard before, till that mysterious iniquity, provoked and troubled at the first entrance of reformation, sought out new limbos and new hells wherein they might include our books also within the number of their damned....

But some will say, what though the inventors were bad, the thing for all that may be good. It may be so; yet if that thing be no such deep invention, but obvious and easy for any man to light on, and yet best and wisest commonwealths through all ages and occasions have forborne to use it, and falsest seducers and oppressors of men were the first who took it up, and to no other purpose but to obstruct and hinder the first approach of reformation; I am of those who believe it will be a harder alchymy than Lullius ever knew to sublimate any good use out of such an invention. Yet this only is what I request to gain from this reason, that it may be held a dangerous and suspicious fruit, as certainly it deserves, for the tree that bore it, until I can dissect one by one the properties it has. But I have first to finish, as was propounded, what is to be thought in general of reading books, whatever sort they be, and whether be more the benefit or the harm that thence proceeds?...

Good and evil we know in the field of this world grow up together almost inseparably; and the knowledge of good is so involved and interwoven with the knowledge of evil, and in so many cunning resemblances hardly to be discerned, that those confused seeds which were imposed upon Psyche as an incessant labor to cull out, and sort asunder, were not more intermixed. It was from out the rind of one apple tasted, that the knowledge of good and evil as two twins cleaving together, leaped forth into the world. And perhaps this is that doom which Adam fell into of knowing good and evil, that is to say, of knowing good by evil....[A substantial portion of the essay is deleted here]....

And if the men be erroneous who appear to be the leading schismatics, what withholds us but our sloth, our self-will, and distrust in the right cause, that we do not give them gentle meeting and gentle dismissions, that we debate not and examine the matter thoroughly with liberal and frequent audience; if not for their sakes, yet for our own? Seeing no man who hath tasted learning but will confess the many ways of profiting by those who, not contented with stale receipts, are able to manage and set forth new positions to the world. And were they but as the dust and cinders of our feet, so long as in that notion they may yet serve to polish and brighten the armory of Truth, even for that respect they were not utterly to be cast away. But if they be of those whom God hath fitted for the special use of these times with eminent and ample gifts—and those perhaps neither among the priests, nor among the pharisees—and we in the haste of a precipitant zeal shall make no distinction, but resolve to stop their mouths because we fear they come with new and dangerous opinions (as we commonly forejudge them ere we understand them); no less than woe to us while, thinking thus to defend the Gospel, we are found the persecutors...

This I know, that errors in a good government and in a bad are equally almost incident; for what magistrate may not be misinformed and much the sooner, if liberty of printing be reduced into the power of a few; but to redress willingly and speedily what hath been erred, and in highest authority to esteem a plain advertisement more than others have done a sumptuous bribe, is a virtue, honored Lords and Commons, answerable to your highest actions, and whereof none can participate but greatest and wisest men.

On Liberty   *The other classic essay on freedom of expression is John Stuart Mill's* On Liberty. *Written in 1858, a little more than two centuries after Milton produced* Areopagitica, *Mill dealt with the challenges to individuality and individual liberty in an increasingly complex age. The Industrial Revolution was irrevocably under way. Government, of course, but industrial and other social institutions as well were becoming much more sophisticated, and more dominatingly consequential in the lives of individuals. Cities were growing, and life was becoming more complicated in all ways. It was in these circumstances that Mill provided us with his great defence of individual freedom, especially freedom of expression. What follows are excerpts from the much longer work.*

CHAPTER II
OF THE LIBERTY OF THOUGHT AND DISCUSSION

The time, it is to be hoped, is gone by, when any defence would be necessary of the "liberty of the press" as one of the securities against corrupt or tyrannical government. No argument, we may suppose, can now be needed, against permitting a legislature or an executive, not identified in interest with the people, to prescribe opinions to them, and determine what doctrines or what arguments they shall be allowed to hear. This aspect of the question, besides, has been so often and so triumphantly enforced by preceding writers, that it needs not be specially insisted on in this place. Though the law of England, on the subject of the press, is as servile to this day as it was in the time of the Tudors, there is little danger of its being actually put in force against political discussion, except during some temporary panic, when fear of insurrection drives ministers and judges from their propriety; and, speaking generally, it is not, in constitutional countries, to be apprehended, that the government, whether completely responsible to the people or not, will often attempt to control the expression of opinion, except when in doing so it makes itself the organ of the general intolerance of the public. Let us suppose, there-fore, that the government is entirely at one with the people, and never thinks of exerting any power of coercion unless in agreement with what it conceives to be their voice. But I deny the right of the people to exercise such coercion either by themselves or by their government. The power itself is illegitimate. The best government has no more title to it than the worst. It is as noxious, or more noxious, when exerted in accordance with public opinion, than when in opposition to it. Were an opinion a personal possession of no value except to the owner; it to be obstructed in the enjoyment of it were simply a pri-vate injury, it would make some difference whether the injury was inflicted only on a few persons or on many. But the peculiar evil of silencing the expression of an opinion is, that it is robbing the human race; posterity as well as the existing generation; those who dissent from the opinion, still more than those who hold it. If the opinion is right, they are deprived of the opportunity of exchanging error for truth; if wrong, they lose, what is almost as great a benefit, the clearer perception and livelier impression of truth, produced by its collision with error.

It is necessary to consider separately these two hypotheses, each of which has a distinct branch of the argument corresponding to it. We can never be sure that the opinion we are endeavouring to stifle is a false opinion; and if we were sure, stifling it would be an evil still.

[T]he opinion which it is attempted to suppress by authority may possibly be true. Those who desire to suppress it, of course deny its truth; but they are not infallible. They have no authority to decide the question for all mankind, and exclude every other person from the means of judging. To refuse a hearing to an opinion, because they are sure that it is false, is to assume that *their* certainty is the same thing as *absolute* certainty. All silencing of discussion is an assumption of infallibility. Its condemnation may be allowed to rest on this com-mon argument, not the worse for being common.

Unfortunately for the good sense of mankind, the fact of their falli-bility is far from carrying the weight in their practical judgment which is always allowed to it in theory; for while every one well knows himself to be fallible, few think it necessary to take any pre-cautions against their own fallibility, or admit the supposition that any opinion, of which they feel very certain, may be one of the exam-ples of the error to which they acknowledge themselves to be liable... [It] is as evident in itself, as any amount of argument can make it, that ages are no more infallible than individuals; every age having held many opinions which subsequent ages have deemed not only false but absurd; and it is as certain that many opinions now general will be rejected by future ages, as it is that many, once general, are rejected by the present...

When we consider either the history of opinion, or the ordinary conduct of human life, to what is it to be ascribed that the one and the other are no worse than they are? Not certainly to the inherent force of the human understanding; for, on any matter not self-evident, there are ninety-nine persons totally incapable of judging of it for one who is capable; and the capacity of the hundredth person is only comparative; for the majority of the eminent men of every past generation held many opinions now known to be erroneous, and did or approved numerous things which no one will now justify. Why is it, then, that there is on the whole a preponderance among mankind of rational opinions and rational conduct? If there really is this preponderance—which there must be unless human affairs are, and have always been, in an almost desperate state—it is owing to a quality of the human mind, the source of everything respectable in man either as an intellectual or as a moral being, namely, that his errors are corrigible. He is capable of rectifying his mistakes, by discussion and experience. Not be experience alone. There must be discussion, to show how experience is to be interpreted. Wrong opinions and practices gradually yield to fact and argument; but facts and arguments, to produce any effect on the mind, must be brought before it. Very few facts are able to tell their own story, without comments to bring out their meaning. The whole strength and value, then, of human judgment, depending on the one property, that it can be set right when it is wrong, reliance can be placed on it only when the means of setting it right are kept constantly at hand. In the case of any person whose judgment is really deserving of confidence, how has it become so? Because he has kept his mind open to criticism of his opinions and conduct. Because it has been his practice to listen to all that could be said against him; to profit by as much of it as was just, and expound to himself, and upon occasion to others, the fallacy of what was fallacious. Because he has felt, that the only way in which a human being can make some approach to knowing the whole of a subject, is by hearing what can be said about it by persons of every variety of opinion, and studying all modes in which it can be looked at by every character of mind. No wise man ever acquired his wisdom in any mode but this; nor is it in the nature of human intellect to become wise in any other manner. The steady habit of correcting and completing his own opinion by collating it with those of others, so far from causing doubt and hesitation in carrying it into practice, is the only stable foundation for a just reliance on it: for, being cognisant of all that can, at least obviously, be said against him, and having taken up his position against all gainsayers—knowing that he has sought for objections and difficulties, instead of avoiding them, and has shut out no light which can be thrown upon the subject from any quarter—he has a right to think his judgment better than that of any person, or any multitude, who have gone through a similar process.

It is not too much to require that what the wisest of mankind, those who are best entitled to trust their own judgment, find necessary to warrant their relying on it, should be submitted by that miscellaneous collection of a few wise and many foolish individuals, called the public. If even the Newtonian philosophy were not permitted to be questioned, mankind could not feel as complete assurance of its truth as they now do. The beliefs which we have most warrant for have no safeguard to rest on, but a standing invitation to the whole world to prove them unfounded. If the challenge is not accepted, or is accepted and the attempt fails, we are far enough from certainty still; but we have done the best that the existing state of human reason admits of; we have neglected nothing that could give the truth a chance of reaching us: if the lists are kept open, we may hope that if there be a better truth, it will be found when the human mind is capable of receiving it; and in the meantime we may rely on having attained such approach to truth as is possible in our own day. This is the amount of certainty attainable by a fallible being, and this the sole way of attaining it.

Strange it is, that men should admit the validity of the arguments for free discussion, but object to their being "pushed to an extreme;" not seeing that unless the reasons are good for an extreme case, they are not good for any case. Strange that they should imagine that they are not assuming infallibility, when they acknowledge that there should be free discussion on all subjects which can possibly be *doubtful* but think that some particular principle or doctrine should be forbidden to be questioned because it is so *certain*, that is, because *they are certain* that it is certain. To call any proposition certain, while there is any one who would deny its certainty if permitted, but who is not permitted, is to assume that we ourselves, and those who agree with us, are the judges of certainty, and judges without hearing the other side.

In the present age—which has been described as "destitute of faith, but terrified at scepticism"—in which people feel sure, not so much that their opinions are true, as that they should not know what to do without them—the claims of an opinion to be protected from public attack are rested not so much on its truth, as on its importance to society. There are, it is alleged, certain beliefs so useful, not to say indispensable, to well-being that it is as much the duty of governments to uphold those beliefs, as to protect any other of the interests of society. In a case of such necessity, and so directly in the line of their duty, something less than infallibility may, it is maintained, warrant and even bind, governments to act on their own opinion, confirmed by the general opinion of mankind. It is also often argued, and still oftener thought, that none but bad men would desire to weaken these salutary beliefs; and there can be nothing wrong, it is thought, in restraining bad men, and prohibiting what only such men would wish to practise. This mode of thinking makes the justification of restraints on discussion not a question of the truth of doctrines, but of their usefulness; and flatters itself by that means to escape the responsibility of claiming to be an infallible judge of opinions. But those who thus satisfy themselves, do not perceive that the assumption of infallibility is merely shifted from one point to another. The usefulness of an opinion is itself matter of opinion: as disputable, as open to discussion, and requiring discussion as much as the opinion itself. There is the same need of an infallible judge of opinions to decide an opinion to be noxious, as to decide it to be false, unless the opinion condemned has full opportunity of defending itself. And it will not do to say that the heretic may be allowed to maintain the utility or harmlessness of his opinion, though forbidden to maintain its truth. The truth of an opinion is part of its utility. If we would know whether or not it is desirable that a proposition should be believed, is it possible to exclude the consideration of whether or not it is true? In the opinion, not of bad men, but of the best men, no belief which is contrary to truth can be really useful: and can you prevent such men from urging that plea, when they are charged with culpability for denying some doctrine which they are told is useful, but which they believe to be false? Those who are on the side of received opinions never fail to take all possible advantage of this plea; you do not find *them* handling the question of utility as if it could be completely abstracted from that of truth: on the contrary, it is, above all, because their doctrine is "the truth," that the knowledge or the belief of it is held to be so indispensable. There can be no fair discussion of the question of usefulness when an argument so vital may be employed on one side, but not on the other. And in point of fact, when law or public feeling do not permit the truth of an opinion to be disputed, they are just as little tolerant of a denial of its usefulness. The utmost they allow is an extenuation of its absolute necessity, or of the positive guilt of rejecting it.

In order more fully to illustrate the mischief of denying a hearing to opinions because we, in our own judgment, have condemned them, it will be desirable to fix down the discussion to a concrete case; and I choose, by preference, the cases which are least favourable to me—in which the argument against freedom of opinion, both on the score of truth and on that of utility, is considered the strongest. Let the opinions impugned be the belief in a God and in a future state, or any of the commonly received doctrines of morality. To fight the battle on such ground gives a great advantage to an unfair antagonist; since he will be sure to say (and many who have no desire to be unfair will say it internally), Are these the doctrines which you do not deem sufficiently certain to be taken under the protection of law? Is the belief in a God one of the opinions to feel sure of which you hold to be assuming infallibility? But I must be permitted to observe, that it is not the feeling sure of a doctrine (be it what it may) which I call an assumption of infallibility. It is the undertaking to decide that question *for others*, without allowing them to hear what can be said on the contrary side. And I denounce and reprobate this pretension not the less, if put forth on the side of my most solemn convictions. However positive any one's persuasion may be, not only of the falsity but of the pernicious consequences—not only of the pernicious consequences, but (to adopt expressions which I altogether condemn) the immorality and impiety of an opinion; yet if, in pursuance of that private judgment, though backed by the public judgment of his country or his contemporaries, he prevents the opinion from being heard in its defence, he assumes infallibility. And so far from the assumption being less objectionable or less dangerous because the opinion is called immoral or impious, this is the case of all others in which it is most fatal. These are exactly the occasions on which the men of one generation commit those dreadful mistakes which excite the astonishment and horror of posterity. It is among such that we find the instances memorable in history, when the arm of the law has been employed to root out the best men and the noblest doctrines; with deplorable success as to the men, though some of the doctrines have survived to be (as if in mockery) invoked in defence of similar conduct towards those who dissent from *them*, or from their received interpretation.

Mankind can hardly be too often reminded, that there was once a man named Socrates, between whom and the legal authorities and public opinion of his time there took place a memorable collision ...This acknowledged master of all the eminent thinkers who have since lived—whose fame, still growing after more than two thousand years, all but outweighs the whole remainder of the names which make his native city illustrious—was put to death by his countrymen, after a judicial conviction, for impiety and immorality. Impiety, in denying the gods recognised by the State; indeed his accuser asserted (see the "Apologia") that he believed in no gods at all. Immorality, in being, by his doctrines and instructions, a "corruptor of youth." Of these charges the tribunal, there is every ground for believing, honestly found him guilty, and condemned the man who probably of all then born had deserved best of mankind to be put to death as a criminal.

To pass from this to the only other instance of judicial iniquity, the mention of which, after the condemnation of Socrates, would not be an anti-climax: the event which took place on Calvary rather more than eighteen hundred years ago. The man who left the memory of those who witnessed his life and conversation such an impression of his moral grandeur that eighteen subsequent centuries have done homage to him as the Almighty in person, was ignominiously put to death, as what? As a blasphemer. The feelings with which mankind now regard these lamentable transactions, especially the later of the two, render them extremely unjust in their judgment of the unhappy actors. These were, to all appearance, not bad men—not worse than men commonly are, but rather the contrary; men who possessed in a full, or somewhat more than a full measure, the religious, moral, and patriotic feelings of their time and people: the very kind of men who, in all times, our own included, have every chance of passing through life blameless and respected. The high-priest who rent his garments when the words were pronounced, which, according to all the ideas of his country, constituted the blackest guilt, was in all probability quite as sincere in his horror and indignation as the generality of respectable and pious men now are in the religious and moral sentiments they profess; and most of those who now shudder at his conduct, if they had lived in his time, and been born Jews, would have acted precisely as he did. Orthodox Christians who are tempted to think that those who stoned to death the first martyrs must have been worse men than they themselves are, ought to remember that one of those persecutors was Saint Paul...

The Canadian Charter of Rights and Freedoms

The Canadian Charter of Rights and Freedoms *The Charter is Part 1 of Canada's Constitution Act, 1982. It represents the great attempt by modern Canadians to give formal recognition and definition to their basic freedoms, including the important sections on freedom of media and expression. The Charter is beginning to shape Canadian law in a significant way, as more and more cases invoking its provisions are brought before the courts. Journalism and its purposes in society are clearly being influenced in the process, and thus the Charter is included in this appendix.*

Whereas Canada is founded upon principles that recognize the supremacy of God and the rule of law:

Guarantee of Rights and Freedoms

1. The *Canadian Charter of Rights and Freedoms* guarantees the rights and freedoms set out in it subject only to such reasonable limits prescribed by law as can be demonstrably justified in a free and democratic society.

Fundamental Freedoms

2. Everyone has the following fundamental freedoms: (a) freedom of conscience and religion; (b) freedom of thought, belief, opinion and expression including freedom of the press and other media of communication; (c) freedom of peaceful assembly; and (d) freedom of association.

Democratic Rights

3. Every citizen of Canada has the right to vote in an election of members of the House of Commons or of a legislative assembly and to be qualified for membership therein.

4. (1) No House of Commons and no legislative assembly shall continue for longer than five years from the date fixed for the return of the writs at a general election of its members.

(2) In time of real or apprehended war, invasion or insurrection, a House of Commons may be continued by Parliament and a legislative assembly may be continued by the legislature beyond five years if such continuation is not opposed by the votes of more than one-third of the members of the House of Commons or the legislative assembly, as the case may be.

5. There shall be a sitting of Parliament and of each legislature at least once every twelve months.

Mobility Rights

6. (1) Every citizen of Canada has the right to enter, remain in and leave Canada.

(2) Every citizen of Canada and every person who has the status of a permanent resident of Canada has the right (a) to move to and take up residence in any province; and (b) to pursue the gaining of a livelihood in any province.

(3) The rights specified in subsection (2) are subject to (a) any laws or practices of general application in force in a province other than those that discriminate among persons primarily on the basis of province of present or previous residence; and (b) any laws providing for reasonable residency requirements as a qualification for the receipt of publicly provided social services.

(4) Subsections (2) and (3) do not preclude any law, program or activity that has as its object the amelioration in a province of conditions of individuals in that province who are socially or economically disadvantaged if the rate of employment in that province is below the rate of employment in Canada.

Legal Rights

7. Everyone has the right to life, liberty and security of the person and the right not to be deprived thereof except in accordance with the principles of fundamental justice.

8. Everyone has the right to be secure against unreasonable search or seizure.

9. Everyone has the right not to be arbitrarily detained or imprisoned.

10. Everyone has the right on arrest or detention (a) to be informed promptly of the reasons therefor; (b) to retain and instruct counsel without delay and to be informed of that right; and (c) to have the validity of the detention determined by way of *habeas corpus* and to be released if the detention is not lawful.

11. Any person charged with an offence has the right (a) to be informed without unreasonable delay of the specific offence; (b) to be tried within a reasonable time; (c) not to be compelled to be a witness in proceeding against that person in respect of the offence; (d) to be presumed innocent until proven guilty according to law in a fair and public hearing by an independent and impartial tribunal; (e) not to be denied reasonable bail without just cause; (f) except in the case of an

offence under military law tried before a military tribunal, to the benefit of trial by jury where the maximum punishment for the offence is imprisonment for five years or a more severe punishment; (g) not to be found guilty of account of any act or omission unless, at the time of the act or omission, it constituted an offence under Canadian or international law or was criminal according to the general principles of law recognized by the community of nations; (h) if finally acquitted of the offence, not to be tried for it again and, if finally found guilty and punished for the offence, not to be tried or punished for it again; and (i) if found guilty of the offence and if the punishment for the offence has been varied between the time of commission and the time of sentencing, to the benefit of the lesser punishment.

12. Everyone has the right not be be subjected to any cruel and unusual treatment or punishment.

13. A witness who testifies in any proceeding has the right not to have any incriminating evidence so given used to incriminate that witness in any other proceedings, except in a prosecution for perjury or for the giving of contradictory evidence.

14. A party or witness in any proceedings who does not understand or speak the language in which the proceedings are conducted or who is deaf has the right to the assistance of an interpreter.

Equality Rights

15. (1) Every individual is equal before and under the law and has the right to the equal protection and equal benefit of the law without discrimination and, in particular, without discrimination based on race, national or ethnic origin, colour, religion, sex, age or mental or physical disability.

(2) Subsection (1) does not preclude any law, program or activity that has as its object the amelioration of conditions of disadvantaged individuals or groups including those that are disadvantaged because of race, national or ethnic origin, colour, religion, sex, age or mental or physical disability.

Official Languages of Canada

16. (1) English and French are the official languages of Canada and have equality of status and equal rights and privileges as to their use in all institutions of the Parliament and government of Canada.

(2) English and French are the official languages of New Brunswick and have equality of status and equal rights and privileges

as to their use in all institutions of the legislature and government of New Brunswick.

(3) Nothing in this Charter limits the authority of Parliament or a legislature to advance the equality of status or use of English and French.

17. (1) Everyone has the right to use English or French in any debates and other proceedings of Parliament.

(2) Everyone has the right to use English or French in any debates and other proceedings of the legislature of New Brunswick.

18. (1) The statutes, records and journals of Parliament shall be printed and published in English and French and both language versions are equally authoritative.

(2) The statutes, records and journals of the legislature of New Brunswick shall be printed and published in English and French and both language versions are equally authoritative.

19. (1) Either English or French may be used by any person in, or in any pleading in or process issuing from, any court established by Parliament.

(2) Either English or French may be used by any person in, or in any pleading in or process issuing from, any court of New Brunswick.

20. (1) Any member of the public in Canada has the right to communicate with, and to receive available services from, any head or central office of an institution of the Parliament or government of Canada in English or French, and has the same right with respect to any other office of any such institution where (a) there is a significant demand for communications with and services from that office in such language; or (b) due to the nature of the office, it is reasonable that communications with and services from that office be available in both English and French.

(2) Any member of the public in New Brunswick has the right to communicate with, and to receive available services from, any office of an institution of the legislature or government of New Brunswick in English or French.

21. Nothing in sections 16 to 20 abrogates or derogates from any right, privilege or obligation with respect to the English and French languages, or either of them, that exists or is continued by virtue of any other provision of the Constitution of Canada.

22. Nothing in sections 16 to 20 abrogates or derogates from any legal or customary right or privilege acquired or enjoyed either before or after the coming into force of this Charter with respect to any language that is not English or French.

Minority Language Educational Rights

23. (1) Citizens of Canada (a) whose first language learned and still understood is that of the English or French linguistic minority population of the province in which they reside, or (b) who have received their primary school instruction in Canada in English or French and reside in a province where the language in which they received that instruction is the language of the English or French linguistic minority population of the province, have the right to have their children receive primary and secondary school instruction in that language in that province.

(2) Citizens of Canada of whom any child has received primary or secondary school instruction in English or French in Canada, have the right to have all their children receive primary and secondary school instruction in the same language.

(3) The right of citizens of Canada under subsections (1) and (2) to have their children receive primary and secondary school instruction in the language of the English or French linguistic minority population of a province (a) applies wherever in the province the number of children of citizens who have such a right is sufficient to warrant the provision to them out of public funds of minority language instruction; and (b) includes, where the number of those children so warrants, the right to have them receive that instruction in minority language educational facilities provided out of public funds.

Enforcement

24. (1) Anyone whose rights or freedoms, as guaranteed by the Charter, have been infringed or denied may apply to a court of competent jurisdiction to obtain such remedy as the court considers appropriate and just in the circumstances.

(2) Where, in proceedings under subsection (1), a court concludes that evidence was obtained in a manner that infringed or denied any rights or freedoms guaranteed by this Charter, the evidence shall be excluded if it is established that, having regard to all the circumstances, the admission of it in the proceedings would bring the administration of justice into disrepute.

General

25. The guarantee in this Charter of certain rights and freedoms shall not be construed so as to abrogate or derogate from any aboriginal, treaty or other rights or freedoms that pertain to the aboriginal peoples of Canada including (a) any rights or freedoms that have been recognized by the Royal Proclamation of October 7, 1763; and (b) any rights or freedoms that may be acquired by the aboriginal peoples of Canada by way of land claims settlement.

26. The guarantee in this Charter of certain rights and freedoms shall not be construed as denying the existence of any other rights or freedoms that exist in Canada.

27. This Charter shall be interpreted in a manner consistent with the preservation and enhancement of the multicultural heritage of Canadians.

28. Notwithstanding anything in this Charter, the rights and freedoms referred to in it are guaranteed equally to male and female persons.

29. Nothing in this Charter abrogates or derogates from any rights or privileges guaranteed by or under the Constitution of Canada in respect of denominational, separate or dissentient schools.

30. A reference in this Charter to a province or to the legislative assembly or legislature of a province shall be deemed to include a reference to the Yukon Territory and the Northwest Territories, or to the appropriate legislative authority thereof, as the case may be.

31. Nothing in this Charter extends the legislative powers of any body or authority.

Application of Charter

32. (1) This Charter applies (a) to the Parliament and government of Canada in respect of all matters within the authority of Parliament including all matters relating to the Yukon Territory and Northwest Territories; and (b) to the legislature and government of each province in respect of all matters within the authority of the legislature of each province.

(2) Notwithstanding subsection (1), section 15 shall not have effect until three years after this section comes into force.

33. (1) Parliament or the legislature of a province may expressly declare in an Act of Parliament or of the legislature, as the case may be, that the Act or a provision thereof shall operate

notwithstanding a provision included in section 2 or sections 7 to 15 of this Charter.

(2) An Act or a provision of an Act in respect of which a declaration made under this section is in effect shall have such operation as it would have but for the provision of this Charter referred to in the declaration.

(3) A declaration made under subsection (1) shall cease to have effect five years after it comes into force or on such earlier date as may be specified in the declaration.

(4) Parliament or a legislature of a province may re-enact a declaration made under subsection (1).

(5) Subsection (3) applies in respect of a re-enactment made under subsection (4).

Citation

34. This Part may be cited as the *Canadian Charter of Rights and Freedoms.*

Code of Ethics of the American Society of Newspaper Editors

North American journalism has made a number of efforts in this century to formalize an ethical and professional place for itself in society, while at the same time seeking to protect journalism's essential and traditional freedoms. Often such efforts have taken the form of expressing values as codes of ethics for journalists. One of the earlier and more influential examples is that of the American Society of Newspaper Editors which was prepared in 1923, and is here reproduced in full.

The primary function of newspapers is to communicate to the human race what its members do, feel and think. Journalism, therefore, demands of its practitioners the widest range of intelligence, or knowledge, and of experience, as well as natural and trained powers of observation and reasoning. To its opportunities as a chronicle are indissolubly linked its obligations as teacher and interpreter.

To the end of finding some means of codifying sound practice and just aspirations of American journalism, these canons are set forth:

I.

RESPONSIBILITY—The right of a newspaper to attract and hold readers is restricted by nothing but considerations of public welfare.

The use a newspaper makes of the share of public attention it gains serves to determine its sense of responsibility, which it shares with every member of its staff. A journalist who uses his power for any selfish or otherwise unworthy purpose is faithless to a high trust.

II.

FREEDOM OF THE PRESS—Freedom of the press is to be guarded as a vital right of mankind. It is the unquestionable right to discuss whatever is not explicitly forbidden by law, including the wisdom of any restrictive statute.

III.

INDEPENDENCE—Freedom from all obligations except that of fidelity to the public interest is vital.

1.   Promotion of any private interest contrary to the general welfare, for whatever reason, is not compatible with honest journalism. So-called new communications from private sources should not be published without public notice of their source or else substantiation of their claims to value as news, both in form and substance.

2.   Partisanship, in editorial comment which knowingly departs from the truth, does violence to the best spirit of American journalism; in the news columns it is subversive of a fundamental principle of the profession.

IV.

SINCERITY, TRUTHFULNESS, ACCURACY—Good faith with the reader is the foundation of all journalism worthy of the name.

1.   By every consideration of good faith a newspaper is constrained to be truthful. It is not to be excused for lack of thoroughness or accuracy within its control, or failure to obtain command of these essential qualities.

2.   Headlines should be fully warranted by the contents of the articles which they surmount.

V.

IMPARTIALITY—Sound practice makes clear distinction between news reports and expressions of opinion. News reports should be free from opinion or bias of any kind.

1.   This rule does not apply to so-called special articles unmis-

takably devoted to advocacy or characterized by a signature authorizing the writer's own conclusions and interpretation.

VI.

FAIR PLAY—A newspaper should not publish unofficial charges affecting reputation or moral character without opportunity given to the accused to be heard; right practice demands the giving of such opportunity in all cases of serious accusation outside judicial proceedings.

1. A newspaper should not invade private rights or feeling without sure warrant of public right as distinguished from public curiosity.

2. It is the privilege, as it is the duty, of a newspaper to make prompt and complete correction of its own serious mistakes of fact or opinion, whatever their origin.

DECENCY—A newspaper cannot escape conviction of insincerity if while professing high moral purpose it supplies incentives to base conduct, such as are to be found in details of crime and vice, publication of which is not demonstrably for the general good. Lacking authority to enforce its canons the journalism here represented can but express the hope that deliberate pandering to vicious instincts will encounter effective public disapproval or yield to the influence of a preponderant professional condemnation.

(Adopted 1923 and still unchanged)

The Canadian Publishers' Code *Finally, it is useful to recognize that a journalistic code of ethics for Canadian journalists was prepared by the Canadian Daily Newspaper Publishers Association in 1977. The full text of this document follows.*

A STATEMENT OF PRINCIPLES FOR CANADIAN DAILY NEWSPAPERS

1. ETHICS

Newspapers have individual codes of ethics and this declaration of principles is intended to complement them in their healthy diversity. As individual believers in free speech they have a duty to maintain standards of conduct in conformance with their own goals.

II. FREEDOM OF THE PRESS

Freedom of the press is an exercise of the common right to freedom of speech. It is the right to inform, to discuss, to advocate, to dissent.

The Press claims no freedom that is not the right of every person. Truth emerges from free discussion and free reporting and both are essential to foster and preserve a democratic society.

III. RESPONSIBILITY

The newspaper has responsibilities to its readers, its shareholders, its employees and its advertisers. But the operation of a newspaper is in effect a public trust, no less binding because it is not formally conferred, and its overriding responsibility is to the society which protects and provides its freedom.

IV. ACCURACY AND FAIRNESS

The newspaper keeps faith with its readers by presenting the news comprehensively, accurately and fairly, and by acknowledging mistakes promptly.

Fairness requires a balanced presentation of the relevant facts in a news report, and of all substantial opinions in a matter of controversy. It precludes distortion of meaning by over- or under-emphasis, by placing facts or quotations out of context, or by headlines not warranted by the text. When statements are made that injure the reputation of an individual or group those affected should be given the earliest opportunity to reply.

Fairness requires that in the reporting of news, the right of every person to a fair trial should be respected.

Fairness also requires that sources of information should be identified except when there is a clear and pressing reason to protect their anonymity. Except in rare circumstances, reporters should not conceal their own identity. Newspapers and their staffs should not induce people to commit illegal or improper acts. Sound practice makes clear distinction for the reader between news reports and expressions of opinion.

V. INDEPENDENCE

The newspaper should hold itself free of any obligation save that of fidelity to the public good. It should pay the costs incurred in gathering and publishing news. Conflicts of interest, and the appearance of conflicts of interest, must be avoided. Outside interest that could affect, or appear to affect, the newspaper's freedom to report the news impartially should be avoided.

VI. PRIVACY

Every person has a right to privacy. There are inevitable conflicts between the right to privacy and the public good or the right to know about the conduct of public affairs. Each case should be judged in the light of common sense and humanity.

VII. ACCESS

The newspaper is a forum for the free interchange of information and opinion. It should provide for the expression in its columns of disparate and conflicting views. It should give expression to the interests of minorities as well as majorities, and of the less powerful elements in society.

Adopted by the Canadian Daily Newspaper Publishers Association April, 1977.

INDEX